LEVINAS AND BIBLICAL STUDIES

Society of Biblical Literature

Semeia Studies

Number 43

LEVINAS AND BIBLICAL STUDIES

LEVINAS AND
BIBLICAL STUDIES

Edited by
Tamara Cohn Eskenazi,
Gary A. Phillips,
and
David Jobling

Society of Biblical Literature
Atlanta

LEVINAS AND BIBLICAL STUDIES

Library of Congress Cataloging-in-Publication Data

Levinas and biblical studies / edited by Tamara Cohn Eskenazi, Gary A. Philips, and David Jobling
     p. cm. — (Society of Biblical Literature Semeia studies, 43)
    Includes bibliographical references.
    ISBN 1-58983-073-3 (paper binding : alk. paper)
    1. Bible. O.T.—Criticism, interpretation, etc., Jewish. 2. Levinas, Emmanuel—Contributions in biblical studies. I. Eskenazi, Tamara Cohn. II. Phillips, Gary Allen. III. Jobling, David. IV. Series: Semeia studies.
    BS1186 .L485 2003b
221.6'092—dc21   2003001673

11 10 09 08 07 06 05 04 03   5 4 3 2 1

Printed in the United States of America
on acid-free paper

CONTENTS

ABBREVIATIONS

AB	Anchor Bible
BibInt	*Biblical Interpretation*
BN	*Biblische Notizen*
BRev	*Bible Review*
ET	English translation
ETL	*Ephemerides theologicae lovanienses*
HBT	*Horizons in Biblical Theology*
IB	*Interpreter's Bible.* Edited by G. A. Buttrick et al. 12 vols. New York: Abingdon, 1951–57.
IBC	Interpretation: A Bible Commentary for Teaching and Preaching
Int	*Interpretation*
JAAR	*Journal of the American Academy of Religion*
JBL	*Journal of Biblical Literature*
JQR	*Jewish Quarterly Review*
JSJ	*Journal for the Study of Judaism in the Persian, Hellenistic, and Roman Periods*
JSNTSup	Journal for the Study of the New Testament Supplement Series
JSOT	*Journal for the Study of the Old Testament*
JSOTSup	Journal for the Study of the Old Testament Supplement Series
OBS	Oxford Bible Series
OBT	Overtures to Biblical Theology
OTL	Old Testament Library
VT	*Vetus Testamentum*
ZAW	*Zeitschrift für die alttestamentliche Wissenschaft*

INTRODUCTION—FACING THE TEXT AS OTHER: SOME IMPLICATIONS OF LEVINAS'S WORK FOR BIBLICAL STUDIES

Tamara Cohn Eskenazi
Hebrew Union College-Jewish Institute of Religion, Los Angeles

Some ten years ago Edith Wyschogrod, then president of the American Academy of Religion, titled a brief, introductory essay "Who Is Emmanuel Levinas?" (1992). In it she contrasted the widespread recognition and esteem bestowed upon Buber already during his life, in the 1950s, with the surprising silence over Levinas in North America. She wrote: "apart from a small coterie of professional philosophers interested in recent continental thought and literary critics of a post-modern bent" (1992: 65), only few Americans know the name, or the work, of Emmanuel Levinas. She concludes that "One reason for the relative obscurity of perhaps the most important Jewish thinker of the second half of the twentieth century is geographical and cultural" (ibid.).

In Europe, Levinas has been influential for the last seventy years. Already in the 1930s, he was "one of the first to introduce Husserl's work into what by now can properly be called the French phenomenological school" (Wyschogrod 1974: viii). The young Jean-Paul Sartre read Levinas's work on phenomenology and as a result (according to Simone de Beauvoir) reoriented his own philosophy along the lines that mark his distinct contribution. Another famous figure, the brilliant and provocative literary critic Jacques Derrida, has been responsible for stimulating the interest of American readers in Levinas. As a result, Levinas's obscurity has begun to be dispelled in the United States. Around 1993 Levinas's reputation began to spread rapidly and widely. His books, some written in the 1960s and available in English since the 1970s, suddenly began to go out of print and back into print in quick succession, a sure sign of a growing number of avid readers. Thus, writing in 2000, Wyschogrod observes that interest in Levinas has grown exponentially. "It goes without saying that Levinas's thought has influenced discussion in ethics and the philosophy of religion. His vision of alterity, of responsibility for the Other, has also spilled over into literary and cultural analysis, political philosophy, and social thought.... To risk a cliché, Levinas would seem to be a philosopher for the next century" (2000: ix).

Because Levinas's major work has been as a philosopher, his impact on biblical studies has been thus far limited, at least in this country. His concerns and categories, however, have influenced how one reads texts in general and, like Buber's and Rosenzweig's hermeneutics, also have impact on reading the Bible. I will describe some of Levinas's contributions to the ways we might think about the world, each other, and the Bible and suggest some specific, distinct understandings of biblical texts that flow from his work.

This introduction aims to familiarize the uninitiated reader with some of Levinas's central ideas. The first part surveys some of his key works and ideas (with an eye to their impact on our understanding of the Bible). The second part offers a few reflections on consequences for interpreting the Bible that Levinas himself does not propose.

The volume as a whole represents a conversation with the work of Levinas. The essays that follow include a sample of Levinas's own work, essays that expound his thought and explore the implications (Aronowicz and Hennessy), essays that apply his insights to biblical texts (Beal, Bongmba, Havea, Linafelt, and Srajek), and essays that wrestle with his interpretation, especially regarding gender issues (Eskenazi and Shapiro). The volume concludes with a response to some of these essays (Chalier).

1

Levinas was born in Lithuania in 1905, studied with Husserl and Heidegger in Freiburg (1928–1929), and earned his doctorate as a phenomenologist. His work gained influence early in Europe, especially in France. As one interpreter points out, Levinas's status as "one of the leading philosophers in France was confirmed with the publication of *Totality and Infinity* (*Totalité et infini*) in 1961" (Davis: 1). Initially Levinas served as the Director of a Jewish school, Ecole Normale Israélite Orientale. In his mid-1950s he received his first university appointment, and in 1973, after years at the universities at Poitiers and Nanterre, he was appointed Professor of Philosophy at the Sorbonne. Levinas died in 1995, mourned by a new generation of thinkers many of whom he himself trained and others whom he shaped from afar. For a moving, personal testimony to his legacy, see Derrida's *Adieu to Emmanuel Levinas* (1999).

The very titles of Levinas's books disclose already his persistent concerns:

Time and the Other both honors and subverts Heidegger's *Being and Time* and the Kantian emphasis on time and space. The book explores the nature of human existence in terms of relation with the Other. In contrast to Hegel, Levinas insists on the irreducibility of the Other (1987c; orig. 1947).

Totality and Infinity (here abbreviated *TI*) opposes what Levinas sees as the dangerous drive to unity, unification that leads to the closed, inevitably destructive, system of totality that has characterized Western philosophy and ultimately expressed itself in the Holocaust (1969; orig. 1961).

Otherwise Than Being or Beyond Essence also takes up the Heideggerian project of *Being and Time* but reorients the subject, the self, the person. It is not Being but being otherwise, directing oneself toward the other, that is the prior reality constituting a self (1981; orig. 1974).

Ethics and Infinity is philosophically Levinas's response to Heidegger, replacing the categories of *Being and Time* with ethics and infinity (1985; orig. 1982).

Difficult Freedom develops the consequences of Levinas's teachings especially in Jewish terms. This, among all the titles I mention, is the only work where the Bible and other Jewish texts explicitly play a role (1976; orig. 1963).

Proper Names captures Levinas's insistence on the particularity of the person, coalesced in facing the other and organized around a proper name (1996b; orig. 1975).[1]

Each work, in title and content, challenges the major assumptions and contributions of Western philosophy, especially in its continental mode. Levinas both appropriates the contributions of philosophers such as Hegel and Heidegger and radically alters them in the name of other, more humane, categories that I would suggest are both explicitly and implicitly biblical.

---

1 The list is partial. Levinas's work in English and French is quite extensive, and the literature about Levinas is voluminous, although only a portion of it appears in English (and mostly since the 1990s). A comprehensive list of Levinas's writings and works about him up to 1989 is available in Burggraeve.

Levinas's most important categories for the purposes of this volume are:

1. Infinity, which he also addresses as eschatology, fecundity, and paternity.

2. Ethics, understood, as we shall see, in biblical terms.

3. A self who is formed through facing the Other by saying "Here I am" (*me voici*), which biblical scholars can recognize as the *hinneni*.

4. The Other.

5. The face.

Levinas's "to be," as facing the Other, invokes key revelatory moments in the Bible, such as Sinai or Jacob's transformative wrestling in Gen 32, but is concretized, for Levinas, in the "orphan, the widow, and the stranger." Yet when Levinas speaks that way he does not claim that he is interpreting the world in biblical categories. He uses this terminology when interpreting the world as a philosopher. His conversation partners are Heidegger, Husserl, Buber, Hegel, Kant, Marx, Sartre and Derrida—not Barth, Bultmann, Niebuhr, or von Rad. But, of course, biblical scholars recognize the vocabulary and the implicit references. It is exhilarating to see this biblical "vocabulary" (i.e., frames of reference) and basic ideas applied to an interpretation of reality that extends beyond the confines of specifically biblical or even religious discourse.

Levinas's claims are based not on the authority of the biblical texts (he has at most three references to the Bible in *Totality and Infinity*; Gibbs: 261 n. 6) but on an analysis of phenomena rooted in the most sophisticated approach to metaphysics.[2] The religious person might not require such confirmation of biblical claims from philosophy, but the scholar and the secularist, within us and in the wider community, have been provided thereby with another access to the meanings of these texts.

As biblical scholars, then, we might rejoice when we see key biblical ideas "infiltrate" and influence other disciplines with a seriousness that may in fact be eroding within scholarly biblical studies. Even if this were

---

2 This is not to say that Levinas does not use the Bible in his other writings His writing on Jewish texts and his hermeneutics are deeply intertwined with the Bible. See, e.g., *Difficult Freedom*.

all that Levinas accomplished, we would or should be content and say, as Jews say during Passover: *daynu*, "it is sufficient for us." But there is much more in Levinas for biblical scholars.

Levinas highlights aspects of the Bible and transforms our understanding of them. He makes us see the face anew. He exposes the larger and deeper meanings of those key passages where *panim el panim* ("face to face") occurs, or *hinneni* ("Here I am"), or the fecundity of the injunction to be fruitful and multiply in, for example, Gen 1. He grapples with the corporeality and concreteness of the human life in tension with universal claims, as Jacob wrestles with his mysterious adversary in Gen 32 (see esp. Aronowicz: xxx). By doing so, Levinas places this struggle in the context of the entire Western philosophical tradition. Most of all he places ethics as the first philosophy and interprets ethics in a distinctly biblical way, as the obligation to the one who commands me, the Other whom I face. He thereby replaces autonomy by heteronomy.

Levinas's ideas implant biblical categories not merely in modern philosophy but, more intriguingly, in postmodern philosophy, where one would have least expected it and where its impact may be all the more dramatic. Some of this may be a direct result of the fact that the Holocaust irrevocably stands before Levinas's mind's eye. In many ways his writings respond to the probing questions that haunt us since the Holocaust.

Totality and Infinity, written in 1961, contains many of Levinas's key ideas. The title (like his other titles) is emblematic of his entire philosophy. It criticizes Western imperialist thought that posits and thereby creates a totalizing system of reality. Living through the Holocaust and having been directly shaped by it, personally and philosophically, Levinas is keenly aware of the relation between philosophy and politics and the consequences of certain philosophical systems. He is troubled especially by the quest for totality, so prevalent in Western thought, leading as it did, inevitably, to totalitarianism. He saw already in 1934 the dreaded consequences for such a philosophy and wrote about it then. But it took World War II and the Holocaust, as well as other forms of imperialism over the third world, to expose the consequences fully.

In opposition to totality, Levinas posits infinity. As Levinas develops it, "infinity" is neither endless time nor simply an inexhaustible future. As we shall see, it has specific biblical roots and applications and charts a discontinuous path into the future.[3] (I will say more about infinity shortly.)

---

3 Infinity honors *time* as the juncture where one's being becomes meaningful. The biblical scholar, of course, immediately recalls that the demarcation of time plays a central role in the biblical version of reality, starting with Gen 1. Indeed, such focus on temporality is often

Underlying Levinas's analysis is the question of what is real and what this implies about being human, a question no less urgent today. *Totality and Infinity* begins as follows: "Everyone will readily agree that it is of the highest importance to know whether we are not duped by morality" (21). Levinas observes that war suspends morality, makes mockery of it. "War is not only one of the ordeals—the greatest—of which morality lives; it renders morality derisory" (ibid.). In war "the trial by force is the test of the real." Violence not only annihilates or injures but makes "people play roles in which they no longer recognize themselves, making them betray not only commitments but their own substance, making them carry out actions that will destroy every possibility of action.... The visage of being that shows itself in war is fixed in the concept of totality, which dominates Western philosophy" (ibid.).

According to Levinas, "the twentieth century teaches ... that hunger and fear can prevail over every human resistance and every freedom! There is no question of doubting this human misery.... But to be a [hu]man is to know that this is so. Freedom consists in knowing that freedom is in peril. But to know or to be conscious is to have time to avoid and forestall the instant of inhumanity. It is this perpetual postponing of the hour of treason ... that implies the disinterestedness of goodness, the desire of the absolutely other" (*TI:* 35).

It is, then, the "how" and "why" of our becoming human—in light of all the horror that has been disclosed—that occupies Levinas's work.

Totality dehumanizes by erasing the particular. In totality, Levinas maintains, "The meaning of individuals ... is derived from the totality. The unicity of each present is incessantly sacrificed to a future appealed to to bring forth its objective meaning. For the ultimate meaning alone counts; the last act alone changes beings into themselves" (*TI:* 22). The concept of "Totality" is not only destructive, says Levinas, but also false. It fails to account for that surplus and forever reduces it (ibid.). It is contradicted by the reality of infinity or eschatology (sometimes he calls it "prophetic eschatology").

"Eschatology," Levinas says, "institutes a relation with being *beyond the totality* or beyond history.... It is a relationship with a surplus" (*TI:* 22, Levinas's emphasis). This surplus, plenitude, draws being into a future. It is also a calling forth to full responsibility. Levinas's eschatology thus does not diminish the meaningfulness of the present tense and the

---

used to differentiate the Hebrew Bible from the other ancient Near Eastern creation traditions. Infinity, along with fecundity and paternity and Levinas's notion of plentitude, enable him to describe transcendence in a way that is new but, I think, also articulates certain biblical views of transcendence.

meaningfulness of the person; it does not subsume them to some master narrative. His notion of eschatology, in contrast to Hegel's (who saw rationalization in the judgment of history), "implies that beings have an identity 'before' eternity, before the accomplishment of history, before the fullness of time, while there is still time; implies that beings exist in relationship, to be sure, but on the basis of themselves and not on the basis of totality" (23). They can "speak rather than lending their lips to an anonymous utterance of history" (ibid.).

Infinity is not some vague, subjective idea but a reality "more objective than objectivity" (*TI*: 26). *Totality and Infinity*, says Levinas, is a "defense of subjectivity, but it will apprehend the subjectivity not at the level of its purely egoist protestation against totality, nor in its anguish before death, but as founded in the idea of infinity" (ibid.).

For Levinas, infinity is not construed as something without limits, endless. On the contrary, it is precisely about boundaries and the crossing of boundaries. Infinity is produced by bound and bonded persons. The "I" contains "in itself what it can neither contain nor receive solely by virtue of its own identity. Subjectivity realizes these impossible exigencies—the astonishing feat of containing more than it is possible to contain. This book will present subjectivity as welcoming the Other, as hospitality" (*TI*: 27). Infinity is produced in the relationship of the same with the other (26). It does not preexist.

As he develops them, Levinas's ideas expose and express, concretely and precisely, biblical notions of person and history, not to mention the role of God. He calls "metaphysics" that which is "turned toward the 'elsewhere' and the 'otherwise' and the 'other'" (*TI*: 33), thereby summing up in three words key aspects of the Hebrew Bible:

1. The "elsewhere" can describe the Hebrew Bible's predominant shape as striving to reach elsewhere—the promised land, which is but a hope both at the end of the Torah and at the end of the entire Hebrew canon (see 2 Chr 36:22–23);

2. The "otherwise" appears as the prophetic critique and its messianic aspirations;

3. The "other" leads to the otherness of God and fellow humans who must be encountered in the face-to-face meeting.[4]

---

4 It is hard to avoid reading the opening lines of *Totality and Infinity* as a philosophical retelling of the Abrahamic tradition: "The metaphysical desire does not long to return, for it is desire for a land not of our birth, but for a land foreign to every nature, which has not been our fatherland and to which we shall never betake ourselves" (*TI*: 35).

The notion of the Other is central to Levinas.[5] "The dimension of the divine opens forth from the human face.... The proximity of the Other, the proximity of the neighbor, is in being an ineluctable moment of the revelation of an absolute presence ... which expresses itself. His very epiphany consists in soliciting us by his destitution of the face of the Stranger [sic], the widow, and the orphan" (TI: 78).

"God arises to his supreme and ultimate presence as a correlative to the justice rendered unto men. The direct comprehension of God is impossible" (TI: 78). For Levinas, "There can be no 'knowledge' of God separated from the relationship with men. The Other is the very locus of metaphysical truth, and is indispensable for my relation with God. He [the Other] does not play the role of a mediator. The other is not the incarnation of God, but precisely by his face ... is the manifestation of the height in which God is revealed" (78–79).[6]

Otherness and Infinity resist totality. "Infinity does not permit itself to be integrated. It is not the insufficiency of the I that prevents totalization, but the Infinity of the Other" (TI: 80).[7] "[I]nevitably across my idea of the Infinite the other faces me—hostile, friend, my master, my student.... The face to face remains an ultimate situation" (81).

Levinas understands "Infinity" or transcendence (as he defines transcendence) also as fecundity or paternity (and in *Otherwise Than Being* he also speaks of maternity). In fecundity, "Being is produced as multiple and as split into same and other; this is its ultimate structure" (TI: 269). "In the I [through encounter with the feminine Other] being can be produced as infinitely recommencing, that is, properly speaking, as infinite" (272). "Fecundity evinces a unity that is not opposed to multiplicity, but, in the precise sense of the term, engenders it" (273).

---

5 "To recognize the Other is therefore to come to him across the world of possessed things, but at the same time to establish, by gift, community and universality" (TI: 76). "Things are not, as in Heidegger, the foundation of the site, the quintessence of all the relations that constitute our presence on the earth (and 'under the heavens, in the company of men, and in the expectation of the gods'). The relationship between the same and the other, my welcoming of the other, is the ultimate fact, and in it the things figure not as what one builds but as what one gives" (76–77). "Revelation is discourse; in order to welcome revelation a being apt for this role of interlocutor, a separated being, is required.... To hear the divine word does not amount to knowing an object; it is to be in relation with a substance overflowing its own idea in me" (77).

6 "It is from moral relationships that every metaphysical affirmation takes on a 'spiritual' meaning" (TI: 79).

7 "Totality and the embrace of being, or ontology, do not contain the final secret of being. Religion, where relationship subsists between the same and the other despite the impossibility of the Whole—the idea of Infinity—is the ultimate structure. It expresses the inevitability of the Other" (TI: 80).

In contrast to the typical Western notion of transcendence, rooted in a unitary sense of self that essentially seeks to expand, to connect itself to the other and to the future, trying to escape finitude, Levinas accepts and even celebrates finitude. Through fecundity, "the subject enters into relation with what is absolutely other ... with what remains other in the relation and is never converted into 'mine'" (*TI:* 276). Likewise in paternity, "The son is not only my work, like a poem or an object, nor is he my property. Neither the categories of power nor those of knowledge describe my relation with the child. The fecundity of the I is neither a cause nor a domination. I do not have my child.... Paternity is a relation with a stranger who while being Other *is* me, a relation of the I with a self which yet is not me" (277).[8]

Yet, whereas most discussion of notions such as paternity revel in the continuity that it establishes, and the ways procreation ensures my participation in the future, Levinas values paternity (or fecundity) primarily because of discontinuity, for its production of an Other, for the new beginning that opens up possibilities.

As Handelman points out, for Levinas, "eschatology is the time of the other, and depends on the gratuitous work of the self toward the other" (204). "Paternity, then, is a mode of triumph over fate and age through the very discontinuity of the child. For the child also breaks with the parent, allows a recommencement that changes the past; in fecundity, time brings something new" (206). There must be both a "rupture of continuity and continuation across this rupture" (*TI:* 284). "Levinas finds in fecundity as the discontinuous time-of-the-other a positive relation to the infinity of the future"; he finds "something that enables a *nonnostalgic*, nonfated, nonmythical relation to the past" (Handelman: 206–7). "Fecundity is a recommencement that has the potential to bring pardon, healing, correction of the past. Unlike forgetting, which nullifies the past, pardon acts upon the past, repeats and purifies, but conserves the event in the present" (Handelman: 207; see *TI:* 283).

THE FACE

Although very few explicit biblical references appear in *Totality and Infinity*, one could read Levinas's chapters on the face as an extensive

---

8 In parentheses, Levinas adds: "And you shall say to yourself, 'who can have borne me these? I was bereaved and barren' (Isaiah 49)." The prophet in the book of Isaiah puts these words in the mouth of a female persona. It is ironic that Levinas uses this as a reference for "paternity," not "maternity." See my essay "Love Your Neighbor As an Other" in this volume.

exegesis on Gen 33, a meditation on Jacob's words to Esau, "to see your face is like seeing the face of God" (Gen 33:10 JPS). For Levinas, "The facing position, opposition par excellence, can be only as a moral summons. This movement proceeds from the other. The idea of infinity, the infinitely more contained in the less, is concretely produced in the form of a relation with the face" (*TI*: 196).[9]

Then again, his chapters on "the face" equally qualify as an exegesis on "you shall not commit murder," the biblical verse that recurs in *Totality and Infinity* (e.g., 199, 262):

> This infinity, stronger than murder, already resists us in his face, is his face, is the primordial *expression*, is the first word: "You shall not commit murder." The infinite ... gleams in the face of the Other, in the total nudity of his defenceless eyes, in the nudity of the absolute openness of the Transcendent. There is here a relation ... with something absolutely *other*: ... The epiphany of the face is ethical.... Infinity presents itself as a face in the ethical resistance that paralyses my powers and from the depth of defenceless eyes rises firm and absolute in its nudity and destitution. The comprehension of this destitution and this hunger establishes the very proximity of the other. (*TI*: 199–200)

The being that expresses itself imposes itself. However, "the being that imposes itself does not limit but promotes my freedom, by arousing my goodness.... It is thus the irremissible weight of being that gives rise to my freedom" (*TI*: 200). The commanding face of the Other founds my freedom in responsibility (203): "the face opens the primordial discourse whose first word is obligation" (201). "The Other who dominates in his transcendence is thus the stranger, the widow, and the orphan, to whom I am obligated" (215).

Levinas, as a phenomenologist, attempts to describe reality without reverting to Hegel's and Heidegger's legacy of dehumanization. It is his gift to biblical scholars that the categories he employs often reflect and refract biblical teachings. He shows, thereby, how we can draw from such teachings insights for resisting the legacy of dehumanization. His formulations articulate possibilities for interpreting the Bible in ways that are simultaneously religious, "spiritual," ethical, and nondogmatically philosophical. He grounds his ethics in the transformative face-to-face encounter, not in the prior authority of the text or doctrine. In the face-to-face encounter "resides the rational character of the ethical relation and of

---

9 "And the idea of infinity alone maintains the exteriority of the other with respect to the same, despite this relation.... The idea of infinity exceeds my powers (not quantitatively, but, we will see later, by calling them into question)" (*TI*: 196).

language. No fear, no trembling could alter the straightforwardness of this relationship, which preserves the discontinuity of relationship, resists fusion" (*TI*: 202–3).[10]

As Robert Gibbs observes,

> Levinas' phenomenology climaxes in the moment I am face to face with another person. The face is the experience that lies at the root of ethics for Levinas.... My obligation to be for the other rests in his human face, not as a cluster of nose and eyes, etc., but as announcement of my responsibility for him, my duties. The separation between the other and myself is an inassimilable difference proclaimed in the other's face. I cannot make him mine, nor reduce him to my cognition of him. (Gibbs: 165).[11]

"The face is prior to every question about the 'what' of things, the 'what is it?' The face refers to the question 'who is it?'" (Handelman: 209; see *TI*: 177). "The face is the very 'interface' of self and world. One sees and is seen" (Handelman: 210).[12]

Gibbs paraphrases Levinas's position this way:

> I am in my body in such a way that I am not merely a member of a species, but experience all my life firsthand. My work with the world is one of assimilation, and my desire for something objective is constantly thwarted as I find that everything I touch I make mine. ...
>
> And then some person meets me. This other commands me with her face. For the vulnerability of the other prohibits me from murder, and along with this command comes the astonishment that I cannot comprehend the other. I may not kill, and I cannot assimilate, the other.... The isolated self has been interrupted by an other, by the intentionality of someone else, and so the self is extroverted.
>
> ... And so I find myself not the center, the ruler, of my life, but accused. Levinas puns that this is an indeclinable accusative, because the "me" that is bound to this other cannot shake the responsibility. (181–82)

---

10 "[T]he face in which the other—the absolutely other—presents himself does not negate the same, does not do violence to it as do opinion or authority or the thaumaturgic supernatural ... it remains terrestrial. This presentation is preeminently nonviolence, for instead of offending my freedom it calls it to responsibility and founds it" (*TI*: 203).

11 As Handelman observes, "The 'welcome of the face' is distinguished from Heideggerian 'disclosure' or bringing to light. Levinas wants to insist upon a relation between the same and other that is not reducible to *knowledge* of other by the same, or even revelation of the other to the same" (209, referring to *TI*: 28).

12 "[T]he face is the ethical inversion of the Hegelian gaze—the very gaze of philosophy itself. For the presence before a face, my orientation toward the Other, can lose the avidity proper to the gaze only by turning into generosity, incapable of approaching the other with empty hands. (TI: 50)" (Handelman: 211).

Other statements further elucidate Levinas's position: "I am I because I am responsible for others" (Gibbs: 184). "I become myself through the other.... For Levinas there is no gap between the encounter with the other and the self-sanctification before God: the two moments are entwined in the experience of the face of the other" (187).

As Gibbs further notes, Levinas has constructed a decentered self, a notion of special interest in postmodern discourse where the very possibility of ethics for a decentered self has been in question. Levinas shows not only that ethics is possible for a decentered self but that ethics constitutes the very self capable of responding in a postmodern world.[13]

> It is ironic that, long before the current hubbub called postmodernism, the de-centered self was already discovered—and in an explicitly ethical context. Dialogical philosophers found that interpersonal ethics was the foundation of the self, or rather, that the subject was not its own foundation, but dependent upon others in order to be itself. And perhaps less ironic, the theme of that interpersonal self, that de-centered self, is directly correlate with traditional religious concepts. The antireligious agenda of postmodernism is not a necessary conclusion from the decentered self. (Gibbs: 193)

For Levinas, this decentered self is the heteronomous self, the one who says "Here I am" to the Other, the one whose motto is *"hinneni."*

2

Levinas's passionate moral voice is also preeminently a biblical voice. In his philosophical writings Levinas reclaims biblical teachings, such as the I who says *hinneni*, for philosophy and for the wider culture. He also reassesses other teachings such as eschatology and fecundity to release meanings hitherto overlooked in biblical studies. Let me turn, then, to some ramifications of his views for reading the Bible. There are many ways to go. One could review some of Levinas's own biblical reflections on revelation, covenant, or messianism, for example. But since Levinas develops these ideas explicitly in works such as *Difficult Freedom* and *Nine Talmudic Readings,* I will examine instead some implications that he himself does not address directly.

---

13 "The logic of uniqueness displaces the focus of our thought from the self to the other. But responsibility requires a self who retains at least the capacity to respond. In the currents of postmodernism, the modern philosophical subject seems adrift, if not already drowned and vanished. Can any sense still be made of the concept of responsibility without such a subject? Can ethics survive the fracturing, de-centering, deconstructing of the self?" (Gibbs: 193).

As Handelman notes, Levinas uses the

> images of exile and desert to explain his paradoxical concept of "het-eronomous experience"—experience of the absolutely other. There are, he maintains, "movements" and "attitudes" toward the other that cannot be converted into a category and a return to self; these are found in modes of goodness and work that are one-directional offerings with-out expectation of reciprocal return. One of his favored illustrations is the biblical Abraham's departure from his homeland of Ur contrasted to Ulysses' ultimate return home to Ithaca. As "one-directional action," such movements require a temporality and a patience which ultimately mean "to renounce being contemporary of his accomplishments, to work without entering the promised land." Work so oriented toward the other is work oriented toward the future, a work for "being beyond my death." This "being-*beyond*-death" is meant, of course, to challenge Hei-degger's idea of "being-*toward*-death." For Levinas, the triumph will come in a "time without me," a time beyond my horizon of my time which is "eschatology without hope for self or liberation from my own time." (Handelman: 203–4, referring to Levinas 1966: 36)

This, for Levinas, is Abraham. "Ulysses, on the other hand, 'returns home' and symbolizes for Levinas the course of Western philosophy—the iden-tity, sameness, and egoism which is ultimately protected, not exiled, called outside, broken up" (Handelman: 265); Abraham is preeminently that het-eronomous self who says "Here I am" to the other.

Levinas replaces Descartes's "I think therefore I am" (which founds modern philosophy) by the "biblical 'here I am' of subjectivity and ethics" (Handelman: 266).[14] "*Hineni*, is the I possessed by the other" (ibid.).[15] "Here I am," as Levinas develops it, is, of course, the *hinneni* of biblical narrative, most noted in passages such as the binding of Isaac (Gen 22:1, 7, 11) and the response of Moses to God (Exod 3:4). For Lev-inas—and also for the Bible—it is also related to what he calls eschatology, eschatology *as the time of the other*, the one who is not me.

Let me augment his example by extending it in ways Levinas himself does not explore but that are nonetheless consistent with his interpretation.

---

14 As Handelman puts it, Levinas's "description of the subject in *OTB* [*Otherwise Than Being*] culminates in the French expression *me voici:* 'The word I means here I am [me voici] answering for everything and everyone' (*OTB:* 114).... Those familiar with the Hebrew Bible recognize these words as the oft-repeated Hebrew phrase *hineni*" (Handelman: 265–66).

15 Drawing upon the Song of Songs, Levinas redefines love and philosophy "The 'here I am' is another kind of love that would be the most profound level of the ethical as first phi-losophy: 'Philosophy is wisdom of love at the service of love'" (Handelman: 266, quoting Levinas 1981: 161).

The eschatology that Levinas describes not only characterizes the Abraham narrative or messianic passages in the prophets but in fact shapes the entire Hebrew Bible. The story of Moses and Israel makes the same central point. The entire Torah, that is, Pentateuch, replays this notion of eschatology. Moses' efforts from the start are efforts on behalf of the other, climaxing with his lifelong commitment to a future he will not see, a future in which he, Moses himself or his own biological descendants, will have no promised role (in contrast to Abraham, whose own children are the heart of the promise, or even Aaron, whose descendants receive eternal priesthood).

With Deut 34, the Torah ends on the brink of fulfillment to underscore this point. Likewise, the shape of the Hebrew Bible as a whole reiterates this emphasis on the future, on what is to come, resisting totality, reproducing instead Levinas's infinity, that is, the birth of a new possibility and the reproduction of responsibility. The Hebrew Bible, now canonized in the Jewish tradition as the Tanak (Torah, Nevi'im, Ketuvim; or Torah, Prophets, Writings), thus ends in mid-sentence that opens to a future. The book of Chronicles reproduces a segment of Cyrus's decree. In Ezra-Nehemiah, which precedes Chronicles in the Hebrew Bible, the decree is given in full, as it were (Ezra 1:1–4). The edict commissions the people to build the house of God in Jerusalem. In Ezra-Nehemiah, the edict is followed by detailed descriptions of how the people in fact accomplished all that. But 2 Chronicles only includes the commissioning, and only a portion of it (2 Chr 36:22). As a result, the Hebrew Bible ends in mid-sentence that states, "Let him go up." This exhortation invites the people addressed—the Bible's early audiences and contemporary readers as well—to embark on a journey, to rebuild anew what has been destroyed.

Levinas's notion of infinity offers also a key for understanding some puzzling features of biblical genealogies. Obviously "infinity" as fecundity, paternity, or maternity is inscribed in the biblical story already in chapter 1 of Genesis, as the first commandment, "be fruitful and multiply" (Gen 1:28). This theme pervades the book of Genesis and launches (by way of fulfillment) the book of Exodus (Exod 1:7). But biblical genealogies, *toledot*, have been an irritant to literary critics. They do not culminate as we would wish; they defy tidy ordering. They disrupt. They refuse to lead to closure. Some seemingly lead nowhere—elsewhere.

Levinas helps us understand new things about such genealogies, an addition to all that historians and now anthropologists have been able to say about them. He enables us to see that such genealogies defy finality and in this very movement disclose their meanings: they inscribe Levinas's infinity into the biblical texts. They open up, in a seemingly unsystematic way, the future. They lead not to anywhere specific but to an uncharted future of the Other. In Genesis, this move is doubly an affirmation of the

Other, the one who is not me, not a member of the community reading this book; in the genealogies of Esau, for example (note the 30 verses devoted to Esau's line in Gen 36).

The entire Hebrew Bible is in fact framed by such an infinity, from the several distinct *toledot*, genealogies that structure Genesis (see, e.g., the book of *toledot*, i.e.,"genealogies," in Gen 5:1–32), to the nine chapters of genealogies that open the final book in the Jewish canon, namely, Chronicles (1 Chr 1–9). Moreover, Levinas's emphasis on the particular, on proper names, remembered, rehearsed, and thus reclaimed, further illuminates the significance of such genealogies with their repetition of names even when no stories are attached.

Levinas's notion of infinity also helps explain another feature of biblical narrative: the resistance of biblical narrative to closure, to ring composition. It is common to seek chiastic patterns and other symmetries in biblical narrative. It is my view that such constructs are usually forced and unconvincing. The major convincing example of chiasm or ring composition, Gen 11:1–9 as Fokkelman reads it (11–45), is among the exceptions that prove the rule. Biblical narrative more typically moves toward infinity, not totality. Genesis 11:1–9 utilizes a structure of totality to break totality open, to move from the one to the many, in both space and time: space in the story of the Tower of Babel itself, and time in the lengthy genealogies that frame it (Gen 10:1–32 and 11:10–32).

Let me conclude with comments about "the face." When one reads Levinas's eloquent explication of the meaning of the face, it dramatically and inescapably colors how one then faces the Bible as a whole. Levinas has charged the already powerful face-to-face encounters in the Bible with new vitality and intense force.

Levinas's word, *visage*, face, of course translates the Hebrew *panim*. As biblical scholars we are already aware of the drama and power of the references to the face in the face-to-face of key biblical moments: in Jacob's struggle with the mysterious man on the River of Jabbok (Gen 32); in Moses, asking to see God face to face (Exod 34); in Deuteronomy's recollection that God addressed all Israel face to face (*panim befanim*) at Sinai (Deut 5:4); or in the announcement that the face-to-face encounter with God was reserved for Moses alone (Deut 34:10); the face is also decisive in the so called Levitical blessings (Num 6:26–27) and in the laments and protests about God's hiding the face (e.g., Job 12:24; Ps 27:8–9).

Undoubtedly this is the highest form of encounter. For Levinas, this meaning must be extended and recognized in the meeting with the human Other, with the orphan, the widow, the stranger who confront us with the nakedness of their face. But there is more to perceive. The face is more present, far more demanding in its calling us forth in the Hebrew Bible. The Hebrew *panim* offers meanings not contained in the French.

Note, for example, that the Hebrew word "within," *pnim or pnima,* likewise comes from the same root, *pnh,* linking the innermost part with the face—a connection that Levinas makes on phenomenological grounds but without connecting it to a fundamental Hebrew or biblical terminology.

But the meaning that Levinas bestows on the face can be linked further in the Hebrew Bible, this time with the preposition "before," *lifne* in Hebrew. This word also comes from the root *pnh* that forms "the face" (*panim*). Thus, this familiar preposition (as Gibbs already observed) literally means "to the face" or "before." "The significance of standing in front of someone (before the other's face) has a particular resonance in Hebrew and in the Bible. It is the set of related meanings of the preposition (before) and the noun (face) that Levinas 'translates' in the concept of the face" (Gibbs: 165).

The preposition "before" is small, frequent, often mundane. Yet, when we listen to Levinas, it also always charged with the full force of that encounter that makes us human. Every "before" becomes a possible facing. When one pays attention to the literal possibilities embedded in the Hebrew underlying "before" but obscured in the English, this pervasive proposition regains its force. Interestingly, English, not French, also lends itself to communicating the full force of Levinas's meanings of the face as reflected in biblical Hebrew. Let us consider the English word "before," which we use to translate *lifne.* When we consider it as a compound word of "be" and "for," namely, being *for* someone, that is, "be-for," Levinas's insight comes through and permeates the text—and life. It is, then, as this ordinary preposition, *lifne,* before, that Levinas's face reaches us from every page of the Bible and, potentially, at most moments of our life.[*]

---

[*] This paper was originally delivered as a Presidential Address at the annual meeting of the Pacific Coast Region-Society of Biblical Literature, on March 14, 1994. At that time I dedicated it to my husband David Eskenazi, who so fully embodied Levinas's teaching, devoting his life to facing the Other in small and large ways, lovingly and generously. David's death in 1996 is a great loss. I rededicate the paper to him with love and with gratitude for all that he exemplified in deeds, not merely in words.

ON THE JEWISH READING OF SCRIPTURES

Emmanuel Levinas

It is not a question here of drawing up an inventory of the figures of Jewish hermeneutics of the Bible. This would require a vast amount of research, taking into account the diversity of epochs and tendencies. It would also mean determining the credibility of the interpreters measured less by any consensus than by the intelligence of each person and his familiarity with tradition. R. Ishmael's often-quoted "Thirteen figures of the interpretation of the Torah," or the famous four levels of reading: *peshat* (plain meaning), *remez* (allusive meaning), *derash* (solicited meaning), *sod* (secret meaning), whose vocalized acronym gives the word *pardes* (orchard), call in their turn for exegesis, and constitute only aspects of rabbinism in its relation to the text. Only the modern formulation of this relation, which has yet to be done, might put an end to the improper teachings where traditional sources are quoted as if, beneath the Hebrew letters that conceal them, they all derived from the same depth.

Our more modest intention is to illustrate, by examples, certain ways of reading. We shall do this by presenting a Talmudic extract which produces, in the form of arguments, the exegesis of biblical verses. Nevertheless, in doing this we shall find ourselves being led to some propositions of a more general character, for the chosen extract, in its final section, concerns precisely the scope of exegesis. Exegesis of the exegesis, a privileged text, even if it does not exclude different insights into the same subject. This is in keeping with the characteristic pluralism of rabbinical thought, which paradoxically aspires to be compatible with the unity of the Revelation: the multiple stances of the scholars would constitute its very life, all of them being the "words of the living God."

The Talmudic passage that we shall comment upon will also introduce us in particular to the meaning that, for Jewish religious consciousness, commentary of the Scriptures can take on as the path towards transcendence. It is, perhaps, essential to the actual creation of this notion.

But a Talmudic text that comments on verses requires an interpretation in its turn. What it intends to do is not immediately apparent in terms which, for an inexperienced reader, may seem unusual, and which in fact allow for several levels and dimensions. Hence a third stage in the final section of our commentary: an interpretation of the Talmudic exegesis of the exegesis. This reading of the Talmud would not be possible for us without recourse to a modern language—in other words, without touching on the problems of today. Admittedly, it too is not the only possible reading, but it has the value of a testimony. It testifies to at least one of the ways in which contemporary Jews understand traditional Jewish hermeneutics, and above all to the way in which they understand it when they ask it for food for thought and teachings on the content.

Preliminary Remarks

The text we shall comment upon is taken from one of the last pages of the Tractate Makkoth in the Babylonian Talmud. This short Tractate of about fifty pages deals with judicial punishments of which one, in reference to Deuteronomy 25:2–3, is flogging (*makkoth* = blows). The passage dealing with the exegesis of page 23b has as its immediate context a theologico-legal discussion: is it possible, through the penalty of flogging, inflicted by a human tribunal, to make atonement for the punishment known as being "cut off from among their people," decided, according to the Talmud, by the "celestial tribunal"? Being "cut off from among their people," the most serious theological punishment, means being excluded from the "world to come," which designates the eschatological order in its ultimate terms, whereas the "Messianic epoch," still belonging to History, constitutes a penultimate stage of the "end of times." How can a human decision—in the case of flogging atoning for being "cut off"—intervene in a domain which exceeds man? How can it be guaranteed to be in keeping with the divine will? These questions imply transcendence and a relation which passes through this absolute distance. They touch on the problem of the possibility of such a relation, which also arises in the exegesis examining divine thought.

Before tackling the text, it would be useful to make some general remarks which, for a reader coming from outside, are called for by the particular or outdated nature of being flogged or cut off. This whole evocation of "blows," of the transgression and guilt it presupposes, may wound our liberal souls; just as the reference to a "celestial tribunal" may go against our modern minds by the dated or questionable "vision of the world" which it implies.

But in order to move towards a meaning which is retained despite an apparently antiquated language, it is necessary first of all to accept patiently—as one accepts the conventions of a fable or a stage setting—

the particulars of the text in their specific universe. It is necessary to wait for them to set themselves in motion and free themselves from the anachronisms and local colour on which the curtain rises. In no way must this "exotic" or "outmoded" language stop thought by its picturesque elements, or by the immediate meaning of the things and deeds it names. This will change. Often from apparently incongruous or insignificant questions. Without fading before their concepts, things denoted in a concrete fashion are yet enriched with meanings by the multiplicity of their concrete aspects. This is what we call the paradigmatic modality of Talmudic reflection: notions remain constantly in contact with the examples or refer back to them, whereas they should have been content as springboards to rise to the level of generalization, or they clarify the thought which scrutinizes by the secret light of hidden or isolated worlds from which it bursts forth; and simultaneously this world inserted or lost in signs is illuminated by the thought which comes to it from outside or from the other end of the canon, revealing its possibilities which were awaiting the exegesis, immobilized, in some way, in the letters.

The Tribunal and the Love of One's Neighbour

Let us come back now to the principal points of a discussion on flogging, being "cut off from among their people," and the punishments of the human and celestial tribunal. Let us accept these figures of speech and the legal formal nature of the words.

According to R. Hananiah b. Gamaliel, those who are guilty of certain transgressions that the Law of the Pentateuch punishes by cutting them off obtain remission from this damnation if they submit to the flogging imposed by the earthly tribunal. The human tribunal would thus have to be aware of sins which expel human beings from the human (the decision of God's tribunal would measure the seriousness of the sin), and would thereby have to repair the irreparable. Can the tribunal do as much as celestial compassion or mercy? Is mercy shown at the tribunal? Reference is made by R. Hananiah to Deuteronomy 25:3: "Forty stripes may be given him, but not more; lest, if one should go on to beat him with more stripes than these, your brother be degraded in your sight." The word "brother" would be essential here. It is a matter of punishing without degrading: would the tribunal and justice have the secret of the extreme measure of a difference which is a differential? In any case, R. Hananiah breaks with the dark mythological fatality whose eventuality would indicate a religious tyranny, in order to proclaim that no sin exists in relation to Heaven which cannot be expiated among men and in the light of day. The tribunal would thus also be the place where the divine regenerative will is revealed. Admittedly, there is violence. But it is an act without a spirit of violence, contempt or hatred. A fraternal act, without passion. It proceeds from a responsibility for others. To be the guardian of others, contrary to the vision of the world according to Cain, defines fraternity. For the tribunal which reasons and weighs up, the love of one's neighbour would be possible. Justice dispensed by the just becomes compassion—not in uncontrollable indulgence, but through a judgement. God speaks with a compassion that is born in the severity of the tribunal. Excessiveness? It certainly is. But pure indulgence, free forgiveness, is always at the expense of someone innocent who does not receive it. The judge is allowed such indulgence only if he personally assumes the costs.[1] But it is proper for the earthly judge, for man, for the brother of the guilty party, to restore to human fraternity those who have been excluded. To be responsible to the point of being answerable for the other's freedom. This heteronomy among the conditions of autonomy in human fraternity is acutely thought in Judaism with the category of divine paternity as its point of departure. Divine justice arrays itself in fraternity by revealing itself in a human tribunal.[2]

R. Hananiah b. Gamaliel's second argument is an "*a fortiori.*" If the transgression of certain interdicts "cuts off a human being from his people," then all the more reason for his carrying out the Law to return him to them. Now, to suffer the flogging decided on by the tribunal is to obey the Law to which a guilty person is subject. But why "all the more reason"?[3] Because divine compassion is still more certain than its severity. A theme that is present throughout rabbinical thought, and to which R. Hananiah implicitly refers. Is it not written (Exodus 34:7):

---

[1] "In rendering legal judgment, [the judge] used to acquit the guiltless and condemn the guilty; but when he saw that the condemned man was poor, he helped him out of his own purse [to pay the required sum], thus executing judgment and charity..." Tractate Sanhedrin 6b. [*Translator's note:* Levinas indicates that he is quoting from the translation into French by the Great Rabbi Salzer.]

[2] It is against the paganism of the notion of the "Oedipus complex" that it is necessary to think forcefully about apparently purely edifying verses such as that in Deuteronomy 8:5: "Know then in your heart that, as a man disciplines his son, the Lord your God disciplines you." Paternity here signifies a constituent category of what has meaning, not of its alienation. On this point, at least, psychoanalysis testifies to the profound crisis of monotheism in contemporary sensibility, a crisis that cannot be reduced to the refusal of a few dogmatic propositions. It conceals the ultimate secret of anti-Semitism. Amado Lévi-Valerusi has insisted throughout her work on the essentially pagan character of the myth of Oedipus.

[3] [*Translator's note:* The Soncino edition of the Babylonian Talmud renders the *a fortiori* argument as "how much more should one..."]

[The Lord keeps] steadfast love for thousands [of generations], forgiving iniquity and transgression and sin, but who will by no means clear the guilty, visiting the iniquity of the fathers upon the children and the children's children, to the third and the fourth generation...?

And the Rabbis gloss "thousands" as at least two thousand! For at least two thousand generations steadfast love granted to merit is handed down; for four generations iniquity cries out for justice: compassion is thus five hundred times greater than divine severity. Behind this arithmetic of mercy there is moral optimism: the triumph of evil has one time only; nothing is ever lost from the triumph won over evil or from good.

From this point onwards, R. Simeon intervenes with the merit attached to the obedience to the interdicts. An intervention which, above and beyond the theological meaning of the terms, defines a certain conception of human life: "One who desists from transgressing is granted reward like one who performs a precept." The constraint imposed on the spontaneity of life, such as is provided for in the negative commandments of Leviticus 18 (whose sexual interdicts appear as the privileged example of negative commandments), is asserted by R. Simeon as the guarantee of "rewards." The negative commandment is the constraint *par excellence*, restraining the tendencies where life is lived in its spontaneity as an "outgoing force," and in particular the blind abundance of sexual desire. It would be the promise of rewards, if we are to believe R. Simeon. Certainly one can expect from this promise what simple and unquestioning faith expects: longevity, eternal life or earthly happiness—just as one can denounce its spirit of repression which abuses that faith. But as a reward for a life accepting limitations, one can also understand the nature of this very life: the limitation of the wild vitality of life, through which this life wakes from its somnambulant spontaneity, sobers up from its nature and interrupts its centripetal movements, in order to be opened up to what is other than self. A life in which Judaism is recognized, limiting through the Law this wild, animal vitality, accepting this restriction as the best share—that is, as a "reward."[4] The

---

4 Curiously, in the final paragraphs of the pages we are studying in the Tractate Makkoth, the distant noise of unsuppressed and triumphant life, the noise of Rome, is heard. "Long ago, as Rabban Gamaliel b. Eleazar b. 'Azariah, R. Joshua and R. Akiba were walking on the road, they heard the noise of the crowds at Rome (on travelling) from Puteoli, a hundred and twenty miles away. They all fell aweeping, but R. Akiba seemed merry. Said they to him: Wherefore are you merry? Said he to them: Wherefore are you weeping? Said they: These heathens who bow down to images and burn incense to idols live in safety and ease, whereas our Temple, the 'Footstool' of our God, is burnt down by fire, and should we then not weep? He replied: Therefore, am I merry. If they that offend Him fare thus, how much

plenitude of a sense of responsibility and justice is preferred to life intox-
icated with its own essence, to the invasion of the unharnessed appetite
of desire and domination where nothing, not even other people, can
stand in its way.

R. Simeon b. Rabbi deduces the reward reserved for those who do not
transgress the interdicts from the promise made in Deuteronomy 12:23–5 to
the person who refrains from eating blood: if the abstinence consonant with
a natural loathing is rewarded, how much more so is the resistance against
what is desirable! Perhaps the horror of blood here has a meaning which is
not only of a gastronomic nature. Resistance to sexual excesses and to the
taste for plunder is, *a fortiori*, worthy of merit. And yet this is the "true life,"
if we follow the literary writers of the great Metropoles! All this accounting
of merits and rewards has a wider meaning. Life as it is lived, natural life,
begins, perhaps, in naivety, in tendencies and tastes which are still in keeping with a code of ethics; but if it is allowed to run its course unhindered, it
ends in loveless debauchery and plunder established as a social condition,
and in exploitation. The human begins when this apparently innocent but
virtually murderous vitality is brought under control by interdicts. Does not
authentic civilization, however it may be marked by biological failures or
political defeats, consist in holding back the breath of naive life and remain-
ing fully awake in this way, "for generations and generations to come, to the
end of all generations"?[5]

We can now understand R. Hananiah b. 'Akashia's thought which
closes the *Mishnah:* "The Holy One, blessed be He, desired to make Israel
worthy, therefore gave he them the law (to study) and many commandments (to do)"; and "[the Lord made] the law great and glorious" (Isaiah
42:21). This is certainly not to create artificial merits or to put up hurdles
deliberately. It is for the greatness of justice and for his glory that commandments are necessary against a life lived as an "outgoing force."
Even in cases—such as the horror that may be felt in eating or shedding
blood—where nature seems to protect us from evil! There is no natural

---

better shall fare they that do obey Him!" How much more shall we one day be rewarded or
how much better do we who are just fare already, despite our misfortunes? When we are
walking on the road and are tired, whether or not we are Rabban Gamaliel, R. Eleazar b.
'Azariah and R. Joshua, the greatest of the great, the sounds of Rome may for a moment
cause us to question, in our minds and in our nerves, the soundness of the just life. R. Akiba
alone is able to be merry: despite the failures, he is certain of receiving the best share. He is
certain of it not through painful empirical experience, but through an *a fortiori* reasoning that
is not here the guarantee of a promise, but of a value.

5 These are the words with which R. Simeon b. Rabbi closes his intervention in the Talmudic text we are commenting upon: "One who refrains therefrom [shall] acquire merit for
himself and for generations and generations to come, to the end of all generations!"

tendency that is healthy enough not to be able to be inverted. Holiness is necessary for the healthiness of the healthy.[6]

But the greatness of justice evoked by R. Hananiah b. 'Akashia, which is conditioned by a life obeying the many commandments, is also the glory of the tribunal and the judges. To make the law glorious! Only the judges who themselves practise the many commandments can form the glorious council to which God's will aspires. The judge is not just a legal expert of laws; he obeys the Law he administers, and he is trained by this obedience; the study of the Law is itself the essential form of this obedience.[7] Such a situation is necessary in order for earthly punishment to reduce celestial punishment; for it to be rightfully thought, with the Psalmist, that "God has taken his place in the divine council," and that "in the midst of the gods [judges] he holds judgement" (Psalms 82:1). It is necessary in order simply to justify man's judgement passed on man and the punishment inflicted by one on the other—that is to say, the responsibility of one person for the other. This is the strange ontological structure presupposed by this responsibility whereby one person assumes the destiny and the very existence of another, and is answerable for this other in a way, however, that is not characteristic of him. It is a responsibility that precedes freedom, which would mean precisely belonging to God, a

---

[6] On the subject of the interdicts, it would be interesting to quote the lines which figure in what follows in our text of pages 23a and 23b of the Tractate Makkoth: "R. Simlai when preaching said: Six hundred and thirteen precepts were communicated to Moses, three hundred and sixty-five negative precepts, corresponding to the number of solar days (in the year), and two hundred and forty-eight positive precepts, corresponding to the number of the members of man's body. Said R. Hamnuna: What is the (authentic) text for this? It is, Moses *commanded us torah, an inheritance of the congregation of Jacob* (Deuteronomy 33:4), 'torah' being in letter-value, equal to six hundred and eleven, 'I am' and 'Thou shalt have no (other Gods)' (not being reckoned, because) we heard from the mouth of the Might (Divine)." [*Translator's note:* The ending of Levinas's translation differs substantially from that given here: "If one adds to this the first two commandments of the Decalogue pronounced at Sinai and which we heard from the very mouth of the Lord, that makes six hundred and thirteen."] A bizarre sort of accounting! In actual fact, it gives at least three lessons:

(a) Every day lived under the sun is potential depravity and thus requires a new interdict, a new vigilance which yesterday's cannot guarantee.

(b) The life of every organ of the human body, of every tendency (the accuracy or arbitrariness of the anatomy or physiology counting two hundred and forty-eight matters little, since the number of "positive" precepts divulges the secret of this figure), is the source of possible life. A force that is not justified in itself. It must be dedicated to the most high, to serving.

(c) The code containing the six hundred and thirteen precepts is not met by the number given by the breakdown of the numerical value of the letters making up the word Torah. It is not a system justified uniquely by its coherence. It institutes the order of life only because its transcendent source is personally asserted in it as word. True life is inspired.

7 Cf. *Quatre lectures talmudiques* [*Four Talmudic Readings*].

unique belonging which, anterior to freedom, does not destroy freedom and thereby defines, if one may say so, the meaning of the exceptional word: God. God appearing *through* a council of the just, itself called divine; God as the actual possibility of such a council. And, conversely, a council of the just which is not only the ultimate source of his judgement: a different will wills within it, the judge's judgement is inspired and exceeds or overflows human spontaneity. This is what our text will say further on. Justice cannot be reduced to the order it institutes or restores, nor to a system whose rationality commands, without difference, men and gods, revealing itself in human legislation like the structures of space in the theorems of geometricians, a justice that a Montesquieu calls the "logos of Jupiter," recuperating religion within this metaphor, but effacing precisely transcendence. In the justice of the Rabbis, difference retains its meaning. Ethics is not simply the corollary of the religious but is, of itself, the element in which religious transcendence receives its original meaning.

Transcendence and Exegesis

In the Talmudic extract we are commenting upon, the text relating to transcendence comes immediately after the one that discusses the powers a human tribunal would have in order to modify the decisions of Heaven in some way, and to be certain of agreeing with the absolute Tribunal. Here are the terms in which the problem is put: "Said R. Joseph: Who has gone up (to Heaven) and come (back with this information)?"

The answer is supplied by another scholar, Abaye, in the name of a Tanna master, R. Joshua b. Levi:

> "Three things were enacted by the (mundane) Tribunal below, and the Celestial Tribunal on high have given assent to their action"; (we might also exclaim,) who has gone up (to Heaven) and come (back with this information)? Only, we (obtain these points by) interpreting certain texts; and, in this instance too, we so interpret the texts.

R. Joshua b. Levi would thus entrust to the interpretation of texts, what the Rabbis call *Midrash* (exposition of meaning), the ability to force open the secret of transcendence.

Here are the three "things" which are said to have been instituted by the earthly tribunals whose exegesis would prove to have the assent of the celestial will. First of all, the established custom under the magistracy of Mordecai and Esther, of the liturgical reading of the "Scroll of Esther" on the Feast of Purim. It would find its justification in a biblical verse (Esther 9:27): "They confirmed, and the Jews took upon them and

their seed [the Jews acknowledged and accepted]." Why two almost synonymous verbs in this verse? Because confirmation [acknowledgement]
and taking upon themselves [acceptance] were two distinct acts: acceptance below, acknowledgement in Heaven.

Then the authorization of saluting another person with the Divine
Name: in Ruth 2:4, Boaz (whom the Rabbis class among the judges) greets
the reapers: "The Lord be with you!"; and in Judges 6:12 the angel says to
Gideon: "The Lord bless thee, thou mighty man of valour."

Finally, the prescription of bringing the tithe (due to the Levites) to
the Temple chamber, established as a custom by Ezra according to
Nehemiah 10:39. It is confirmed by the prophet Malachi (3:10): "Bring ye
the whole tithe unto the store house that there may be food in My house,
and try Me herewith, saith the Lord of Hosts, if I will not open you the
windows of heaven and pour you out a blessing, until there be no
enough." And the Talmud adds: "What means: 'until there be no
enough'? Said Rami b. Rab: (It means), until your lips weary of saying
'Enough, enough'!"

Do not such "proofs" imply the inspired origin of the whole biblical
canon? Does it not present the notions of height and transcendence as
established, and the very idea of God as clear and distinct?

Unless R. Joseph's question, in its apparent naivety, is an extremely
audacious one, questioning the mythological meaning of transcendence
and the revelation it seems to acknowledge. Unless, in questioning the
idea of someone "going up to Heaven," he goes so far as to concern the
great man called upon in Exodus 24:12: "Come up to me on the moun-
tain, and wait there; and I will give you the tables of stone, with the law
and the commandment." A calling upon whose reality in fact would be
vouched for, ultimately, only by a text which itself already belongs to the
statement of the truth which it ought to be able to establish: *petitio prin-
cipii* which would hint at the whole of historical criticism today. But does
not Abaye's reply indicate that he already understands his interlocutor
on this higher level? Instead of establishing exegesis on some dogmatism
of traditional metaphysics adopted as a truism, does not Abaye's reply
consist in basing a new meaning for transcendence, and the old vocabulary, on the structure of the Book of books inasmuch as it allows for
exegesis, and on its privileged status of containing more than it contains—
in other words, of being, in this sense exactly, inspired?

The reading processes that we have just seen at work suggest, first,
that the statement commented upon exceeds what it originally wants to
say; that what it is capable of saying goes beyond what it wants to say;
that it contains more than it contains; that perhaps an inexhaustible
surplus of meaning remains locked in the syntactic structures of the
sentence, in its word-groups, its actual words, phonemes and letters, in

all this materiality of the saying which is potentially signifying all the
time. Exegesis would come to free, in these signs, a bewitched significance that smoulders beneath the characters or coils up in all this
literature of letters.[8]

Rabbinical hermeneutics is rashly considered as neglecting the spirit,
whereas the aim of the signified by the signifier is not the only way to signify; whereas what is signified in the signifier, according to its other
modes, answers only to the mind that solicits it and thereby belongs to
the process of signification; and whereas interpretation essentially
involves this act of soliciting without which what is not said, inherent in
the texture of the statement, would be extinguished beneath the weight of
the texts, and sink into the letters. An act of soliciting which issues from
people whose eyes and ears are vigilant and who are mindful of the
whole body of writing from which the extract comes, and equally attuned
to life: the city, the street, other men. An act of soliciting which issues
from people in their uniqueness, each person capable of extracting from
the signs meanings which each time are inimitable. An act of soliciting
issuing from people who would also belong to the process of the signification of what has meaning. This does not amount to identifying exegesis
with the impressions and subjective reflections left by the word once it
has been understood, nor to including them gratuitously in the "outside"
of meaning. It does, however, amount to understanding the very plurality of people as an unavoidable moment of the signification of meaning,
and as in some way justified by the destiny of the inspired word, so that
the infinite richness of what it does not say can be said or that the meaning of what it does say can be "renewed," to use the technical expression
of the Rabbis. As the people of the Book, for whom the demanding reading of the Scriptures belongs to the highest liturgy, would not Israel also
be the people of continued revelation?

But in the light of this, the language that is capable of containing more
than it contains would be the natural element of inspiration, despite or
before its reduction to the instrument of the transmission of thoughts and
information (if it can ever be entirely reduced to this). One may wonder
whether man, an animal endowed with speech, is not, above all, an animal

---

8 The word of the rabbinical scholars, the word setting out or commenting on the
Torah, can be compared to the "glowing coals," to use a phrase from the Pirqe Aboth in the
Tractate of Principles of the Babylonian Talmud. A remarkable Talmudist, a disciple of the
Gaon of Vilna (one of the last great masters of rabbinical Judaism, on the eve of the nine-
teenth century, the Jewish age "of Enlightenment"), Rabbi Hayyim Volozhiner, interpreted
this remark approximately as follows: the coals light up by being blown on, the glow of the
flame that thus comes alive depends on the interpreter's length of breath.

capable of inspiration, a prophetic animal. One may wonder whether the book, as a book, before becoming a document, is not the modality by which what is said lays itself open to exegesis, calls for it; and where meaning, immobilized in the characters, already tears the texture in which it is held. In propositions which are not yet—or which are already no longer—verses, and which are often verse or simply literature, another voice rings out among us, a second sonorous voice that drowns out or tears the first one. The infinite life of texts living through the life of the men who hear them; a primordial exegesis of the texts which are then called national literature and on to which the hermeneutics of universities and schools is grafted. Above and beyond the immediate meaning of what is said in these texts, the act of saying is inspired. The fact that meaning comes through the book testifies to its biblical essence. The comparison between the inspiration conferred on the Bible and the inspiration towards which the interpretation of literary texts tends is not intended to compromise the dignity of the Scriptures. On the contrary, it asserts the dignity of "national literatures." Yet how is it that a book is instituted as the Book of books? Why does a book become Bible? How is the divine origin of the Word indicated? How is it signed in Scripture? And does not this signature, which is more important for people living today than "the thunderings and the lightnings" of Sinai, betray simple faith?

Inspiration: another meaning which breaks through from beneath the immediate meaning of what is meant to be said, another meaning which beckons to a way of hearing that listens beyond what is heard, beckons to extreme consciousness, a consciousness that has been awoken. This other voice resonating in the first takes control of the message as a result of this resonance coming from behind the first. In its purity of message, it is not just a certain form of saying; it organizes its content. The message as message awakens listening to what is indisputably intelligible, to the meaning of meanings, to the face of the other man.[9] Awakening is precisely this proximity of others.[10] The message as message in its method of awakening is the modality, the actual "how" of the ethical code that disturbs the established order of being, unrepentantly leading its style of being.[11] With its referent as reading, as the book—yet no less wondrous

---

9 The Book *par excellence* of what has meaning. And this is without yet highlighting the testimony given to this book by a people who have existed for thousands of years, or the interpenetration of their history and of this book, even if such communication between history and book is essential to genuine scriptures.

10 Cf. my study "De la conscience à la veille," *Bijdragen*, 3-4 (1974), 235–49.

11 Ethics—appearing as the prophetic—is not a "region," a layer or an ornament of being. It is, of itself, actual dis-interestedness, which is possible only under a traumatic

for all that—do we not have here the original figure of the beyond freed from the mythology of ulterior worlds?[12]

That *ethics* is not determined in its elevation by the pure height of the starry sky; that all height takes on its transcendent meaning only through ethics and the message incessantly breaking (hermeneutically) the texture of the Book *par excellence:* these, undoubtedly, will constitute the teaching to be drawn—one of the teachings to be drawn—from the passage we are commenting upon.

Curiously, the biblical text first cited by R. Joshua b. Levi in consideration of the agreement between the earthly tribunal and the celestial tribunal is taken from the book of Esther from which, it might be said, God has gone so far as to withdraw his name, the word by which he is named. Yet in this book the message emerges from between the events recounted according to their "natural" motivation, the necessities and the casting of lots. That these events, instituted as liturgy by Mordecai and Esther, could have been understood as belonging to holy History is the "miraculous" surplus of their place in the divine plan. There arises the historical order of the facts (their established order), and consciences are awoken at the highest ethical moment in which Esther disturbs royal etiquette and consents to her ruin in order to save other men. The order upset by this awakening is paralleled by the king's insomnia. Does not a Midrash from the Tractate Megillah compare the insomnia of Ahasuerus to the very insomnia of God? As if, in the impossibility of sleeping, the ontological rest of being were to be torn and entirely sobered up. Is not the relation to transcendence this extreme consciousness?

No less remarkable is the second text in which the epiphany of God is invoked in the human face. The face of the other, irreducible difference, bursting into all that gives itself to me, all that is understood by

---

experience whereby "presence," in its imperturbable equality of presence, is disturbed by "the other." Disturbed, awoken, transcended.

12 In the texts invoked, indeed, determined situations and beings—equal to themselves, being held in definitions and boundaries that integrate them into an order and bring them to rest in the world—are passed through by a breath that arouses and stirs their drowsiness or their identity as beings and things, tearing them from their order without alienating them, tearing them from their contour like the characters in Dufy's paintings. The miracle of beings presenting themselves in their being and awakening to new awakenings, deeper and more sober. It cannot be denied that as a disturbing of order, as a tearing of Same by Other, it is the miracle, the structuring—or de-structuring—of inspiration and its transcendence. If purely thaumaturgical miracles seem spiritually suspect to us and acceptable as simple figures of the Epiphany, it is not because they alter the order but because they do not alter it enough, because they are not miraculous enough, because the Other awakening the Same is not yet other enough through them.

me and belongs to my world; an appearance in the world which un-
makes and dis-orders the world, worries me and keeps me awake. That
is what is perceived by bringing together Ruth 2:4 and Judges 6:12. A
transcendence both in the text in which exegesis finds more than the
written seems to say, and in the ethical content, the message, which is
thus revealed.

The third moment—in which the gift of the tithe is transformed by
being brought to the Temple—would signify the transformation of the
very act of giving into an absolutely free act of generosity where the
person giving, not knowing the beneficiary, does not hear the expression
of the latter's personal gratitude.[13] Is that not one of the meanings, the
figure, as it were, of the cult itself? What "strong minds" would be
tempted to mock as duties towards an "empty heaven" is enigmatically
the absolute opening of the soul: the opening of dis-interestedness, of sacrifice without reward, of discourse without answer or echo, which
"confidence in God" and prayer must have the strength to reach. The
opening of self to the infinite that no confirmation can equal, and that is
proven only by its very excessiveness. That would be the abundance for
which lips cannot be enough, drying out through saying "enough," of
which Rami b. Rab speaks in his strange hermeneutic of Malachi 3:10. A
beyond the discourse. This is probably what this sudden transformation
is: in the disinterested generosity of the act of giving, receiving becomes
infinite, the opening on to the infinite.

THE AMBIGUITY

In our reading of the Talmudic passage, inspiration and the exegesis
that discovers it, we have discerned the spirituality of the spirit and the
actual figure of transcendence. Have we been right to do so? Have we
been right to recognize in the ethical code on the level of the tribunal,
understood as a council of the just, the actual place in which the spirit
blows and the Other penetrates the Same? Will a person today not resist
such readings by reducing the transcendence of inspiration, exegesis and
the moral message to man's interiority, to his creativity or his subcon-
scious? Is not ethics basically autonomous? In order to dispute such
modern-day resistance, would it not have been necessary to interpret as
inspiration the reasons of reasoning reason in which philosophy, in its
logic, recognizes the reign of Identity which nothing that is *other* could
disrupt or guide?

---

13 On the importance attached to this modality of the gift, cf. Baba-Bathra 10b.

Now this is precisely what the final section of the Talmudic extract that concerns us wishes to suggest. R. Eleazar intervenes to confirm in his own way the general argument of Makkoth 23b on the possible agreement between earthly courts of law and celestial justice. He refers to Genesis 38:26, where Judah, the son of Jacob, recognizes the injustice of the accusation he had brought against his daughter-in-law Tamar (this "is said to have taken place," according to our text, at the Tribunal of Shem, Noah's son, who was still alive). R. Eleazar refers to I Samuel 12:3–5, where all of Israel testifies at the Tribunal of Samuel to the disinterestedness of the judge Samuel; and he refers to I Kings 3:27, where King Solomon, in his own Tribunal, recognizes the mother among the two women arguing over a child. Confession of the guilty party, testimony of the people, sentence of the king: to each of these human speeches (unquestionably human in the verses quoted), R. Eleazar—in the name of a supremely audacious exegesis, but probably also in the name of a daring thought—lifts out, under various pretexts, the ends of verses which he attributes to the echo of a heavenly voice. Will the holy spirit thus have been present at men's tribunals?

One interlocutor, Raba, questions such extravagance: there is no need to have voices intervening in discourses where reason is sufficient. But it is R. Eleazar's lesson that the Talmudic text retains. It retains it without discussion, in the name of tradition. Inspiration is thus said to be in the exercise of reason itself! The logos would already be prophetic! Through the uncertainties and presumptions of reasoning thought, the light of evidence would come as if under the trauma of the Revelation. A message would be declared in all evidence.

This is true, but it should be emphasized that despite tradition, the redactors of the Talmudic text recorded the opinion that was rejected: Raba's scepticism. It is still written down. As if an ambiguity had to remain in the conclusions of the lofty debate that has just taken place according to the style of the Talmud, with remarks that are apparently without relief and made "without appearing to be made."

Would not the man of today recognize in this ambiguity the alternating movements of his own thought?

To say that the ideas on transcendence and the very idea of transcendence come to us through the interpretation of writings is, admittedly, not to express a subversive opinion. Yet it is less dogmatic to people today. It suggests on the one hand that language, at the hour of its ethical truth—that is, of its full significance—is inspired, that it can therefore say more than it says, and that prophecy is thus not an act of genius, but the spirituality of the spirit expressing itself, the ability of human speech to extend beyond the primary intentions that carry it. This is perhaps possession by God, through which the idea of God comes to us. But this language offered to transcendence is also the object of philology; thus the transcendence that is expressed through it would be just an illusion, the prestige of influences to be demystified by History. Let us prefer, then, the genesis of every text to its exegesis, the certainties of given signs to the hazards of mysterious messages, the combinations of the shadows in the Cave to the uncertain calls from outside! This is also a science, at times an admirable one, to destroy false prophecies.

Alternative or alternation. And even an alternation of alternations before the letters of Scripture. These letters, for those who respect them as for those who mock them, may still support the dogmatic principles of a God, a power stronger than others, who interrupts—like a monstrous force or a heroic person—the necessities of nature. Then, through a science that they nurture with their presence as relics, these letters strike their readers, one and all, and rescue them from the level of asserted or denied mythologies. But in this start that readers receive there is a new alternation of movements: they go from the traumatic experience of the unknown and strange meaning to the grammar which, already operating on another level, restores order, coherence and chronology. And then there is a movement back: from history and philology to the understanding of meaning coming from behind the literature of letters and anachronisms, an understanding that again affects and awakes, forcing us out of the bed of the preformed and customary ideas that protect and reassure.

An alternation which, admittedly, testifies to the hesitation of our little faith, but from which also stems the transcendence that does not impose itself with denials through its actual coming and which, in inspired Scripture, awaits a hermeneutic—in other words, reveals itself only in dissimulation.

THE LITTLE MAN WITH THE BURNED THIGHS: LEVINAS'S BIBLICAL HERMENEUTIC

Annette Aronowicz
Franklin and Marshall College

INTRODUCTION

The first thing that needs to be said about Levinas's biblical hermeneutic is that he never interprets the biblical text directly. Rather, he insists upon the mediation of talmudic commentary, if the biblical reading is to remain within a Jewish perspective.[1] Levinas's approach to the Bible, then, is inaccessible as such. To understand it, we must turn to his interpretation of the rabbis. The hermeneutic he applies to their text, he often claims, is a continuation of the hermeneutic they themselves apply to the Bible. To illustrate this, I would like to turn to one of his talmudic commentaries, "As Old As the World?" (Levinas 1990c: 70–88).[2]

"As Old As the World?" bases itself on a mishnah and gemara (see n. 1) from *b. Sanhedrin* 36b–37a.[3] As the title of the tractate indicates, this

---

[1] What we usually call the Talmud are the rabbinic discussions compiled at the end of the fifth century C.E. and referred to as the Gemara. The Gemara is responding to earlier rabbinic discussions, compiled at the end of the second century C.E., referred to as the Mishnah. On any page of a volume of Talmud, we therefore find the particular mishnah (i.e., the particular discussion of the second century) that the gemara (i.e., the particular discussion of the fifth century) is responding to. But, in addition, a page of Talmud always has a number of other commentators, most prominent among them the great eleventh-century French commentator Rashi and the later medieval commentaries, the Tosafists. There are also later commentators on the bottom of the page. To study Talmud, then, is to place oneself within a whole series of rabbinic readings. Levinas focuses his interpretation on the Mishnah and Gemara at hand, occasionally mentioning some of the other commentators. It has to be assumed, however, that he has taken them into account. All of his readings are based on the Babylonian Talmud, the larger and more frequently studied compilation of rabbinic commentary, the other being the Jerusalem Talmud.

[2] Unless otherwise stated, all page references in this essay are to Levinas 1990c.

[3] I have included the full text that Levinas interprets in this commentary as an appendix to this essay. It might be helpful to the reader to turn to it first, before reading my commentary on Levinas's commentary.

passage centers on the Jewish court of law, the Sanhedrin, and, as Levinas will indicate, it is, although not to the naked eye, a meditation on the nature of justice. Initially, I will simply present Levinas's interpretation of that notion of justice, focusing as he does on the gemara. Once we see what this notion of justice involves, it will be easier to extract the hermeneutical principles that guided Levinas's reading. To extract them, I will return to the mishnah to show them at work. I will conclude with a few words about the implications of this hermeneutic, not only for reading the Bible, but also for reading in general.

JUSTICE

The gemara that Levinas interprets in "As Old As the World?" begins with a question about the preceding mishnah. I will cite this mishnah in full to convey the seemingly technical nature of its concerns:

> The Sanhedrin formed a semi-circle so that its members could see each other.
>   Two clerks of the court stood before the judges, one to the right and one to the left, and they recorded the arguments of those who would acquit and those who would condemn.
>   Rabbi Judah said: "There were three court clerks, one recording the arguments for acquittal, the second the arguments for conviction, and a third both the ones for acquittal and the ones for conviction. Three rows of students of the Law were seated before the judges. Each knew his place, if it became necessary to invest someone, the one appointed was from the first row; in such a case, a student from the second row moved up to the first and a student from the third row to the second. The most competent person in the assembled public was chosen and was placed in the third row. And the last to come did not sit in the place of the first (in the row, who had gone up to the other row) but in the place which was suitable for him." (70)

We can see from this text that the Tannaim, the rabbis who engaged in the discussions comprising the Mishnah, were interested here in details regarding the physical layout of the court, the number of court clerks, the role of the court as a school of law, and so forth. Since this mishnah does not mention where in the Bible its teaching on the Sanhedrin comes from, the gemara begins by asking just that: "From which text does this come?" Rav Aha bar Hanina replies: "We learn from verse 3, chapter 7 (of the Song of Songs): 'Your navel is like a round goblet full of fragrant wine; your belly like a heap of wheat hedged about with roses'" (70).

We seem to be in the presence of a flagrant *non sequitur*. How did the Amoraim, the rabbis speaking in the Gemara, come to the conclusion that the Tannaim derived their knowledge of the Sanhedrin's functioning from a verse of love poetry referring to bellies, navels, and the like? Levinas points out that the gemara's question might not mean exactly what it means. Rav Aha bar Hanina might be asking not so much, "what is the textual legitimation for the mishnah's statement" as "what is the Sanhedrin, the system of justice just mentioned in the mishnah, based on?" Since the text he has chosen is about love, he obviously wants to establish a link between love and the dispensation of justice. But what is this link? Levinas, basing himself on this gemara as a whole, and most especially on the discussion within it of the last part of the verse, claims that the rabbis are suggesting that no justice exists in the world unless the people who sit in judgment upon others know how to bridle their erotic impulses. In other words, justice is founded on the restraint of the passions.

This in itself is hardly a novel idea, and Levinas is quick to acknowledge that the classical Greeks, in texts such as the *Oresteia*, expressed this well enough. We will come back to what he has to say about the classical Greeks. But, for now, suffice it to say that he also points to something very specific in the rabbis' understanding of justice that is not to be found in the Greeks. In order to show this, he focuses mainly on last part of Song 7:3, "hedged with roses," the source of several comments in the gemara at hand.

What would "hedged with roses" have to do with the Sanhedrin? A rabbi answers: "'Hedged with roses': even if the separation is only a hedge of roses, they will make no breach in it" (71). The "they," given the context of the discussion, refers to the judges sitting on the bench, Levinas informs us. The hedge of roses is obviously a barrier, a limit that the judges do not traverse to the other side, the side of evil. Since the entire context of the biblical verse is erotic imagery, what the judges do not fall prey to is their erotic urges. Central to Levinas's commentary is the nature of the barrier that keeps them from falling.

A hedge of roses is not much of an obstacle. In contrast to a wall, machine guns, barbed wire, it is very easily crossed. Thus, the first meaning that Levinas draws from the imagery is that the purity of the judges is not a result of pressure from the outside—fear of punishment, for example. They are able to contain their erotic impulses without any external coercion. Let it be said, in passing, that Levinas is not claiming that the erotic as such is evil but that unbridled indulgence in it is evil in that it prevents justice.

The second meaning Levinas derives from the imagery of the hedge of roses (and he derives several others as well) is that it is the sort of barrier that not only presents no obstacle but also, in a way, encourages evil. Aren't roses enticing in their beauty? To be able to resist crossing a hedge of roses would then mean that the judges are able to resist temptation at

its very heart. They do not cut themselves off from the erotic but live
within it. Yet they are not dominated by the erotic impulse. When Levinas talks about the erotic in this context, he means first and foremost the
sexual urge, as the biblical verse itself refers to it; but the sexual urge is
simply the most basic form of our desire for self-satisfaction and, as such,
it is symbolic of other desires of like nature.

At this point within the rabbinic discussion, a Min, a heretic, someone who does not accept the authority of the rabbis, objects: "You claim
that during her time of impurity a woman forbidden to her husband nevertheless has a right to be alone with him. Do you think there can be fire
in flax without its burning?" (71).

The Min, in his statement, refers to the Jewish law forbidding sexual
relations between man and wife during her menstrual cycle. Yet, according to the law, the couple is allowed to stay together during that time. It is
a misreading of human nature, according to the Min, to expect that
human beings will be able to restrain their urges when given the means
to satisfy them and without external supervision. What the rabbis are
suggesting, namely, the possibility that the judges are human beings who
resist their impulses to self-satisfaction in the midst of temptation, is
simply utopian. If there is fire in flax, it will burn.

The rabbis' reply to the objection seems at first merely to repeat what
they have already said: "Rav Kahana answered: 'The Torah has testified
for us through a hedge of roses; for even if the separation is only a hedge
of roses, they will make no breach in it'" (71).

Rav Kahana, then, asserts that the Torah, in contrast to the Min, claims
that such a human being is indeed possible. But how does the Torah testify through a hedge of roses? Here, according to Levinas, comes one of
the major interpretive turns of this gemara: "Resh Lakish said: It can be
answered on the basis of the following text (Song of Songs 4:3): 'Your
brow (rakkathek) is like a pomegranate.' Even those established as good-
for-nothings among you are full of mitzvot [commandments], as a
pomegranate is full of seeds" (71).

Resh Lakish, Levinas tells us, is finally revealing to us what the hedge
of roses really is: the mitzvot. In other words, what makes it possible to
form a human being who has so internalized a way of behaving that the
erotic does not derail him? It is the practice of the commandments. They
are that frail partition that nonetheless keeps those who practice them
from evil. They are the practice that regulates life in such a way that the
erotic is not abolished but contained.

Their power, claims Levinas, does not derive from any inherent mag-
ical property but from their capacity to educate the instincts. Rituals are a
way of putting a pause between ourselves and nature. They put a brake
on our spontaneity. For instance (the example is mine), if one thinks of

the commandment to wash the hands and say a blessing before the eating of bread, it is clear that the ritual activity stops us from merely hurling ourselves at food, giving in to our appetites. This sort of restraint, in many different areas, can eventually lead to the kind of human beings who can resist their drives as a matter of course. Even the good-for-nothings, although presumably they lapse, still retain the capacity to restrain their instincts, at least on occasion, because of the practice of the *mitzvot*. Here Resh Lakish is speaking not only of what is possible for judges, an elite group in any society, but what is possible for the most ordinary of human beings.

If we were to pause here to ask the question with which the gemara began—"Where does this [that is, justice] come from?"—the answer would be the *mitzvot*. The image of the human being given to us so far is that of someone who does not traverse a hedge of roses, even though it is easy to do so. The emphasis has been on self-control, a self-control that has become so natural that it can coexist with temptation and not give in to it. The rest of the gemara will not continue along exactly the same lines, though. The image of the human being in its latter part shifts somewhat, although there is no contradiction. This new image of humanity is introduced by a shift of text. We are no longer in the Song of Songs but in Genesis.

> Rav Zera said: That is to be deduced from the following text: "Ah, the smell of a field watered by the Lord" (Genesis 27:27). One should not read *begadav* (his clothes) but *bogedav* (his rebels). (71)

It will be easier to follow what Levinas makes of this statement if we first turn to how he interprets the one that follows, also involving Rav Zera:

> About this it is told: some good-for-nothings lived in the neighborhood of Rav Zera. He brought them close to himself so that they could do *Teshuvah* (the return to the good). This irritated the sages. When Rav Zera died, the good-for-nothings said: Until now, the little-man-with-the-burned-thighs prayed for us. Who is going to pray for us now? They thought about it and did *Teshuvah*. (71)

Levinas begins by explaining how Rav Zera got his nickname, "the little-man-with-the-burned-thighs." It happened as a result of a peculiar exercise, which was itself preceded by two exercises quite like it. All three involved fasting for a hundred days, although the reasons for the fasts differed in each case. The first fast occurred because of Rav Zera's determination to overcome his combative style. He had learned this style as a student in the academies of Babylon. When he moved to Jerusalem, he discovered that there students never challenged their teachers. It took him one hundred days of fasting to overcome his desire to challenge them. The second fast was to keep the head of the yeshiva (i.e., head of the rabbinic academy), who was gravely ill, from dying. This would seem very praiseworthy were it not that his motivation was to avoid becoming head of the yeshiva himself. As Levinas puts it, anachronistic on purpose, he didn't want to take time away from his research to become an administrator. The final fast is the one that led to the burning of his thighs, although Levinas suggests this might have been the cumulative outcome of all three of them. Rav Zera determined that he didn't want the fire of hell to have power over him any longer. In the course of his fasting he got so strong that, as proof of his power over hell, he could sit next to a very hot stove and not get burned. One day his colleagues came to look at him. The minute their eyes fell upon him, the fires of hell immediately regained their rights. Hence the burned thighs.

Levinas leaves us to savor this triptych without giving us much interpretation of its details, other than to warn us that "when the eyes of our colleagues are upon us, the fire of hell always regains its rights over us" (87). He does draw out the basic similarity in all three tasks, however. In each case, Rav Zera was concerned with his own purity, with the restraints of his passions as an end in itself. If evil, as represented by the fires of hell, had no power over him, it is because Rav Zera learned to have sufficient self-control to withstand it. But this is not the same Rav Zera who prays for the good-for-nothings in his neighborhood. Here he is with and for others, immediately preoccupied by them, rather than being an isolated figure aiming for some distant self-perfection. His purity is no longer a matter of self-control but of responsibility.

We can now go back to what Levinas makes of Rav Zera's initial statement about Jacob. The reason he smelled so sweet to Isaac is that, by putting on Esau's clothes, he was signaling his responsibility for his brother and, through his brother, for all rebels, for all those who would sell their birthright for a pot of porridge. To don others' clothes, in Levinas's reading, is to put oneself in their place, to agree to take on their responsibility, thus to become responsible for them, to do what they should have done. But to don someone's clothes is also to remain with them, to put oneself in their place, to keep them within what is human. In Levinas's reading of the rabbis here, Rav Zera, in staying close to the good-for-nothings and praying for them, was, in fact, acting in the tradition of Jacob, who took on the responsibility that Esau gave up, who did not divorce himself from the rebels.

Responsibility is, of course, a key term in Levinas's vocabulary. In his interpretation of this gemara, we see it contrasted to an urge for personal purity as an end in itself. Simply resisting the erotic does not bring about justice in the world. It is the movement toward the other, over and beyond restraint of our erotic impulses, on a different plane, that brings it about. As Levinas puts it, in order for morality to start, someone has to go first. There has to be that first gesture of generosity toward someone else (87). Otherwise, everyone remains locked in his or her own self. To operate on this different plane, the plane of generosity expressed in the responsibility toward the other, the *mitzvot* are necessary. In their education of our instincts, in the pause they introduce between ourselves and nature, they form us to responsibility in the sense of Jacob and of Rav Zera of the burned thighs.

We have reached the end of our gemara, whose last few sentences return to the mishnah's description of the students' seating arrangement in the court of law. This reminds us, as Levinas explains, that all these inner dispositions need to be reflected not only in the individual's behavior but also in an objective order, in public institutions whose workings are accepted by the society at large. Justice cannot depend merely on individuals' standards of what constitutes the good. So, although the good depends on its inner appropriation by every individual, it also needs to be given objective expression at the level of a society's functioning, in the very seating arrangement of a court of law, for instance.

LEVINAS'S HERMENEUTICS

Having gotten some idea of what Levinas draws from this rabbinic text, we might now well ask what principles of interpretation guided him in this process. It turns out that the responsibility he discovers as content is the very principle that leads him to this discovery in the first place. To unpack this statement, I would like to turn to the first part of the passage Levinas's commentary is based on, the mishnah previously cited.

It will be recalled that the mishnah briefly describes the physical layout of the court of law—the shape of the seating arrangement, where the court clerk stood, where the students sat. In each and every detail, Levinas will find a meaning pointing to responsibility but also revealing his own responsibility toward the authors of the text. Let us turn, for instance, to the first sentence of the mishnah: "The Sanhedrin formed a semi-circle so that its members could see each other" (70).

Levinas, taking his cue from the reference to the face-to-face that a semi-circle allows, suggests that the Tannaim are here underlining, by the very shape of the seating arrangement, that justice does not come into being from the work of the intellect in isolation. It appears as human beings face each other, respond to each other. Each is accountable to all the others for his decision and each must respond to the decisions of all the others. To be a judge in the Sanhedrin is not to be a member of a joint stock company, Levinas says, but to be in an exchange in which the engagement of your person with other concrete persons is the very medium of the decision-making process.

He comments also on the fact that a semicircle is not a circle. It leaves an opening. This opening, he indicates, is not just an opening to the defendants, plaintiffs, and their witnesses, who present their case within that space. That goes without saying. It is an opening to the outside world, signaling the Jews' need of that world. Closing oneself off from what is "outside," however that outside is interpreted, is not the path to justice.

On the number of court clerks, Levinas gives us the outlines of an entire epistemology. The reason there are always two records is that it takes two people testifying to what they have seen to establish evidence as evidence. In other words, facts are not simply objectively there. They are made by people who are willing to stake their integrity before others. They are made by testimony. While the context is legal, we are given a brief glimpse into the underpinning of all knowledge.

Without going any further, we can already see Levinas's mode of proceeding. The physical description is not eliminated. That is, it remains of utmost relevance how the judges were disposed in the courtroom, where the students were seated, and so forth. But the reason it remains of utmost relevance has to do with the thought it embodies. This is what Levinas wants to bring into the light of day, without dismissing the body that conceals it. He isn't claiming there is only one way to read what this thought is. He himself often offers alternate readings of the same imagery. He insists, however, that there is thought here in need of a formulation that touches us directly.

In this approach to the wording of the text, Levinas's method is remarkably similar to that of the Amoraim, the rabbis of the Gemara. They too pore over every word, not only of the Mishnah, but, in this particular case, of the biblical text itself. For instance, before we get to the famous hedge of roses at the end of Song 7:3 ("Your navel is like a round goblet full of fragrant wine, your belly like a heap of wheat hedged about with roses"), the rabbis have gone over every word.

> "Your navel": that is the Sanhedrin. Why the navel? For the Sanhedrin is in session at the navel of the universe.
> "A goblet" (in Hebrew, *aggan*) because it protects (in Hebrew, *meggin*) the entire universe.
> "Round" (in Hebrew, *sahar*, crescent of the moon), for it resembles the crescent of the moon.
> "Full of drink" (in the text: not lacking in liquid): for if one of its members has to absent himself, it is ensured that twenty-three remain (in session), corresponding to the small Sanhedrin. Otherwise, he cannot leave.

"Your belly is like a heap of wheat": everyone profits from wheat; everyone finds to his taste the reasons adduced for the verdicts of the Sanhedrin. (70–71)

I will not go into the meaning Levinas draws from each of the rabbis' comments, for, of course, they require interpretation. But we can see that his own manner of stopping at every image, every detail, to find the thought lurking within, closely parallels theirs. We can also see that in what the rabbis do with the imagery of the navel, for instance, there is a similar turn to the ethical. The erotic is made to mean on the plane of justice.

But how is the exploring of every detail, to reveal the ethical dimension lurking within, illustrative of responsibility toward the other? How is this like Rav Zera praying for the good-for-nothings or like Jacob, in the rabbis' reading, putting himself in the place of his brother, taking on his tasks?

The link here lies in the vulnerability of the other, be it the good-for-nothings, the rebels, or the rabbis. All human beings are *ipso facto* vulnerable. That is, they are exposed outsiders, other than myself. It is not a question of belonging to another group, although belonging to another group accentuates otherness. It is a question of having a face, a face that can never be the mirror image of me; it comes from the outside, absolutely.

The rabbis are no longer alive, but their voices, recorded in the text, still address us, still confront us with the vulnerability of the other, the one who is not me, who is not us. To respond to that vulnerability is to answer those voices, thus keeping them within the community of the living. To answer those voices is not merely to set them in their historical context: "This is how they thought about justice in the second or sixth century." It is not merely to find patterns in the text, binary oppositions, contradictions, or whatever. In order to serve the authors, vulnerable as only those who can no longer speak for themselves can be, their words need not only to mean, but to mean now and for us, urgently. Historical research or structural analysis is a useful but preliminary step.

Responsibility, however, is also exhibited on a yet prior level to that of finding a universal meaning in the rabbinic texts. It is quite obvious that Levinas has already decided, before he knew the content of the text, that a meaning existed, a meaning for us. For instance, at the beginning of the gemara, when Rav Aha bar Hanina cites the Song of Songs as the source for the Sanhedrin, Levinas immediately sees this as revealing a thought, a thought to be discovered and elaborated, to be sure, but a thought nonetheless. How does he know this? Presumably, upon first reading this text, he hadn't yet figured out what Rav Aha bar Hanina was saying. But, in order for him to take the trouble to figure it out, he must already have decided there was something to find! This decision, made before the act of interpreting itself, lies at the heart of Levinas's hermeneutic. It is the most basic embodiment of its responsibility.

Responsibility, as Levinas explains it, in the cases both of Jacob and of Rav Zera, has to do with generosity without which no morality can start. One needs to make the first move as a response to the vulnerability of the other. To read a text, then, is not merely to find patterns and structure and meaning of all sorts, although it is also that. Prior to all that, prior logically, not chronologically, it is to accept the other as master, to use Levinas's language. *Master*, in French as well as in English, means teacher, as well as one who commands. The mastery of the teacher lies in the ability to command our attention, to lead us to truth. We need to respond to that command, however. Otherwise, no teaching reaches us. In that response lies our responsibility. Our response is not an acquiescence to any specific teaching. It is the acquiescence to the possibility of being taught. Once the content is revealed, we have every right to dispute it.

But couldn't this method—the discovery of responsibility in the details of the text while one is already practicing it oneself—merely be an arbitrary imposition of meaning? After all, hasn't one *already* formulated a notion of responsibility before the act of interpreting begins? Levinas will state that while no reading can ever free itself completely from the suspicion of arbitrariness, his approach is not a willy-nilly forcing of the text in a purely subjective direction. His reading, he indicates, is limited by the imagery of the text, its patterns, its conventions. For instance, when he talks about the meaning of the semicircular formation of the Sanhedrin, the Mishnah itself had already indicated the importance of the face-to-face, in its own wording. It was the gemara itself that presented the hedge of roses as a barrier. Levinas's elaborations take their cue from the wording of these texts, wording that others can substantiate. More importantly, his very emphasis on ethics is *already* the rabbis' emphasis, Levinas will claim. After all, it is not Levinas by himself who turns the discussion of the Song of Songs into a discussion of justice, of *mitzvot*, of Rav Zera of the burned thighs. The links between rabbinic statements may be far from clear. But the turn to the ethical is obviously there. It is up to us, using the language of our times as others have used the language of theirs, to render the links between the parts intelligible and make that ethics accessible.

Still, Levinas will never claim that patterns of meaning are "in" the text and that he is merely bringing them out, for without the hermeneutic of responsibility these patterns remain inaccessible. The ability to extract meaning depends on something outside the text, even as it reflects the very meaning it eventually discovers in the text. Which came first: the hermeneutic or the contents of the text? We are always already too much in the middle of the process of interpreting to be able to answer that question.

In what has been said so far, the stress has been on the reader's responsibility to the author he or she is interpreting. But a commentary such as "As Old As the World?" makes clear that our responsibility extends to other human beings beside the authors. After all, in the act of interpreting we respond not only to the voice in the text but also to other voices from which we have learned, and to the people to whom we are addressing our own words. I would like briefly to indicate how Levinas's notion of responsibility is given shape in regard to these others as well.

Levinas, like the people to whom he is speaking, has been formed to a large degree by Western sources. The heart of these Western sources for him is the classical Greek tradition, as represented primarily by philosophy, but also, occasionally, as in this case, by its great literature. In each of his talmudic commentaries, Levinas will address one or another of these "Greeks," including contemporaries such as Heidegger. Just as the Sanhedrin left a space for what is outside, so does the act of interpretation, according to Levinas, need to confront what is outside the text, because one is already in the world and not in a closed circle. In "As Old As the World?" the main confrontation occurs with Aeschylus's *Oresteia*. In the course of mulling over the gemara's reference to the Sanhedrin as the navel of the universe, he is reminded by one of his study partners that this imagery of the navel as the center of justice occurs in reference to Delphi and also figures prominently in these plays. He rereads Aeschylus and concludes that, indeed, the playwright's notion of justice closely resembles that of the rabbis. Here too the erotic is contained, although not eliminated. He will eventually locate a difference in the Jewish understanding of justice, but the important point is that, rather than dismissing beforehand all exchange with what is non-Jewish, he not only favors such an exchange but also finds it inevitable. In the course of reading one bumps into that other, who is also there.

It could be objected, however, that Levinas's move in the direction of the *Oresteia* is merely rhetorical. Doesn't he dismiss it in the end by claiming that the Jewish texts have a more profound understanding of what is truly human than the Greeks? He definitely claims that the notion of responsibility, as embodied in Rav Zera of the burned thighs, did not occur to the Greeks. The act of unsolicited generosity, the staying with and for the other, is not the emphasis in their texts. Judaism, then, has a particular teaching unavailable elsewhere, not only necessary to the world, but more necessary perhaps than that of the Greek if justice is ever really to be enacted.

But matters are not so simple, for if that were indeed Levinas's sole intention, his very wording betrays him. To give just one example, let us return to what he says about the *mitzvot*.

How do such men [those able to resist temptation] become reality? By means of *mitzvot*. The originality of Judaism consists in confining itself to the manner of being of which Léon Ashkenazi will speak much better than I: in the least practical endeavor, a pause between us and nature through the fulfillment of a *mitzvah*, a commandment. The total interiorization of the Law is nothing but its abolition. (83)

In this passage, the just person is the product of a specific series of practices available only in the Jewish tradition, the commandments. The Greeks, the rest of the nations, do not have them. The real embodiment of justice is available only in Judaism.

On the preceding page, however, we find the following formulation: "This morning it was deplored that we have lost contact with the natural world. But the entire Jewish tradition has wanted to put a time for reflection between natural spontaneity and nature. Ah, that Jewish intellectualism. The fence of roses is the trifling partition of ritual—which stops us" (82).

This passage seems to be pointing in exactly the same direction as the preceding one, except for the introduction of the word "ritual," understood here as that pause between us and nature. Ritual is not a monopoly of the Jewish tradition. It can be found in all traditions. We are thus given a way to understand it, wherever it appears, precisely as that containment of instinct. But, if that's the case, cannot other traditions also produce just individuals, even if they do not have the *mitzvot*?

I am not saying that Levinas addresses this issue directly, at least not in this essay.[4] But the language itself directs us to this issue, and, though I said earlier that it "betrays" him, this is not adequate to Levinas's intention. He states quite clearly in his introduction to the talmudic essays, but also throughout them, that in interpreting classical Jewish texts, we need to resort to "Greek," to the university language that educated Westerners, including Jews, share with each other, because it is the way toward intelligibility, to giving the rabbis' voices their universal dimension (for instance, 1990c: 7–10; see also 1984: 361). Levinas has been accused by some commentators, in fact, of betraying the Jewish tradition because this

---

4 There is a much more direct formulation of the possibility of just human beings outside the Jewish tradition in the commentary entitled "Judaism and Revolution" (1990c: 98–99).

vocabulary leads to the effacing of the very difference Levinas claims he wants to preserve (Handelman: 312–13).

Wherever one wishes to place oneself in this debate, the presence of Western language, the word "ritual," for instance, in conjunction with *mitzvot*, immediately introduces a dialectic. The *mitzvot* are specifically Jewish, and yet they share something with practices from other traditions, hence the word "ritual." Yet they are not ritual in general; they are *mitzvot*. They lead to Rav Zera and not to Orestes. Yet the difference cannot be understood without the commonality, and that commonality cannot become a stopping ground but an impetus for the discovery of yet more difference. The movement cannot come to an end. In that movement, the other, in this case the Greek, is never dismissed for good but pops up again and again. Perhaps the problem of the particular and the universal is not solved this way. But it may not be as important to solve it as it is to resolutely face the other, again and again, rather than rest in either commonality or difference.

An additional other to whom Levinas is responsible in the process of interpreting is, of course, the people he is addressing, his audience. "As Old As the World?" originally delivered as an oral presentation in 1966 at the Colloquium of French-Speaking Jewish Intellectuals held in Paris every year from 1957 to the present, faced an audience of Western-educated Jews. Many of them did not immediately see the need for Jewish sources, hence the title of the essay. The question mark at the end ("As Old As the World?") suggests, in fact, that everything to be found in the Jewish sources has already been thought, is available through other traditions. If the answer to the question is yes, presumably Judaism becomes superfluous. A good Western education, for instance, would be enough to give access to wisdom.

We have already indicated that Levinas's reading of Jewish sources jumps back and forth between traditions. Such a reading challenges the self-enclosedness of both. The responsibility Levinas exercises toward his audience in this way is precisely in breaking its self-containment, the self-containment in which we all live. It involves challenging assumptions so deeply ingrained we do not even recognize them as assumptions.

One example of such a challenge occurs frequently throughout the talmudic commentaries but is particularly prominent in "As Old As the World?" because of the topic at hand. Levinas repeatedly stresses the importance of the practice of *mitzvot*. Without this practice, Levinas warns, the famed Jewish predisposition to justice will eventually vanish. It can sometimes persist a bit after the practice of *mitzvot* has waned, but not beyond a certain point (84). To remind French Jews, living in a society from which they do not wish to differentiate themselves in any way, that the *mitzvot* are key to the formation of a just human being is to judge their assumptions on several different planes at once. The interpretative act has to touch its recipients in their own responsibility to the other, if it is to be complete.

One final instance of this responsibility to the audience manifests itself in yet another way. Levinas never makes his reading of the rabbis too systematic, too tight. There are many lacunae. This, of course, is partially due to the nature of line-by-line commentary, whose logic inevitably is interrupted by the text itself. It cannot be expository in the way of the philosophical argument. But if Levinas chooses this mode rather than the philosophical argument in his reading of the rabbis, it is precisely to preserve a certain looseness. For instance, we might well want to know how self-control and the act of generosity toward the other are related. Is there first self-control and then generosity? Does the kind of generosity Levinas refers to here bypass self-control altogether? Do the *mitzvot* lead to both? All this is left untouched, as is the connection of *mitzvot* and ritual in general, just to mention a few such topics.

Rather than answering such questions, Levinas presents his audience with a few key notions: the restraint of erotic passion, responsibility. These key notions always remain closely linked to the images in the text—the hedge of roses, Rav Zera of the burned thighs. The images are never elaborated exhaustively or systematically, simply because, as images, they bear a surplus of sense. Levinas purposely keeps us aware of this surplus of sense, at the very same time as he begins to expose it logically. His responsibility toward the audience resides in giving them enough room to confront the rabbinic text themselves so that the effort of making sense, that first gesture of generosity, is stimulated rather than repressed. A good reading should never become a substitute for the original text but a way of creating more possibilities for other readings to follow. The chain of responsibility never stops.

In all this, we might have lost sight completely of the original question with which we started: What is Levinas's approach to the Bible? As I indicated from the first, he doesn't have an approach to the Bible as such, although he claims that his approach indirectly derives its inspiration from the Bible. After all, the rabbis whose method he adopts claim to derive their own approach from the Bible's emphasis on the ethical. *Their* manner of entering the Bible claims as much to be consonant with *its* emphasis as Levinas claims to be consonant with the emphasis of rabbinic texts. Thus, the figure of Jacob donning Esau's clothes is refracted through Rav Zera's connection with the good-for-nothings, which is in turn refracted in Levinas's admonition to the assimilated Jews of the France of the 1960s. There is a continuity of inspiration, even if the breath that brings it to life always depends on the last person in the line of interpretation. But where does the strength of the breath come from? We are back in our hermeneutical circle.

Conclusion

In line with Levinas's own universalizing impulse, I would like to conclude by saying that the hermeneutic whose outlines have been drawn here is not limited to any set of texts, be they rabbinic or biblical. It is a hermeneutic *tout court*, an approach to interpretation as such. The rabbis' approach to the Bible provides us with a paradigm for approaching inspired speech everywhere. But is it not the claim of every book that, in some way, it is inspired speech? Reading the Book par excellence has taught us to read books in general.

Appendix: From the Tractate *Sanhedrin*, pp. 36b–37a

Mishna *The Sanhedrin formed a semi-circle so that its members could see each other.*

Two clerks of the court stood before the judges, one to the right and one to the left, and they recorded the arguments of those who would acquit and those who would condemn.

Rabbi Judah said: There were three court clerks, one recording the arguments for acquittal, the second the arguments for conviction, and a third both the ones for acquittal and the ones for conviction. Three rows of students of the Law were seated before the judges. Each knew his place; if it became necessary to invest someone, the one appointed was from the first row; in such a case, a student from the second row moved up to the first and a student from the third row to the second. The most competent person in the assembled public was chosen and was placed in the third row. And the last to come did not sit in the place of the first (in the row, who had gone up to the other row) but in the place which was suitable for him.

Gemara *From which text does this come? Rav Aha bar Hanina said: We learn from verse 3, chapter 7 (of the Song of Songs): "Your navel is like a round goblet full of fragrant wine; your belly like a heap of wheat hedged about with roses."*

"Your navel": that is the Sanhedrin. Why the navel? For the Sanhedrin is in session at the navel of the universe.

"A goblet" (in Hebrew, aggan) *because it protects (in Hebrew,* meggin) *the entire universe.*

"Round" (in Hebrew, sahar, crescent of the moon), for it resembles the crescent of the moon.

"Full of drink" (in the text: not lacking in liquid): for if one of its members has to absent himself, it is ensured that twenty--three remain (in session), corresponding to the small Sanhedrin. Otherwise, he cannot leave.

"Your belly is like a heap of wheat": everyone profits from wheat; everyone finds to his taste the reasons adduced for the verdicts of the Sanhedrin.

"Hedged with roses": even if the separation is only a hedge of roses, they will make no breach in it.

About this, a "Min" [heretic] said to Rav Kahana: You claim that during her time of impurity a woman forbidden to her husband nevertheless has the right to be alone with him. Do you think there can be fire in flax without its burning? Rav Kahana answered: The Torah has testified for us through a hedge of roses; for even if the separation is only a hedge of roses, they will make no breach in it.

Resh Lakish said: It can be answered on the basis of the following text (Song of Songs 4:3): "Your brow (rakkathek) is like a pomegranate." Even those established as good-for-nothings among you are full of mitzvot [commandments], as a pomegranate is full of seeds.

Rav Zera said: That is to be deduced from the following text: "Ah, the smell of my son's clothes is like the smell of a field watered by the Lord" (Genesis 27:27). One should not read begadav (his clothes) but bogedav (his rebels.) [sic]

About this it is told: some good-for-nothings lived in the neighborhood of Rav Zera. He brought them close to himself so that they could do Teshuvah (the return to the good). This irritated the sages. When Rav Zera died, the good-for-nothings said: Until now, the little-man-with-the-burned-thighs prayed for us. Who is going to pray for us now? They thought about it and did Teshuvah.

"Three rows of students. . . " Abaye said: It follows from this that when one moved, they all moved. And when one said: up until now I was in first place and now I am in last place, he was answered, according to Abaye: Be last among lions and do not be first among foxes.

CREATION, CHAOS, AND THE SHOAH: A THEOLOGICAL READING OF THE *IL Y A*

Scott Hennessy
University of Virginia

> *Two things fill the mind with ever new and increasing admiration and awe, the oftener and more steadily we reflect on them: the starry heavens above me and the moral law within me. I do not merely conjecture them and seek them as through obscured in darkness or in the transcendent region beyond my horizon: I see them before me, and I associate them directly with the consciousness of my own existence.*
> —Kant, *The Critique of Practical Reason*

> *Never shall I forget that night, the first night in camp, which has turned my life into one long night, seven times cursed and seven times scaled. Never shall I forget that smoke. Never shall I forget the little faces of the children, whose bodies I saw turned into wreaths of smoke beneath a silent blue sky.*
> —Elie Wiesel, *Night*

What happens when the starry heavens above are obliterated by smoke and the moral law within is silenced? What makes us human? Who decides? If ethics and morality are situational, who speaks on behalf of the poor, the widowed, the orphaned? Can there be a moral law after Auschwitz? How do we speak about ethics and responsibility? How shall we speak of God and morality amidst the smoke and silence of the blue sky?

Out of the silence of the Shoah, Emmanuel Levinas articulates the personal responsibility that one has for another person, a responsibility that precedes and grounds language itself. Writing from within the Western philosophical tradition, Levinas argues for the primacy of ethics over ontology, for the good before and beyond being. He creates a space within the philosophic tradition to hear the call of the good, a good named God. By writing and rewriting, saying and unsaying what has

been said, Levinas echoes the divine call of the good at the heart of language, in the heart of our soul.

In this work, I will trace out Levinas's work as a philosophical response to the Shoah, through the doctrine of creation. In the most direct terms, Levinas describes the creation of community against the chaos of destruction. Amidst the destructive evil of the Holocaust that enabled people to deny the human nature of Jewish men and women, and especially their children, a few people responded to the call of God to reach out and care for them. The simple acts of sheltering and feeding the stranger speak more eloquently of God and humanity than all the liturgies offered to the glory of God in those dark times. The "in the beginning" of creation is not just an event in a pre-archaic past, but an ongoing participation in the goodness of the good against the silence of chaos.

In the Beginning ...

After the event, there is a return to the beginning. After the exile, the story of creation is written in response to the captor's mythology and the memory of destruction. As the book of Job culminates in the revelation of God's creation, so the Bible itself begins with this wisdom as a foundation against the experience of chaos. The ordered world of Israel collapsed into chaos with the destruction of Jerusalem and the temple in 586 B.C.E. Foreseeing the coming disaster, Jeremiah writes:

> I looked on the earth, and lo, it was waste and void;
>   and to the heavens, and they had no light.
> I looked on the mountains, and lo, they were quaking,
>   and all the hills moved to and fro.
> I looked, and lo, there was no one at all,
>   and all the birds of the air had fled.
> I looked, and lo, the fruitful land was a desert,
>   and all its cities were laid in ruins
>   before the LORD, before his fierce anger. (Jer 4:23-26)[1]

The waste and void, the *tohu wa-bohu,* symbolizes the chaotic threat to God's creation. The laying waste to the temple plunged the people of God into a maelstrom of despair. Their divinely ordered world was no longer.

By the rivers of Babylon, the people of Israel learned to sing a new song as they rewrote their theology. Second Isaiah speaks directly of God as creator against the chaos of exile:

---

[1] Scripture quotations are from the NRSV.

For thus says the LORD,
who created the heavens
    (he is God!),
who formed the earth and made it
    (he established it;
he did not create it a chaos,
    he formed it to be inhabited!):
I am the LORD, and there is no other.
I did not speak in secret,
    in a land of darkness;
I did not say to the offspring of Jacob,
    "Seek me in chaos."
I the LORD speak the truth,
    I declare what is right. (Isa 45:18–19)

Seeking to discern God's presence through the silence and night of exile, Isaiah spoke of God acting through history in the person of Cyrus and of God transcending history as the creator of the cosmos. The glory of creation speaks of God's sovereignty. There is no other God besides the God of Israel. Like Job, Second Isaiah situates the present time of suffering within the greater context of God's creation while acknowledging the silence of God during the time of devastation: "Truly, you are a God who hides himself, O God of Israel, the Savior" (45:15). After declaring God's forgiveness to the people of Israel, Second Isaiah then speaks of Israel's redemptive ministry to the world: "It is too light a thing that you should be my servant to raise up the tribes of Jacob and to restore the survivors of Israel; I will give you as a light to the nations, that my salvation may reach to the end of the earth" (49:6). Through this servant God will be glorified, as the servant suffers for us.

In exile, the Priestly writers also reaffirmed the power of God. No longer limited to the land and temple at Jerusalem, Yahweh was now seen as the only God, the creator who transcends the entire world. The creation story of Genesis symbolizes God's providence. Despite the devastating experience of exile, God is majestically in control of all creation. The forces of chaos are held at bay, yet they remain. There is the possibility of creation slipping back out of control. The story of the flood reminds us that the waters of chaos surround the creation. Despite the proclamation of God's victory, the threat of chaos remains.

This view of a struggle between God and chaos is familiar to biblical scholars. Hermann Gunkel began the textual archaeology of the creation account in Genesis from the Babylonian myths of creation. He describes the *Chaoskampf*, the battle with chaos, in his *Schöpfung und Chaos in Urzeit und Endzeit* of 1895. Bernhard Anderson, Bernard Batto, Richard Clifford, Jon Levenson, Susan Niditch, and others have developed further the underlying tension between creation and chaos in the biblical texts. Their readings of Genesis underscore and challenge the traditional understanding of the doctrine of *creatio ex nihilo*. For on the one hand, *creatio ex nihilo* stresses God's sovereignty over matter against the mythic view of a struggle between gods. The Priestly writers emphasized the supremacy of God. But, on the other hand, the traces of a *Chaoskampf* within the biblical texts themselves speak of an unresolved tension regarding creation. In his *Creation and the Persistence of Evil*, Levenson succinctly summarizes the issue:

> Two and a half millennia of Western theology have made it easy to forget that throughout the ancient Near Eastern world, including Israel, the point of creation is not the production of matter out of nothing, but rather the emergence of a stable community in a benevolent and life-sustaining order. (12)

More than accounts of the beginning, creation stories reflect upon the present situation, as Westermann, in his commentary on Gen 1–11, states:

> In order to make clear the proper meaning of the creation declaration, one must takes as one's starting point that each individual creation narrative, each creation myth or each simple sentence that makes a statement about creation, is not directed primarily to saying something about an event in the past, but is spoken to and into the present. We can say this because we have established that the primary motif of the creation narratives was not a question about the origin, but about the world and humanity under threat in the present. (603)

More than a philosophical description, creation narratives address the ongoing struggle with chaos.

This tension between viewing creation either as *creatio ex nihilo* or as *Chaoskampf* runs throughout the work of Emmanuel Levinas. Philosophically, Levinas argues for *creatio ex nihilo*, but his description of the *il y a* (the "there is") echoes the biblical struggle with chaos. Levinas uses creation as a way of undermining the totalizing nature of Western philosophy. His use of creation is not only a strategic approach to philosophy and the origin of the self but also a reflection upon the present threat of totalitarian thought. In an autobiographical description of his work, *Signature*, reprinted in *Difficult Freedom*, Levinas writes: "This disparate inventory is a biography. It is dominated by the presentiment and memory of the Nazi horror" (1990b: 291). It is this horror that rumbles through the night and fog of the *il y a*. Levinas speaks of creation in order to address this horror.

The *Il Y A*

The *il y a*, the "there is," appears throughout Levinas's work. In *Signature* he describes it and uses it to outline his philosophical itinerary:

> Here is the path taken by the author of this book: an analysis which feigns the disappearance of every existent—and even of the *cogito* which thinks it—is overrun by the chaotic rumbling of an anonymous "to exist," which is an existence without existents and which no negation manages to overcome. *There is*—impersonally—like *it is raining* or *it is night*. None of the generosity which the German term *"es gibt"* is said to contain revealed itself between 1933 and 1945. This must be said! Enlightenment and meaning dawn only with the existents rising up and establishing themselves in this horrible neutrality of the *there is*. They are on the path which leads from existence to the existent and from the existent to the Other, a path which delineates time itself. (1990b: 292)

On the one hand, Levinas imagines the destruction of all beings and what is left is the rumbling of silence, the "there is," being itself filling in the void of nothingness. Unlike Heidegger, who envisions being anxiously threatened by nothingness, Levinas conveys the impossibility of escaping being itself. There are no evasions, no exits from existence. The *il y a* is not pure nothingness but rather the silent night of being in general. It is the felt presence of no thing, but of existence in general. Out of this chaotic background, beings arise, but they are never free of the *il y a*.

Levinas first addresses the subject of the *il y a* in one of his earliest essays, *De l'évasion* of 1935. From the mid-1930s on, Levinas realized the danger of Hitler and National Socialism. Jacques Rolland stresses the relationship between the experience of the *il y a* and being Jewish in the 1930s in his introduction and notes to the reprinted essay. Unlike previous persecutions of the Jews, Hitler ultimately made being Jewish a crime. There was no chance for conversion, and only the wealthy could afford to buy their escape. Most did not realize the impossibility of escape, let alone the need for it, until it was too late. This inability of escaping one's being is the background to Levinas's essay. It is the experience of the *il y a*. Individuals no longer matter but are mobilized as automatons, enmeshed within the gears of the system without escape:

> The elementary truth that *there is being*—being that matters and weighs on one—reveals itself in a depth that measures its brutality and seriousness. The pleasant game of life loses its playful character (character of being a game). Not because the sufferings with which it is menaced render it disagreeable but because the depth of the suffering is such that it is impossible to interrupt it or to escape the sharp feeling of being riveted. (1982a: 70; my translation)

As Rolland points outs, this is the same language Levinas uses to describe being Jewish in an article for *Paix et droit* in 1935. Speaking of Hitlerism as the greatest trial, an incomparable ordeal, that Judaism has ever undergone, Levinas writes:

> The affront under its racist form adds to the humiliation a harrowing knowledge of despair. The pathetic fate of being Jewish becomes a fatality. One can no longer flee. The Jew is ineluctably riveted to his Judaism. (reprinted in Chalier and Abensour: 144; my translation)

This experience of the hostility of being, the threat of existence, is the *il y a*. From a biblical perspective, it is the threat of chaos disrupting and overcoming creation. A resurgence of the *tohu wa-bohu*. Throughout his work, Levinas refers to the *il y a*. Time and again, it resurfaces as the "presentiment and the memory of the Nazi horror."

During the Second World War, Levinas was imprisoned in a hard labor camp for Jewish prisoners of war outside of Hanover. Thanks to his French uniform, the rules of the Geneva Convention applied to him. His family in Lithuania, to whom he dedicates his masterpiece, *Otherwise Than Being,* were killed. His wife and daughter in France were saved by the aid of his friend Maurice Blanchot, who helped to hide them in a convent near Orléans. Following the war, Levinas published an article entitled "*IL Y A*" in the journal *Deucalion.* Here, while employing Heideggerian terminology, Levinas begins to distinguish himself from his former teacher. Where Heidegger had revealed the threat of not being as the anxiety of Being-in-the-world, Levinas shows the opposite threat of being unable to escape being. Even nothingness is an experience of being. For even while imagining the return of all beings to nothingness, something still passes, the silence of the night and nothingness: "The anonymous current of being swallows up, submerges every subject, person or thing" (1946: 145; my translation). The experience of the *il y a* is one of being exposed, insecure, delivered in this nocturnal space to being itself, swimming in the chaos of existence. Employing imagery from Pascal, Hoffmann, and Poe, Levinas describes this experience as the night: "The bustling of the *il y a*, is the horror" (149).

Levinas does not mention Conrad's *Heart of Darkness*, but both the title and the work convey the dark experience of the *il y a*: "I was on the point of crying at her, 'Don't you hear them?' The dusk was repeating them in a persistent whisper all around us, in a whisper that seemed to swell menacingly like the first whisper of a rising wind. 'The horror! The horror!'" (Conrad: 79). The horror for Levinas is not an anxiety related to death but the loss of subjectivity. One is immersed, consumed by being. It is to be depersonalized. The *il y a* is the impersonal vigilance of the night, the fear of the dark that haunts the insomniac trapped in the night without exit.

While Levinas presents the *il y a* as an imaginative philosophical exercise, it powerfully conveys the horror of the Final Solution, especially life in the concentration camps. In the camps, people were no longer considered as human beings but rather as numbered property to be worked to death. Hunger, thirst, hard labor, lack of sleep, and the continuous threat of violence rapidly reduced the inmates to depersonalized automatons, existing in the borderland between life and death. The most extreme became the living dead, the *Muselmänner*. Primo Levi describes them in his *Survival in Auschwitz*:

> Their life is short, but their number is endless; they, the *Muselmänner*, the drowned, form the backbone of the camp, an anonymous mass, continually renewed and always identical, of non-men who march and labour in silence, the divine spark dead within them, already too empty to really suffer. One hesitates to call them living: one hesitates to call their death death, in the face of which they have no fear, as they are too tired to understand. (82)

The world of the *Muselmänner* is the *il y a*. With the camps, the Nazis created a system of death that has been called the *univers concentrationnaire*. This universe is literally the de-creation of the world.

In the article "IL Y A," Levinas states that the notion of the *il y a* is the very absence of God. Anthropological descriptions of mystical participation in the sacred that resemble the *il y a* are of a world without God: "The primitives are absolutely before Revelation, before the light" (1946: 150). For Levinas, creation is the birth of the individual existent out of existence. Like God's creation of the universe out of the *tohu wa-bohu*, so individuals rise up out of the *il y a*.

The birth of the subject out of the *il y a* is the central theme of Levinas's first book after the war, *Existence and Existents*. Writing in captivity, Levinas evokes the fatigue and labor of existing. To be an existent, a subject, is to stand up out of the *il y a*. It is to take a position over against existence itself: "To be conscious is to be torn away from the *there is*, since the existence of a consciousness constitutes a subjectivity, a subject of existence, that is, to some extent a master of being, already a name in the anonymity of the night" (1978a: 60). *Existence and Existents* is an extended meditation on the horror of being, the fear of being. But it is a horror that is only revealed when one's world is threatened. To be in the world is to be freed from the *il y a*:

> This circle is the world. In it the bond with care is relaxed. It is in times of misery and privation that the shadow of an ulterior finality which darkens the world is cast behind the object of desire. When one has to eat, drink and warm oneself in order not to die, when nourishment

becomes fuel, as in certain kinds of hard labor, the world also seems to be at an end, turned upside down and absurd, needing to be renewed. Time becomes unhinged. (1978a: 45)

Behind the sincerity of life, the goodness of the world we inhabit, lurks the chaos of the *il y a*. The horrors of our century, symbolized by the *univers concentrationnaire*, resembles the *Chaoskampf* of the ancients.

CREATION AND RESPONSIBILITY

At the heart of Emmanuel Levinas's work is the commandment, "You shall not commit murder." More than a negative prohibition, one is commanded to care for the other person. Confronted by the face of the other, one is literally solicited by God to care for this specific person. From the photos of starving children to the faces of the homeless on our streets, we experience a sense of responsibility for them. I am responsible for this person. I am the one called to help them. I am the one chosen by God to reveal the glory of God in physically caring for this person. Throughout his writings, Levinas seeks to describe this experience that defines who we are as human beings. His philosophical writings are difficult to read because of the great care with which he writes and addresses philosophical problems. But the experience he describes, our responsibility for the other person, is basic to all of us.

The philosophical issues he addresses are familiar to biblical scholars. How does one describe the Goodness of God, the sheer transcendence of God, without reducing God to our level, inscribing God within a system, be it language or theology? How can the very "otherness," what is unique to another person, be maintained in language or thought, without thereby reducing the other person to an object of my thought or perception? Can we think beyond the category of being and nonbeing, or is everything reduced to the limits of this world? How can we even possibly talk about creation, of an event before being and time? These questions and Levinas's attempts to address them are important because each individual person is important. However, if each person is no longer respected as unique, if all are only parts within a system, there remain no guarantees beyond social convention to protect the individual. While Kant's moral law would seem to guarantee the protection of the individual, what happens when a society defines certain members as nonhuman? When, as in Nazi Germany, a group is defined as vermin to be exterminated, who defines humanity? Levinas wants to show within philosophy the sanctity of each individual without appeal to special revelation or theology. He wants to show that ultimately each of us is responsible for the other person. Ethics must precede philosophy.

A student of both Husserl and Heidegger, Levinas pushes the phenomenological method to its limits in order to declare the priority of ethics over ontology. Before philosophy, before language, before even the I of the "I think, therefore I am," one is responsible for the other person. Elected by God before birth, one comes into being already responsible for one's neighbor. Before a choice or a conscious decision, one's self is possessed, obsessed by the command to care for the neighbor. Throughout his work, Levinas has sought a way to express the Good beyond being without thereby implicating God in being itself. How can one speak of what is beyond or before being? How can one trace the passing of the Infinite, the Transcendent?

There is an increasing sophistication and development throughout Levinas's work, but the central themes of responsibility and opposition to totalitarian thinking are present in all his work. His first work to bring him recognition was *Totality and Infinity*. Employing optical imagery, Levinas describes Western philosophy as the primacy of the panoramic that equates truth and disclosure as the essential virtue of being. Everything is brought to the light of the I that surveys and encompasses the world within its gaze. What is foreign, what is exterior, is absorbed into the interior by an idea. The foreign, the other, is neutralized and encompassed by the same. The totality of *Totality and Infinity* is the totality of being. From Plato to Hegel, Descartes to Heidegger, Western philosophy reduces all to the totality of being.

But alongside and within this tradition, there are statements pointing to what is beyond being. In his *Third Meditation*, Descartes described infinity as an idea that could not be conceived by a finite substance, but only received from God: "I would not, nevertheless, have an idea of an infinite substance, since I am a finite being, unless the idea had been put into me by some substance which was truly infinite" (124). Levinas employs this notion of infinity to disrupt the hegemony of Western thought that conceives everything in terms of being. Even nonbeing is defined in relationship to being and therefore is part of the ontological system. But with infinity there is an idea that surpasses the limits of reason, an idea that reason cannot conceive.

By the face of the other, the Infinite commands one to assume responsibility for this person. By the term *face*, Levinas indicates the otherness of the other person, that which resists the absorbing gaze of the I. That which cannot be thematized, that which is outside the totality of being, is the face. More than a visual image, the face is the speech of the other. The face challenges the I's comprehensive vision and freedom. The face of the one speaking exceeds the vision of the I. This overflowing of the face is the divinity of exteriority; it is the beyond being of God. This Good is what commands us not to kill our neighbor. In the face of our neighbor we are summoned by this command to take responsibility for this specific person in front of us.

Levinas wishes to avoid creating a new system or totality that would encompass the face or the relationship between persons. The face-to-face is an "irreducible and ultimate relation" (1969: 295). In describing the face, Levinas is invoking the reader into a face-to-face relationship:

> The description of the face to face which we have attempted here is told to the other, to the reader who appears anew behind my discourse and my wisdom. Philosophy is never a wisdom, for the interlocutor whom it has just encompassed has already escaped it. Philosophy, in an essentially liturgical sense, invokes the Other to whom the "whole" is told, the master or student. (ibid.)

Levinas invites the reader to join him in discovering within oneself the ethical experience. But unlike Kant, he realizes that ethics cannot be grounded in reason or the perfection of God. Responsibility for the other precedes both language and thought. We are free to disavow and ignore this responsibility, and often we subordinate its demands under the system of justice, but this command does not originate from us or being.

Levinas uses the idea of creation *ex nihilo* to express the separation of humanity and the Infinite, but also to reveal the multiplicity of human beings not united into a totality. Each person is unique and not subsumed under a category of being. We are separated from the Infinite. We are free to exist, because the Infinite leaves a place for us:

> Infinity is produced by withstanding the invasion of a totality, in a contraction that leaves a place for the separated being. Thus relationships that open up a way outside of being take form. An infinity that does not close in upon itself in a circle but withdraws from the ontological extension so as to leave a place for a separated being exists divinely. Over and beyond the totality it inaugurates a society. The relations that are established between the separated being and Infinity redeem what diminution there was in the contraction creative of Infinity. Man redeems creation. (1969: 104)

The image of contraction resembles the Kabbalistic notion of *Tsimtsum*. As Gershom Scholem explains in his *Major Trends in Jewish Mysticism*, Isaac Luria developed this notion to explain the possibility of creation:

> How can there be a world if God is everywhere? If God is "all in all," how can there be things which are not God? How can God create the world out of nothing if there is no nothing? This is the question. The solution became, in spite of the crude form which he gave it, of the highest importance in the history of later Kabbalistic thought. According to

Luria, God was compelled to make room for the world by, as it were, abandoning a region within Himself, a kind of mystical primordial space from which He withdrew in order to return to it in the act of creation and revelation. (260-61)

Levinas states that "Man redeems creation." We are responsible for the creation, for each other. Like God, we create a space for the other person by welcoming him or her into our home, by withdrawing our claim to the things of the earth.

Throughout *Totality and Infinity*, the goodness of creation is stressed. Though we are beings needing certain necessities for our existence, we are also capable of enjoying life. Our enjoyment of life, the happiness of living, affirms our being home in the world. But enjoyment is without security. The happiness of enjoyment is threatened by the return of things, food, tools, and the like back into the elemental: "But this identity of things remains unstable and does not close off the return of things to the element. A thing exists in the midst of its wastes. When the kindling wood becomes smoke and ashes the identity of my table disappears" (1969: 139–40). This return to the elemental is the *il y a*. The I at home with itself, enjoying itself, maintains itself against the anonymous, disturbing *il y a*.

The home where one dwells physically separates the I from the elemental while also offering the possibility of hospitality for the other. The other contests one's possessions by the epiphany of his face: "The Other—the absolutely other—paralyzes possession, which he contests by his epiphany in the face.... I welcome the Other who presents himself in my home by opening my home to him" (1969: 171). This hospitality redeems creation for the things enjoyed; the food, the bread from one's own mouth are given and shared with the other. This offering of the world is Transcendence: "Transcendence is not an optics, but the first ethical gesture" (174).

In his masterwork, *Otherwise Than Being: or, Beyond Essence,* Levinas deepens his analysis of language to show how one gives oneself to another in speaking. Language is explored in terms of what is said and the saying of the said. The content, what is said, is not as important as the act of saying. The simple courtesy of saying "After you" reveals the priority of the other person. More than courtesy, this deference to the other reveals one's election to an unlimited responsibility, even to the sharing of the bread from one's mouth. It is a responsibility even "for the faults and misfortunes of others" (1981: 10). But this command to care for the other cannot be situated within time; it cannot be even recalled or remembered.

The election of the self occurs before time. Even before the I of the *cogito,* one's self has been called to responsibility for the neighbor by God.

The I that later comes into being as a person distinguishes himself or herself from the environment, but this I is already defined by language and ontology. The I is derived from seeing and identifying oneself in time. But before the birth of this I, the self has already been called by God. Before the I, as identified by consciousness and defined by thought and philosophy, there is the me addressed by God as revealed in the prophetic response to God, "Here I am, send me."

This me is irreplaceable and unique. Echoing the Suffering Servant of Isaiah, Levinas describes this election:

> In the exposure to wounds and outrages, in the feeling proper to responsibility, the oneself is provoked as irreplaceable, as devoted to the others, without being able to resign, and thus as incarnated in order to offer itself, to suffer and to give. It is thus one and unique, in passivity from the start, having nothing at its disposal that would enable it to not yield to the provocation. (1981: 105)

In the passivity of the self, of the me, one can begin to speak of creation *ex nihilo:* "a passivity that excludes even receptivity, since in creation what would still be able to assume the action of a minimal extent, such as a matter assuming by its potencies the form that penetrates it, arises only once the creative act is completed" (1987a: 136). But how can we speak of a time before our existence? Properly, we can't. Such a thought is beyond the limits of thought and language. Properly, creation cannot be represented because it precedes being and time. To talk about creation or being created already situates this action in the present. But in the guilt or responsibility for the other person that obsesses us, we trace the passage of God; we acknowledge our creatureliness. We have been called before we exist. But this goodness that calls us cannot be reduced to the level of being. It is beyond being and nonbeing:

> In this obedience the subject is elected and retains the trace of election. This value never presents itself as a theme, is neither present nor represented, and, not allowing itself to be thematized, not beginning, is more ancient than a principle. In an immemorial past without a present, through the ambiguity and the antiquity of the trace, it is non-absent. This value is, by an abuse of language, named. It is named God. (1981: 136)

Levinas strictly maintains the transcendence of God, not as a higher level of being, but rather as beyond being. God is not the ground of being but the Good who calls us out of being. Creation *ex nihilo* expresses the separation of the creature from the Creator. God is beyond being or essence. But within the world, we find ourselves already called to serve the other. The glory of God is revealed in obedience to the command to care for the other:

> To bear witness (to) God is precisely not to state this extraordinary word, as though glory would be lodged in a theme and be posited as a thesis, or become being's essence. As a sign given to the other of this very signification, the "here I am" signifies me in the name of God, at the service of men that look at me, without having anything to identify myself with, but the sound of my voice or the figure of my gesture— the saying itself. It is sincerity, effusion of oneself, "extraditing" of the self to the neighbor. Witness is humility and admission; it is made before all theology; it is kerygma and prayer, glorification and recognition. (1981: 149)

God cannot be deduced from the created world, but in taking responsibility for others, God is glorified. Just as he renounces attempts at theodicy, Levinas avoids proving God's existence. The Good cannot be captured in words or represented but comes to pass in the substitution of oneself for the other. Levinas's description of responsibility in the saying, the offering of oneself to another, describes the Suffering Servant:

> In sincerity, in frankness, in the veracity of this saying, in the uncoveredness of suffering, being is altered. But this saying remains, in its activity, a passivity, more passive than all passivity, for it is a sacrifice without reserve, without holding back, and in this non-voluntary—the sacrifice of a hostage designated who has not chosen himself to be hostage, but possibly elected by the Good, in an involuntary election not assumed by the elected one. (1981: 15)

Yet in the saying, the response, "Here I am," that Glory is glorified:

> Glory is but the other face of the passivity of the subject. Substituting itself for the other, a responsibility ordered to the first one on the scene, a responsibility for the neighbor, inspired by the other, I, the same, am torn up from my beginning in myself, my equality with myself. The glory of the Infinite is glorified in this responsibility. (1981: 144)

There are traces of God in acts of goodness, but God is beyond the confines of creation. God is beyond being. The absolute transcendence of God means that ethics cannot be grounded in God or an ethical experience. Ethics is beyond experience, before philosophy. We are free to refuse the command that creates us responsible for the other. Creation *ex nihilo* signifies a world separated from God. It is only in sincerely responding to the other that the glory of the Infinite passes. God does not guarantee ethics. Only in our response to the other person, only in our offering of ourselves to another, does the trace of the glory of God pass within our world.

Throughout his career, Levinas has been consistent in addressing responsibility for the other person. In his earliest writings, the *il y a* plays a prominent role as he describes and characterizes the elemental nature of creation. But the *il y a* moves into the background of his later works as he focuses more and more upon language and the creation of the self. It is a movement from the outdoors to the hospitable home of *Totality and Infinity* to the very interior of the self who says "Here am I" in *Otherwise Than Being*. This journey inward accompanies a deeper and deeper degree of responsibility, from hospitality to being a hostage for the other person. The self is responsible for the faults of the other, for bearing their suffering. Responsibility is an obsession for the other, an obsession not chosen but received before the birth of the I. "I am summoned as some-one irreplaceable. I exist through the other and for the other, but without this being alienation: I am inspired. This inspiration is the psyche" (1981: 114). This inspiration, literally the breathing in of what is outside, speaks of the hollowing or the fission of the self. The self is not for the I, but for the other.

Again, Levinas's description of the psyche parallels the withdrawal, the contraction, the holding of breath of God to make room for creation. The self that suffers for the other creates a space for the other to live:

> In proximity the absolutely other, the stranger whom I have "neither conceived nor given birth to," I already have on my arms, already bear, according to the biblical formula, "in my breast as the nurse bears the nurseling. " He has no other place, is not autochthonous, is uprooted, without a country, not an inhabitant, exposed to the cold and the heat of the seasons. To be reduced to having recourse to me is the homelessness or strangeness of the neighbor. It is incumbent on me. (1981: 91)

This me, the psyche, the self, is responsible for creation: "The self, the subjection or subjectivity of the subject, is the very over-emphasis of a responsibility for creation" (125).

Against every thought or system that would reduce human beings to merely parts of a totality, Levinas seeks to affirm the uniqueness of each person. I am created, called by God before time, before being. My election is my responsibility for the other person. In caring for others, I redeem the created order. The threat of chaos, the *il y a*, that reduces things back to the waste and void of the elemental continually rustles in the background of life. Against this rustling of being that claims every-thing and nothing as part of it, the self passively substitutes itself for the other, denying its own being, its own existence, so that the other might live. Each of us is called to be the Suffering Servant, wounded for the transgressions of others, crushed for their iniquities, and yet out of this anguish to see light. This denial of being, even of one's own being, traces the passage of the Good beyond being.

Throughout the long night of Hitlerian violence, the few people who opened their homes to the persecuted and homeless Jews re-created a world for them. They offered the bread from their mouth to feed the hungry. Against the horror of the *il y a*, the elemental chaos to which National Socialism had reduced Jewish refugees through the weapons of hunger, fear, deportation, and extermination, the Righteous Ones provided shelter. They created a space for them in their own homes, their own hearts. Welcoming the other, they responded "Here I am," and through them the glory of God was shown in that dark night.

FACING JOB

Timothy K. Beal
Case Western Reserve University

The face to face remains an ultimate situation.
—Emmanuel Levinas (1969: 81)

The face remains present in its refusal to be contained.
—Emmanuel Levinas (1969: 194)

What his mind was intent upon was not the ingenious web of imagination but the shudder of thought.
—"Johannes de Silentio" (= Kierkegaard: 26)

The Akedah, or binding, of Isaac: out on Highway 61, Robert Zimmerman (a k a Bob Dylan) made it funny. "God said to Abraham 'Kill me a son.' Abe said 'Man, you must be putting me on.' God said 'No.' Abe said 'What?' God said 'You can do what you want Abe but the next time you see me coming you'd better run.' Abe said 'Where do you want this killing done?' God said 'Out on Highway 61.'" But it's not a funny story. Of course, having a keen sense for the ironic, Zimmerman knew this too. Highway 61 is not a funny place. And the thought that God could demand such a thing —even as a test—is enough to make one shudder.

Johannes de Silentio (a k a Søren Kierkegaard) was haunted by this story, and he imagined that Sarah, Isaac, and especially Abraham would have been haunted by it too, or rather by its God. The Akedah is a story riddled with gaps. What did Sarah know of all this? What did she think? What passed through Isaac's mind when he saw the knife poised above him in his father's hand? What did Abraham think when he first looked up and saw Mount Moriah on the horizon? By way of a "Prelude" to *Fear and Trembling*, Silentio tells a parable of a man obsessed with this story. "His only wish was to be present at the time when Abraham lifted up his eyes and saw Mount Moriah afar off" (26). The man reimagines the story four different ways, each time dwelling on different gaps in the biblical

version. Each time he fills those gaps in such a way that they only open
wider—infinitely wide, it seems. Each time, as we look up at Mount
Moriah with Abraham, we look down into the abyss, for what his mind
was intent upon was not the ingenious web of imagination nor the net-
works of sense-making, not the total vision of how it all comes together
meaningfully. Not what settles, but what disturbs: the "shudder of
thought." In the remembering, in the retelling, Mount Moriah becomes
theology's faultline, the epicenter of its own unsettling ("a tremor passed
through his body" [29]).

There Is

To be honest, the thought that God is dead—anything but unthinkable today—brings no terror, no existential panic, nothing other than a
sense of the ennui that has long settled in and that we have mostly
accommodated in our various fundamental cynicisms. What is truly terrifying, entirely unthinkable today, is the possibility that the
unnameable, incomprehensibly, is.

Levinas knew this too. He knew that "horror is nowise an anxiety
about death" (1989e: 33), my own or God's. Indeed, Levinas's writing
over the past sixty-five years has persistently, even vigilantly, reminded
us of this unthinkable thought, inclining our ears and turning our faces
toward what can be without being understood, without being *made sense*
of. His was a writing, even an invocation, that addressed itself precisely
to what is always out of reach, always beyond. And given his tremen-
dous influence on this century—from legal ethics to psychoanalysis to
feminist theory to talmudic studies to literary theory to Christian theology
to philosophy to ... name a few—he more than any other has presented
us with theological dimensions in the emerging contours of "postmodern" thought. The postmodern condition is traced with his disturbing,
restless, written incantations of the other. And, embarrassing as it is to
some of his interpreters, his persistent preoccupation with an unnameable, distinctly Jewish, biblical, even rabbinic "there is" (*il y a*)—a rustling
alterity that troubles the ingenious webs of imagination and opens to discourses of the religious—will not go away.

What is perhaps most remarkable in Levinas's writing, however, is
that the moment of the shudder is recognized also and even primarily
as an *ethical* moment, brought on by a particularity that resists being
reduced to generalization. For Levinas, much of the history of Western
philosophy has been characterized by a drive to dominate and comprehend all difference through identification and unity, or sameness. The
main force of ontology is that it "reduces the other to the same" (1969:
42). This kind of philosophy is totalitarian: it aims at grasping all things—

containing, controlling, totalizing, making self-present and intelligible. Anything that is nonidentical must be absorbed by force into the identical; otherwise, it must be either exterminated or abjected (cast out of the system of representation as neither subject nor object). But otherness persists in its irreducible particularity. Indeed, the irreducible difference of the other is the precondition of identity, which means that a subject's responsibility to the other must be primary, demanding that one, relentlessly and vigilantly, think the limits of any totalizing system. Thus "the overflowing of an adequate idea" (Levinas 1969: 80) becomes an ethical moment, a moment of obligation to and responsibility for an other.

Levinas draws our attention to the particular that exceeds system and is beyond accommodation by universal categories. It is a particular, moreover, that *in its particularity* opens onto an absolute otherness beyond even formal theology. He does so by attending to supposed mundane moments, in which otherness may be encountered. For example, the moment of insomnia: "Insomnia is disturbed in the core of its formal or categorial *sameness* by the *other*, which tears away at whatever forms a nucleus, a substance of the same, identity, a rest, a presence, a sleep" (Levinas 1989a: 170; cf. 1989e: 30–36). Insomnia is being unable to *just be.* It disturbs the stability of being, tearing away at whatever aggregation of features allows me to imagine that I am whole, one, integrated. It is the embodiment of unrest, the settling in of nonstasis. It is the refusal of rest. Refusal by whom? By my own body, which is somehow, in the experience of insomnia, other than that same body's desire for sleep. Insomnia, then, is the body divided against itself: the refusal of rest by otherness within the subject, a rustling of the *il y a* that calls into question my own identity, my own self-sameness. The irony of the body's refusal of that very same body's desire for sleep elicits a profound sense of self-disaggregation. And this ironic refusal (here life itself is inherently, deeply ironic) becomes an opening to ethics. The stirring of otherness within the one, the same, opens the restless subject to other others.

Or in the face-to-face encounter, where a supposed mundane moment becomes an "ultimate situation." The face of the other, which is present yet resists fitting in, disturbs my desire for a totalizing system of thought that might make sense of everything. Naked and hungry, imploring "do not kill me" (and echoing "'Thou shalt not kill"), the face solicits a critique of the system from within, "a calling into question of oneself, a critical attitude which is itself produced in the face of the other and under his authority" (Levinas 1969: 81). Self-critical reflection becomes accountability, responsibility. There is no reciprocity here, no possibility of simple dialogue. The moment is more freighted, more disturbing, *ultimate.* As Maurice Blanchot writes (1995: 245–46):

Just as others are always higher than I am, closer than I am to God (that unpronounceable name), so the dissymmetrical relation from them to me is the foundation of ethics and puts me under obligation, with an extraordinary obligation that weighs down on me.... It is knowledge that is not merely knowledge. It leads down a more difficult path, because we shall only find ourselves on it if we have gone through an upheaval in philosophy that places ethics at the beginning and even before the beginning. In this way, we discover Others [*Autrui*] not in the happy or laborious equality of friendship, but in a state of extreme responsibility that puts us under obligation, takes us hostage even, revealing to us the strangeness of the dissymmetry between You [*Toi*] and me.

Of course one must not forget that Levinas was Jewish, writing during and after the Nazi Shoah, and that his biography is "dominated by the presentiment and memory of the Nazi horror" (Levinas 1978b: 177). His parents were killed in Lithuania, and he himself, having moved to France as a teenager, only narrowly escaped the same end. When reading Levinas one cannot help but think of the face of the other Jew sentenced to obliteration under the sign of a Nazi "final solution." Here, moreover, the ash is a double-trace: the trace of the other Jew, but also the trace that marks the disappearance—or retreat, as Blanchot put it—of the God of salvific power and justice.

Faultline

The moment of insomnia, the moment of the face-to-face.... These are examples of moments when one encounters particularities that resist the general: epiphanies that resist metaphysics; points in time that resist collapse into the March of History (March of History: oblivion of the particular).

When read vigilantly, as Levinas teaches us to do, the book of Job can elicit such a moment. The particularity of the face of pain, Job's face, and the theological horror written across it, is just such an epiphany. Nowhere else in the Bible is the face of the other in utterly uncontainable pain so carefully and relentlessly attended to than in the book of Job. Nowhere else in the Bible is the voice of utterly senseless disorientation so carefully sustained than in the book of Job. It solicits my attention. It demands that I hear it. And its particular, infinite shrillness, which makes me shudder, insists on posing an ethical dilemma that quickly moves me into philosophical and theological crisis. It is theology's faultline reappearing, as Tod Linafelt has shown, even in the fundamental undecidability of one single word (ברך) that, in Job, doubles itself over blessing and curse. Job is "a crack in biblical discourse where life wells up and death infiltrates, a faultline in religious language that runs to the very character of God" (Linafelt 1995b: 1, cf. 15).

Indeed, the book of Job is like a faultline across the body biblical, for it calls into question the order of justice so rigorously postulated elsewhere, namely, the moral universe founded on the equations righteousness = blessing and wickedness = curse. This interrogation is oftentimes quite explicit. Consider, for example, the book of Job's subversive citations of Deuteronomy in the prologue and epilogue. Deuteronomy 28 recites a long list of curses that will fall on Israel if they refuse to obey YHWH. One of the more grievous afflictions is found in verse 35: "YHWH will strike you with terrible boils ... from the sole of your foot to the top of your head" (יככה יהוה בשחין רע ... מכף רגלך ועד קדקדך). This is precisely, word for word, what YHWH allows to happen to Job in 2:7: "he [who? ha-satan or YHWH?] struck Job" (ויך את־איוב) "with terrible boils from the sole of his foot to the top of his head" (בשחין רע מכף רגלו עד [וער Qere] קדקדו). Why? Because he had not obeyed YHWH? Because he was unrighteous? wicked? So his "friends" conclude. But we know that it is quite the opposite. Job is stricken precisely because he is righteous: "perfect/blameless and upright ... feared God and turned away from evil" (Job 1:1). It appears that Job's perfect righteousness has painted a giant bull's-eye on his forehead. Indeed, one might think of Job as Abraham and Isaac combined: he is the righteous, faithful patriarch, but he is also the one being sacrificed (תם: "perfect," "whole," like the תמים sacrificial offerings in Leviticus; cf. Job 12:4), in this case to a sinister wager —or perhaps for the sake of manifesting the terrible glory of God, which is what finally silences his screams for justice.

This countercitation of the Deuteronomic order of blessing and curse continues in the epilogue of Job (ch. 42). In Deut 30:3 it is promised that, after the people have survived the terrible curses, if they return to YHWH, heart and soul, "then YHWH your God will restore your fortunes" (ושב יהוה אלהיך את־שבותך). Job similarly concludes with a restoration of Job's fortunes, again using the same phrasing as Deuteronomy: "YHWH restored Job's fortunes" (ויהוה שב את־שבית [שבות Qere] איוב) (42:10). Why? Because he returned to God? He never left! (Though at times he wishes God would leave him alone—divine absence is not Job's problem.) The overall shape of Job moves, like Deuteronomy and other biblical passages, from blessing to curse and back, but Job renders the logic that elsewhere founds that pattern (do right, get blessed; do wrong, get cursed) at best senseless and at worst (in the hands of his friends) menacing.

The book of Job is a biblical faultline. It can cause a tremor to pass through the rest of Scripture, interrogating most profoundly its systems and strategies for making theological sense out of pain.

Here I want to focus on one particular epicenter along this fault-line, namely, the face-to-face encounter between Job and his friends in chapter 21, located at the conclusion of the book's second round of discussion (Job 15–21). In this round of discussion there is a pattern to the individual speeches that is worth noting, because it says a great deal about what is at stake in the relation (or nonrelation) between Job's particular voice of pain and the friends' generalizing voices of moral order.

First, every speech in this round begins with a second-person ("you") direct address. The friends begin each of their speeches by addressing Job directly and then invariably turn away from direct address to elaborate, in graphic detail, on the divinely ordained and executed fate of the wicked.

Chapter 15 (Eliphaz): "you" (vv. 1–16)
                        fate of the wicked (vv. 17–35)

Chapter 18 (Bildad):   "you" (vv. 1–4)
                        fate of the wicked (vv. 5–21)

Chapter 20 (Zophar):   "you" (vv. 1–3)
                        "Poem on the Fate of the Wicked" (vv. 4–29)

Moreover, the numerous allusions to Job's particular suffering in these discourses on the fate of the wicked make it clear that they increasingly see Job's fate as the fate of the wicked, and that Job is, therefore, wicked.

Job's responses all begin in similar fashion, addressing the friends directly with second-person speech. Rather than turning to the subject of the fate of the wicked, however, each of Job's speeches turns instead to graphic descriptions of *his own* pain and suffering, which he believes God is inflicting on him without reason.

Chapters 16–17 (Job): "you" (16:1–5)
                        "me" as God's victim (16:6–17:16)

Chapter 19 (Job):   "you" (vv. 1–6)
                        "me" as God's victim (vv. 7–29)

Chapter 21 (Job):   "you" (vv. 1–6)
                        the good fortune of the wicked, contrasted
                        with "my" own ill fortune and suffering
                        (vv. 7–34)

So, the friends' speeches move from "you" to an ill-fated "him" (the wicked, implying Job), whereas Job's speeches move from "you" to an ill-fated "me." The friends are especially good at offering graphic depictions of the generalized *wicked* person's suffering, whereas Job is especially good at offering graphic depictions of *his own* suffering. They do agree on one thing: God is the doer of the deeds. In all of these speeches, God is the subject of all the verbs of affliction. Beyond that, however, what these two voices represent is a radical and irreducible conflict between generalizing elaborations of a universal moral order on the one hand and the irreducible, senseless voice of pain in its particularity on the other. The friends' voices of the moral order speak in the impersonal third-person about "him" or "them" or "it," thereby locating and justifying suffering according to the rules of their grand, theodic scheme. God makes the wicked suffer because they deserve it, and if your suffering fits the description, then you must be wicked. The voice of personalized pain, on the other hand, speaks from its particularity, a particularity that does not fit within the moral universe of the friends. This voice makes no sense according to the rules of *any* order but rather appears as a mark of the absence of divine justice. The moral universe of the friends is a totalizing strategy of containment and, as their recitations on the fate of the wicked grow increasingly extravagant and forceful, the possibility that they will sacrifice Job to it becomes increasingly likely.

In 21:5, Job's resistance reaches a desperate climax in language that is highly suggestive of Levinas's writing on the face-to-face encounter:

Face me [פְּנוּ־אֵלַי] and be appalled. Put your hand over your mouth.

This is a most literal confrontation by the face of the other, for פְּנוּ (commonly translated "look at") is a verbal form of the Hebrew noun פָּנֶה, "face." In this encounter, the other's face presents itself within the friends' moral order as an anomaly. The face of senseless pain and suffering is present precisely in its refusal to be contained within that order. Job insists that this be faced and that it be allowed to interrogate their universalist claims and even to demolish them.

This is a moment of intentionality, an ethical moment. The friends could face him in his particularity—a particularity that is, in horrifying ways, "higher ... closer ... to God" than they are. If that were to happen, if they were to let this anomaly sink in, it would make their own faces grow pale.

The verb שָׁמַם, here translated in the imperative as "be appalled," carries a range of connotations from "appalled" to "horrified" to "devastated." The entire range may be applied here, as the face of pain should elicit the very sense of relentless terror and utter demolishment that Job has given voice to again and again throughout the dialogues. Here, then, appalment, horror, and devastation open a possibility for ethical trans-formation: a devastation of the friends' system for forcing sense from senseless suffering at the expense, and even sacrifice, of the other, whose epiphany here is Job's boil-ridden, stench-breathed, sleepless, and bleary-eyed face. This face, Job insists, has become the site of a divine rampage that is absolutely inexplicable by anything like traditional theodicy. It solicits rupture within the system and demands that the end-less droning of the friends be, *ultimately*, shut up: "Put your hand over your mouth."

At the same time, the thought of it all sends shudders through Job's own body: "When I think of it, I am terrified [or dismayed], and shud-dering seizes my flesh" (21:6). Silentio's Abraham looked up to Mount Moriah. Job need only look at himself. The shudder of thought is inextri-cably bound to the body in pain.

Job knows that "horror is nowise an anxiety about death" (Levinas 1989e: 33). Indeed, he longs for death as if for rest:

Why did I not die at birth? ...
Now I would be lying down in peace.
    I would be sleeping. I would be at rest. ...
Why is light given to the miserable,
    and life to the bitter-souled,
who long for death when it isn't there,
    and dig for it more than for hidden treasure,
who are extremely joyful
    and glad when they find the grave?
Why is light given to one who cannot see the way,
    whom God has hedged in? ...
Truly that which I fear is overcoming me,
    and what I dread is befalling me.
I am not at ease, nor am I quiet.
    I have no rest, but trouble comes. (Job 3:11, 13, 20–23, 25–26)

Job knows that "in suffering," as in insomnia, "there is an absence of all refuge.... The whole acuity of suffering lies in the impossibility of retreat.... In this sense suffering is the impossibility of nothingness (Levinas 1989d: 40). Job longs for rest, for stability, for security, but there is none. There is only senseless suffering. And remember (Job is always reminding us) that the problem is brought on not by the absence of God but rather by the oppressive ever-presence of divine power without divine justice. Theologically speaking, Job embodies the "shud-der of thought" that threatens to tear the friends' "ingenious [and insidious] web" of theodic sense-making.

Two-Faced Conclusion

This terror at divine *presence* is far from the guiding, comforting gaze of God in Ps 139:5–12:

> You shut me in behind and before,
>> and put your hand on me.
> Such knowledge is beyond me.
>> It is so high I cannot attain it.
> Where can I escape from your spirit?
>> Where can I flee from your presence?
> If I go up to heaven, there you are.
>> If I go down to Sheol, you are there too.
> If I take wing with the morning,
>> and settle at the far limits of the sea,
> even there your hand will lead me;
>> your right hand will hold me tight.
> If I say, "Surely darkness will hide me,
>> and the light around me will become night,"
> even the darkness is not dark to you.
>> Night is as the daylight.
>> Darkness and light are the same.

Levinas comments on this psalm in his lecture on Tractate *Berakot* 61a from Talmud Bavli (on the creation of the human in Gen 2). In that tractate, a rabbi invokes Ps 139 ("you shut me in behind and before ... where can I flee from your presence?") in order to support his reading of the original human creation as two-faced, that is, having one face in front and one in back. God faces the human both coming and going. In explicating this Levinas offers a meditation on Ps 139 in relation to the two-faced human:

> It is impossible to escape from God, not to be present before his sleepless gaze. A gaze which is not experienced as a calamity, in contrast to the terror felt by Racine's Phaedra! ... In the biblical passage, certainly God's presence means: to be besieged by God or obsessed by God. An obsession which is experienced as a chosenness. Everything is open.... With only a single face, I have a place in the rear of the head, the occiput, in which my hidden thoughts and my mental reservations accumulate. Refuge which can hold my entire thought. But here, instead of the occiput, a second face! Everything is exposed.... *You are always exposed! But in this spirited psalm you are discovered with joy; it is the exaltation of divine proximity that this psalm sings: a being exposed without the least hint of shadow.* (Levinas 1990a: 167; my emphasis)

The sleepless gaze seems here to arouse an insomnia without any of the terror of the *il y a* so striking in Levinas's philosophical discourse, or for that matter so striking in Job (who, by the way, alludes to Psalm 139 with deep irony). Indeed, for Job divine ever-presence is terrifying. Job experiences it as a ceaseless pursuit, exposure, and torment that leaves him longing for rest, sleep, even and especially a final sleep. For Job, unlike the psalmist (as Levinas recalls him), death is refuge from divine besiegement and divine obsession.

> Why is light given to the miserable ...
> who are extremely joyful
>   and glad when they find the grave?
> Why is light given to one who cannot see the way,
>   whom God has hedged in? (Job 3:20, 22–23)

To transpose Levinas: in Job's vexed realm, you are discovered with terror; it is the dread of divine proximity that Job screams: a being exposed without the least hint of shadow.

So is this reading of Job a citation of Levinas against Levinas? Does it oppose Levinas the philosopher to Levinas the Talmudist? Perhaps. Some might say that they are opposed. Yet anyone who reads Levinas the philosopher and Levinas the Talmudist carefully will quickly recognize the one in the other, for there is "a *sameness* that these *others* had in common" (Levinas 1990a: 172). I would prefer, therefore, to think of them as two sides, two *faces,* if you will, of an irreconcilable tension within which Levinas teaches us to live, vigilantly, sleeplessly. This, I think, is a heritage Levinas has left us. To follow him, we might sing with the psalmist one moment and then, the next moment, clasp our hands over our blabbering mouths as we face Job, in all our deep-set irony, in all our uncontainable vacillations between exaltation and dismay.*

---

* This essay was written in the weeks following Levinas's death in 1995.

ESCHATOLOGY: LEVINASIAN HINTS IN A PREFACE[1]

Elias Bongmba
Rice University

This paper is a meditation on the hints Levinas provides on eschatology. I do not plan to do a full-length exegesis of a particular biblical
text or a reading of Levinas's talmudic meditations. I focus on his view
that the intersubjective journey is and should be an eschatological experience. As background to the discussion, I comment on Levinas's views
on the relationship between philosophy and theology. In addition, I
present in brief Heidegger's reading of Paul's First Letter to the Thessalonians, to highlight Heidegger's reading of that epistle on the issue of
the Parousia so as to provide a sharp contrast with the remarks Levinas
made on eschatology. In the conclusion, I also bring Levinas's understanding of eschatology into a conversation with the work of the
African scholar John Mbiti. Levinas has not developed a full-blown
eschatology in the sense theologians talk about, but he has indicated in
the preface to *Totality and Infinity* that the intersubjective journey is a
morality that will be ushered in through the eschatology of messianic
peace (1969: 22). Levinas offers suggestive remarks elsewhere, but I will
return to Levinas's remarks in the preface of *Totality and Infinity* toward
the end of this essay.

I must begin by pointing out that a meditation on a theological
theme that Levinas has not developed fully is a risky business for two
reasons. First, Levinas is a philosopher and as such has articulated his
thoughts in dialogue with other philosophers—Heidegger, Marcel, Berg-
son, Husserl, Hegel, Kant, Descartes, Plato, Parmenides, and so
forth—and not with theologians. Second, in addition to his philosophical
works, Levinas's religious works come out of the Jewish tradition. His
Jewish background is so important that without it his philosophy would
not have been possible (Peperzak 1983: 298). It is clear that Levinas has

---

1 I want to thank Tamara Eskenazi for reading an earlier draft of this paper and giving me helpful insights.

attempted to articulate his philosophy with these influences without compromising philosophical discourse. Yet Levinas's enterprise goes further than Alan Megill's claim that even though Levinas uses "a philosophical language and method, the dominant preoccupation of his thought arises within the perspective of a certain kind of Judaism" (Megill: 308). Were Megill right, Levinas would be engaged in theology instead of philosophy.

The question then is, Why attempt to tease out hints on eschatology from Levinas's words? Levinas himself, in his essay "God and Philosophy," has argued that philosophy cannot ignore God (1993a: 154). The difficulty of bringing God into philosophical reflection lies in the fact that any attempt to make the notion of God meaningful runs into difficulties because "as soon as [God] is conceived, this God is situated within being's move" (154). Aware of this, Levinas proceeds along the path on which he has anchored his philosophy, the idea of alterity and of going beyond being, intelligibility, and rationalism in order to address the problematics of God and philosophy (154–55). Levinas underscores the importance of religious ideas but argues that religious thinking has some affinity to philosophy because it is founded on experience.

> A religious thought which appeals to religious experiences allegedly independent of philosophy already, inasmuch as it is founded on experience, refers to the "I think," and is wholly connected to philosophy. The "narration" of religious experience does not shake philosophy and cannot break with presence and immanence, of which philosophy is the emphatic completion. (158–59)

Levinas argues that even in Descartes's substantialist metaphysics, the idea of God breaks out, as it were, of a *cogitatio,* overturning "the universal validity and primordial character of intentionality. We will say that the idea of God breaks up the thought which is an investment, a synopsis and a synthesis, and can only enclose in a presence, re-present, reduce to presence or let be" (160). Reflecting on Cartesian meditations, Levinas demonstrates that the thought of the infinite that Descartes writes about interrupts the thought of the "I" bringing in a second moment of consciousness that was not there before. Levinas recognizes the presence of God that questions self's recollecting and assuming activity. Levinas also interprets this manifestation of the infinite to the thinking subject as a holding back. This manifestation defies re-presentation and contemporaneity. It designates an immeasurable depth, "a dazzling in which the eye takes in more that it can hold" (163). Robert Manning argues that the God whose presence Levinas evokes here is not the God of natural theology, the mysterious, the God of mysticism, nor the God some people think of as the most excellent being.

> For Levinas, God is the absolutely unknowable, absolutely transcendent, and wholly other God of traditional Judaism. What isn't so traditional about Levinas's God, what isn't so commonplace about Levinas's "certain kind of Judaism," however, is his insistence that God can be known only through the ethical command.... "the knowledge of God comes to us as a commandment, as a Mitzvah." (147)

Manning's point about the Otherness of God in Levinas is correct; however, it seems to me that Levinas's argument that God can be known only through the ethical command is commonplace in Judaism because the emphasis on the ethical places Levinas squarely in the prophetic tradition. Levinas is clear that the presence of such a God awakens a praxis, which Levinas calls a desire. It is a desire that cannot be satisfied in the ordinary sense. It is a "desire for that which is beyond being, is disinterestedness, transcendence—desire for the Good" (1993a: 163). This desire for the Good is not service to the transcendent being, but a human interaction in desire which then reveals God.

> The God of the Bible cannot be defined or proved by means of logical predictions and attributions. Even the superlatives of wisdom, power and causality advanced by medieval ontology are inadequate to the absolute otherness of God. It is not by superlatives that we can think of God, but by trying to identify the particular inner human events which open towards transcendence and reveal the traces where God has passed. (Kearney: 67)

Divine transcendence is here placed beyond human wisdom. The idea is that human beings cannot establish divine presence through thought because the divine remains absolute alterity and stands outside human schematization. However, human events, that is, actions undertaken for and on behalf of others, can open the path to God. Levinas argues that history has called into question the Western ontological view of God, which has made people see God as a player in the unfolding human drama with God as an ontological adventurer (for a fuller discussion of this point, see Manning: 150). Levinas resists such constrictions on the idea of God. "We have wondered if the Revelation might not lead us to precisely this idea of inequality, difference and irreducible alterity which is uncontainable within gnoseological intentionality, a mode of thought which is not knowledge but which, exceeding knowledge, is in relation with the Infinite or God" (1989c: 208). Why then does such a God not fit into the more familiar picture of the great miracle worker in the drama of history? The danger here is turning theology into theodicy. The problem here is that the experience of suffering, such as the Holocaust, makes it difficult to hold to a traditional, ontological view of God or make it meaningful or bearable (Manning: 151). According to Levinas, what was witnessed in the camps was Nietzsche's notion of the death of God (1993a: 161–62). But his line of reasoning at this point is not intended to dismiss religion. Instead, he indicates that out of the ruins of theodicy, the ruins that destroyed the traditional conception of God which cannot be employed in a traditional theodicy to talk about a happy ending, we can still affirm morality. Given these circumstances, Manning says, Levinas invites all to think of God in terms of the moral law. "God must be conceived strictly in ethical terms because this is the only way to think God, through the face of the sufferer whose suffering is beyond all theodicy. The trace of God, says Levinas, is in the face's commandment to be responsible for and love the other" (Manning: 153).

So far Levinas makes the case that philosophy and God are not incompatible. He strengthens his case by drawing from the Cartesian experience to indicate that subjectivity is aware of this alterity, this Other that is in subjectivity. Levinas goes on to show that it is this presence or awareness of this alterity that makes love and ethics possible. Ethics is possible because of the transcendental structure that we find in the idea of the infinite. Ethics establishes a relationship between the finite and the Infinite without any contradictions. Levinas goes back to the Hebrew Bible to locate the mode of discourse that defines this relationship—it is the prophetic word. The prophetic word brings life to hearers. It is a transcendent word that cannot be objectified. It issues an invitation to engage in the ethical deed.

Richard Cohen has pointed out that in laying down his position, Levinas does not intend to avoid or reduce conflict but attempts to find a solution by going beyond the polarity between the God of reason and the God of Abraham, Isaac, and Jacob, by thinking a personal God philosophically (174). Cohen has brought together in a very compelling manner Levinas's positions on this question. I mention them here without discussing them in detail. First, in Cohen's view, Levinas's notion of atheism conditions a relationship with God (180). Second, the human face opens to us dimensions of divinity. Third, the human face should not be seen as the incarnation of God but as the height, which makes possible the revelation of God. Fourth, the best expression and demonstration of the presence of God is to render justice to other people (Levinas 1969: 78, cited in Cohen: 188). Fifth, cries for justice come out of proximity with the other (Levinas 1981: 158, cited in Cohen: 190). Sixth, Levinas posits a third party that is constantly checking asymmetry and proximity in the face-to-face relationship. Seventh, it is only in the context of proximity that we can understand justice, society, the state, its institutions, exchanges, and work.

Levinas, like Kant, recognizes the importance of religion and the affinity of ethics with religion (Kant 1965: 122). In an interview with Edith

Wyschogrod, Levinas confirms that the *mise en scène* of religion is similar to that of ethics (Wyschogrod: 106). Having said that, I should point out that Levinas, like Heidegger before him, indicates that he has given up on philosophical theology and the theology of faith in order to emphasize the relation with the Other (108). There is a subtle distinction that one must make here. Heidegger warned against turning to philosophy in the hope that philosophy can rescue theological thinking. In his *Introduction to Metaphysics* he stated the matter very clearly. "Only epochs which no longer fully believe in the true greatness of the task of theology arrive at the disastrous notion that philosophy can help to provide a refurbished theology if not a substitute for theology, which will satisfy the needs and tastes of the time" (1961: 7). However, I remain convinced that this very negation of theology in both Heidegger and Levinas opens up new avenues for theological exploration. Manning has rightly suggested that Levinas has contributed to religion by employing language that demands that knowledge of God should be subordinated to ethical responsibility for the Other. This shift in focus is primary and challenges preoccupation with merely studying and understanding God (Manning: 162–63). Furthermore, Manning suggests that Levinas's philosophy makes a significant contribution in the domain of ecumenical discussions among different religious traditions (128). In addition, by rejecting theological discourse that stresses knowing God, Levinas argues for an ethical relation with another human being. Our knowledge of God is defined by our relationship to another human being.

> The comprehension of God taken as a participation in [his] sacred life, and allegedly direct comprehension, is impossible, because participation is a denial of the divine, and because nothing is more direct than the face to face, which is straightforwardness itself. A God invisible means not only a God unimaginable, but a God accessible in justice. Ethics is the spiritual optics. (1969: 78)

The dichotomy that Levinas sets in the above passage is between comprehension and a face-to-face confrontation. The idea here is not so much the issue of God's absence as the importance Levinas attaches to how one gets to God. That path lies in justice, and such justice is understood only in ethics, which Levinas calls in one of his memorable phrases, "spiritual optics." In this move away from comprehension, Levinas problematizes and rejects theological discourse that is compartmentalized into theory and practice (Meskin: 139–40). Such a procedure misses the idea of transcendence. "Transcendence happens when I give, when I leave my own self-centered pleasure and minister to the other's need. The transcendence which giving or hospitality produce is neither theoretical nor practical" (140). Thus by paying attention to the ethical, Levinas invites us to a different way of thinking theologically. To read Levinas with this in mind is to catch the *double entendre* in his religious discourse, which rejects a theologizing that focuses on comprehension for comprehension's sake, yet invites readers to a rigorous engagement in ethics as a way of seeing the human and divine. It is in this light that one has to read his terse comments on eschatology as an intersubjective enactment.

In the rest of this paper, I will meditate on what Levinas contributes to the understanding of eschatology. In order to do that, I begin with a detour into Heidegger's remarks on themes that are related to eschatology. I do so because Levinas draws from and reacts against the ontology of Heidegger. Furthermore, it will become clear that in reacting against Heidegger, Levinas offers the prospect of a public eschatology rather that a private resoluteness in the face of one's death as a way of moving into the future.

HEIDEGGER ON PAULINE ESCHATOLOGY

Heidegger's work in this area has not received the attention his other writings have been given. The remarks I present here are taken from "Heidegger's Introduction to the Phenomenology of Religion, 1920–21" by Thomas Sheehan. There is a sense in which one could say that these lectures are the closest Heidegger ever got to his Catholic roots, even though he was influenced at this time by Protestant theologians such as Schleiermacher, Luther, and Pascal (Ingraffia: 11). Heidegger rejected Catholicism as a movement and joined instead what was called the "Free Christianity" movement, whose membership included the influential philosopher Edmund Husserl. They championed nondogmatic Protestant views. It is during this phase of Heidegger's "faith" journey that he gave his lectures of 1920 in Freiburg (Ingraffia: 112).

Sheehan points out that Heidegger in these lectures addressed Christianity's approach to facticity of life (experience). Heidegger believed that the Christian understanding of the future was rooted in temporality while the Greek approach focused on the disclosure of truth (Sheehan: 315). In undertaking this exposition, Heidegger hoped to return to the *Vorfragen*, which for him dealt with factical life, because Heidegger was convinced that "philosophy as universal phenomenological ontology takes its departure from the hermeneutic of *Dasein* which ties all philosophical inquiry down to the point where it arises and to which it returns: existence" (316). Factical experience was the coming to grips with the world of meaning; "meaningfulness is lived experientially in what Heidegger calls *Bekümmerung* ... what *Being and Time* will later call *Besorgen* and *Sorge*" (317).

Heidegger approached his task historically, questioning what is experienced and how it is experienced. This procedure was at the heart of Heidegger's understanding of the task of phenomenology, which was to "thematize the very temporal enactment of the event of meaning, and not primarily that-which-it-intends nor the relations established in intentionality" (318). His goal was to recover being in its various forms, a task which necessitated the understanding that all relationality is undertaken in a "time-determined character" involving the negative "not yet" (318). It is thus clear that Heidegger, in effect, was introducing a new approach to the philosophy of religion by stressing factical life experience in temporality, historicity and that very experience itself. The historical situation then became the door for approaching Paul's eschatology in his First Letter to the Thessalonians.

According to Heidegger, the message of this epistle was based on the concrete situation of the apostle's preaching. Heidegger focused on the Greek terms *genesthai* and *eidenai* and stressed presence and one's experiential knowledge of the situation. Thus in the communication of Paul to Christians at Thessalonica, Paul stresses that their daily experience involved their own knowledge of their existential situation. Their situation involved tribulation and joy. Sheehan rightly remarks that in locating this knowledge in affectivity, Heidegger brought together the body and mind as an early indication of the existential structures of *Being and Time* (321). Heidegger drew from Paul to argue "that the original Christian experience generates primordial temporality and lives out of it" (321).

The actions of the Thessalonians demonstrated that they were aware of their temporality. Hegel would have said the Thessalonians were conscious of their situation. Heidegger interpreted the verbal expressions "turning, serving and waiting" (1 Thess 1:9–10) as activities of temporality (321). They waited for the coming of Jesus, the Parousia. Heidegger did not address the time of the Parousia directly but focused instead on Paul's comment to the Thessalonians about their foreknowledge. Heidegger believed that by emphasizing their foreknowledge, Paul wanted to show that this knowledge was already part of their existence. "The question of temporality in Christian religious experience becomes a matter of how one lives one's facticity. This is not a matter of moralism but fundamentally of temporality" (322). Paul made it concrete by contrasting two groups of people. The first cried for peace and security. This was false security because they depended on the world. The second group lived in the fight of the day, which Heidegger interpreted as self-comprehension and the day of the Lord. It also indicated that these people were living in the wakefulness of the Parousia. What Heidegger emphasized was not so much waiting as the presence of God, with Pauline immanence which seemed to indicate that "the how of factical life ... [is] uncertainty." An important shift takes place here from waiting for the future event, or expecting the future, into an emphasis on the presence before God. *Vollzugszusammenhang mit Gott* then becomes one's way of living one's life of uncertainty before an unseen God (Ingraffia: 115). The idea of expectation in Pauline eschatology is superseded by an existential kairotic moment, an eternal present. Sheehan rightly sums up Heidegger's reading of eschatology as an interpretation of the temporality of *Dasein*.

> From out of this context of the enactment of factical life-experience before the unseen God (i.e. being awake) there is generated primordial temporality. The meaning of facticity is temporality and the meaning of temporality is determined from one's basic relation to God. One is becoming, in the uncertainty of the future, what one has already become. Moreover, Christian religious life is nothing other than the living out of this unique temporality and, correlatively, only from out of this temporality can the meaning of God (whatever it might be) be determined. And no objectivist conceptions of time can ever touch this kind of temporality. (322)

Although Heidegger's exposition priorizes temporality, he gives a forceful twist to his perspective that early Christianity interpreted the Parousia as an individualizing experience. According to Sheehan, Heidegger's early lectures and writings stress singularity, an idea that would be a constant theme of *Being and Time*. One senses even in these early reflections an attempt by the individual to renounce the future. Brian Miclot points out that this is Heidegger's interpretation of other writings in the Pauline corpus where "orientation toward factical life consists in the renouncing of having any 'special' grace and taking upon one's own [fate] by one's self" (34). It is noteworthy that Heidegger does not engage in any speculation about the future at this point, nor does he attempt to deal with life after death. His interpretation of Paul addresses, in the main, the early Christian understanding of existence.

LEVINASIAN HINTS ON ESCHATOLOGY

Unlike Heidegger, Levinas has not devoted a particular work to the Parousia. But what Levinas says about the future and his brief remarks on eschatology at the beginning of *Totality and Infinity* give us some grounds for reflections on eschatology. I will introduce those comments with brief remarks on Levinas's discussion of time and the future. Levinas's early reflections on time focus on the future in response to Heidegger (Miclot: 34). Let us recall that Heidegger interprets existence as temporality. Rather than discuss the time of the Parousia, he stresses wakefulness in the light of an uncertain future. In *Being and Time,* Heidegger introduced *Dasein*'s concern about the future through its concern for death. Whereas in the lectures inauthentic existence is described as entanglement with the things of this world and false belief in peace and security, inauthentic existence in *Being and Time* is living the agenda of the herd or what Heidegger calls *Das Man* (they), which teaches *Dasein* to believe that it can avoid death. In the lectures, authentic living was a wakefulness resulting from knowledge of one's condition vis-à-vis God, whose presence one awaits in uncertainty; authenticity in *Being and Time* is owning up to one's facticity and facing death boldly. Heidegger does not see death in biological terms, nor does he see it as something that comes at the end of one's life on earth. Instead, death is constitutive of *Dasein* (Macquarrie: 33–35). Death is *Dasein*'s and *Dasein*'s alone (Heidegger 1962: 284, 294; see Bongmba 2000). Manning points out that "death individualizes *Dasein* by calling it back from its lostness in the *they* to realize itself as a solitary being. ... when *Dasein* stands before death as its ownmost possibility, 'all its relations to any other *Dasein* have been undone" (69; Heidegger 1962: 294).

Levinas, in opposition to Heidegger, demonstrates that it is not death that defines the future, but love (1987c: 76; 1969: 28). Levinas does not see death as something that one anticipates nor as a process of authenticating one's self. Instead death is foreign, uncertain, something we cannot quite grasp or lay hold of (1987c: 71). This is not a denial of death. Levinas says that death is what is "absolutely unknowable ... foreign to all light" (70). One senses in the phrase an attack on the goals of phenomenology, the search for comprehension and its practice which involves bringing all things to the searching light of the knowing subject. But more than that, it is clear from Levinas's perspective that I do not possess death, in the Heideggerian sense of "mineness." It is not mine because Levinas sees death as absolute violence (1969: 233).

Given this perspective, Levinas argues that death is Other. It comes from outside and seizes me, intrudes into my privacy and solitude. When death comes I cannot return to my own base and face it alone as Heidegger suggests (1987c: 74). In this light, the future is also other and comes to me from the outside. Therefore, time is not my own (79). Levinas talks of time by connecting the future to the present. That connection is not intended to do away with the future but to demonstrate that I can have an understanding of time and hence the future when I encounter otherness in the form of another human being rather than my own singular death.

All this is quite a contrast to what we have seen in Heidegger. In the lectures, Heidegger demonstrated that out of the early Christian world, existence is coming to terms with one's temporality, finding meaning in one's world by living authentically in the knowledge of what one is (God's). Such knowledge of existence consists of waiting in the face of the uncertainty of the future. In pursuance of the *Seinsfrage* in *Being and Time,* Heidegger demonstrated that authentic *Dasein* moves into the future by owning up to its utmost possibility and does so by facing its own death. Levinas on the contrary argues that death pulls me violently and hence is other, as also is the future it brings. I can only understand that future if I can turn now and see Otherness, not of death, but another human being to whom I should respond in love.

In *Totality and Infinity* as well as his other works, Levinas calls for a relation with the Other that is grounded on love. The future comes to us from outside. Rather than recoil and face our own death as authentic human beings, Levinas calls on us to be open to the future that is other and to respond to it differently. Levinas talks of fecundity as that which can give hope, and spells out the otherness of the future. Levinas reminds us through the notion of fecundity that there is continuity after the disruption of death, but we cannot determine it.

I have been struck at how the Nigerian writer Wole Soyinka demonstrates this notion of an overpowering future that defies the manipulative schemes of the subject. In his play *Death and the King's Horseman,* which is based on an event that took place in Oyo in 1946, the character Elesin, the King's Horseman, is being pursued by praise singers and drummers because, according to the local custom, the horseman was supposed to accompany the king to the next world (Soyinka: 7; see author's note). Therefore, when the town was ready to bury the dead king, his horseman was also going to be buried alive, with the king. The sound of the praise singers alerts everyone's attention, including the houseboy's, to the colonial district officer who tells his master the meaning of this action in the tradition (Soyinka: 26). The district officer, who is outraged by this custom, intervenes to stop the enactment of this ritual by putting Elesin in jail so that the people cannot apprehend and bury him alive. Since this is an important ritual, Elesin's son, who has just returned from England, dies in the place of his father. His father, who has been put in jail by the colonial official to prevent the community from burying him alive with the king, hears that his son has died and commits suicide. It turns out that in anticipation of his departure from this world during the burial of the king, Elesin had decided to take a new bride and have a son with her because he wanted to go to his death knowing that "my vital flow, the last from this flesh, is intermingled with the promise of future life" (40). This plan does not work. As an indication that no one controls the future, and as an indication that even fecundity is Other, Elesin makes this confession to his bride.

First I blamed the white man, then I blamed my gods for deserting me. Now I feel I want to blame you for the mystery of the sapping of my will. But blame is a strange peace offering for a man to bring to a world he has already wronged, and to its innocent dwellers. Oh little mother, I have taken countless women in my life, but you were more than a desire of the flesh. I needed you as the abyss across which my body must be drawn, I filled it with earth and dropped my seed in it at the moment of preparedness for my crossing.... I confess to you my daughter, my weakness came not merely from the abomination of the white man who came violently into my fading presence, there was also the weight of longing on my earth-held limbs. I would have shaken it off, already my foot had begun to lift but then, the white ghost entered and all was defiled. (65)

The passage is an eloquent repudiation of the subject's ability to manipulate the future or for that matter even manipulate fecundity (for further discussion on fecundity, see Eskenazi's introduction to this volume). As for Levinas, the future is a mystery we cannot control. Levinas foresees an eternity devoid of *Dasein*'s repetition because the future always brings in something new. Levinas will spell out this notion later on in *Totality and Infinity* when he discusses fecundity as a relationship with the future. In opposition to the reiteration of the "I" in fecundity,

the tedium of this repetition ceases; the I is other and young, yet the ipseity that ascribed to it its meaning and orientation in being is not lost in this denouncement of self. Fecundity continues history without producing old age. Infinite time does not bring eternal life to an aging subject; it is better across the discontinuity of generations, punctuated by the inexhaustible youth of the child. (1969: 268)

What are contained in this passage are notions of newness, youth, society, community, intersubjectivity. Thinking eschatologically rules out self-projections.

Levinas argues that the future comes to us as surprise, inviting us to respond, a response that is different from Heidegger's notion of withdrawing into ourselves to face our own death. We can now return to his early remarks about eschatological peace offered in the preface of *Totality and Infinity*. Levinas opens his preface with a rather chilling remark on war. War destroys morality. Conceiving war and coming up with the strategy to win lies in the domain of politics (1969: 21). "War does not manifest exteriority and the other as other; it destroys the identity of the same" (21). Hence, Levinas indicates that he intends to address morality that opposes the politics of totality and war. It is a morality that can become universal "when the eschatology of messianic peace will have come to superpose itself upon the ontology of war" (22).

Levinas indicates that some philosophers have no trust in eschatology, even though they want to "profit from it to announce peace also" (22). However, they still treat eschatology as a "subjective and arbitrary divination of the future, the result of a revelation without evidences, tributary of faith [and] belong[ing] naturally to opinion" (22). Kisiel has pointed out that Heidegger's reading of eschatology focused more on methodology and, we might add, stressed the existence of self and a self-authentication process (1988: 40). Ingraffia argues that Heidegger's reading of eschatology detheologizes the Christian conception of humanity (121). By contrast, Levinas has in mind "prophetic eschatology" that does not attempt to win support through philosophical evidence. What Levinas envisions as eschatology rejects the ontology of war. The aim of such an eschatology is not to engage is the construction of a teleological system or stress a linear orientation of history (1969: 22). The question then is: What does Levinas mean?

First, Levinas links eschatology to relationality. He sees eschatology as that which "institutes a relation with being beyond totality or beyond history, and not with being beyond the past and the present" (22). What are immediately introduced here are themes that carry the argument of *Totality and Infinity,* such as exteriority. It is a surplus exteriority, which makes the fullness of being look empty. It is something that comes from beyond; hence, it is transcendent and is infinite in its scope. These themes are discussed in Levinas as a distinct mode of relating to a human other who is different, transcendent, and beyond my control. Breaking away from the totality of war means instituting in its place dialogue with this human Other. It is dialogue that invites me to the teaching of the other and orders me to accept my responsibility to be ethical. From this perspective, eschatological peace is not recoiling into myself and facing my own death. It is not anticipating or speculating about a future utopia some day. Eschatological peace, according to Levinas, is a human relationship established with a genuine human Other. Eschatology happens now.[2]

Second, eschatology opposes totality. Levinas foresees eschatology as experience with other people. This vision of eschatology spells relationality and involves judgment on history. Prophetic eschatology does not allow one to recoil into oneself and wait for the coming era. Instead, it challenges one to recognize and relate ethically to the Other. History is judged for violence exhibited in wars. Contrary to Christian eschatology,

---

2 As Eskenazi points out, Levinas is articulating a position whose roots go back to the Hebrew Bible and to Jewish interpretations of the Hebrew Bible. See Eskenazi's introduction to this volume.

which stresses the importance of last judgments, Levinas says: "it is not the last judgment that is decisive, but all the judgments of all the instants in time, when the living are judged" (23). It is important from Levinas's perspective to recognize that history is not a grand notion but a human engagement. It is an engagement of human beings who exist in time and have relationships determined by themselves and not totality. Existence as engagement with other people implies speaking—and it is important that people speak for themselves rather than endorse the violence of history. This eschatological vision breaks up totality. Although Levinas emphasizes the particularity of each person, he rejects Heidegger's reading of the future in individual terms. One can also see an attack on Hegel's patronizing grand schemes. Both Hegel's and Heidegger's views of experience are to be supplanted in *Totality and Infinity* with an eschatological and moral vision that proclaims that "the experience of morality does not proceed from this vision—it consummates this vision; ethics is optics" (23).

Third, Levinas argues that eschatology is a condition for peace. Levinas acknowledges that the evidence of history shows the preponderance of violence and war instead of peace. This ought to refute eschatology. Levinas nevertheless argues for the possibility of this view of eschatology and promises to demonstrate it phenomenologically by tracing the experience of totality to a point where it breaks up. This point is "the transcendence of the face of the Other" (24). Later on in the preface Levinas defends subjectivity, arguing that it provides the basis for an intersubjective relation in which the face of the Other breaks totality and replaces it with responsibility.

Fourth, Levinas irrevocably ties eschatological peace to justice in society. In a discussion on the Other and others in society Levinas attempts to show that at a primordial level my relationship with the Other is a reflection of my relationship with other people in the society (Peperzak 1993: 166). Levinas has articulated an asymmetrical relationship between the subject and the Other, but he also argues that such a relationship does not rule out society and politics (166). What Levinas articulates is the presence of a third person who watches me as I undertake my obligations to the Other. Under the watchful eye of a third party, I am obligated toward the poor, exile, stranger, widow, and the like. Carrying out these responsibilities requires structures that will make this obligation possible, hence political society. In such a society I am responsible for the Other, and the Other is also responsible for or is servant of another third or fourth who is Other of my Other. It is in such a situation that justice can be done. Such justice does not come out of a community of reciprocal relationships, but from obligations I have toward the Other (172). I am commanded by the Other, a transcending activity that engenders solidarity concretized in speech because a new

kinship, community, and fraternity have been born. This is an understanding of intersubjectivity that rules out exclusive love.

Although Levinas uses the example of the third "man," which structures justice and peace, he argues that facing the future that way is
openness to prophetic eschatology through which individuals share the
message of peace (1993a: 15–24, 25–46).[3] This message of peace takes root
in society whose future lies in fecundity, where desire and responsibility
make it possible to address evil (199). The notion of fecundity breaks out
of being's temporality and self-centeredness into a future that is given
and where there are possibilities for new beginnings. Ecstatic infinition,
the existential mode of existence that reaches into the future through an
authenticity that recoils inward and allows the individual to face his or
her own death, cannot contain this future. Furthermore, beings' infinition
cannot contain eschatological peace, which requires what Peperzak calls
"sealed or completed time, an eternity of 'messianic' peace" (1993: 200).
Levinas stops short of giving a philosophical exposition of what eternal
time might mean here. His talmudic reflections indicate that prophetic
messianism can be of help in pointing in that direction (1990c).

In his reflections on time and eschatology, the African scholar John
Mbiti has focused on the "present" to articulate a preliminary critique of
missionary eschatology in his controversial study, *New Testament Eschatology in an African Background: A Study of the Encounter between New
Testament Theology and African Traditional Concepts*. By all accounts,
Mbiti's project is very different from Levinas's understanding of time,
because in an earlier work, *African Religions and Philosophy*, Mbiti argues
that African people recognize only a long past, which in Swahili is
zamani, and a present, which is called in Swahili *sasa* (1969: 17). *Sasa*
includes a future, but one so short that it is not significant enough to talk
about as a future. This claim is too sweeping, because there are other
peoples in Africa who do have a concept of the future.[4] Nevertheless
Mbiti points out that missionary proclamation underscored the centrality
of Christian eschatology in everything. The progress of Christianity was
anchored to the view that everything was moving toward some specific

---

3 The essays in Levinas 1993 that I refer to are "Freedom and Command" and "Ego and
Totality." See also Peperzak's discussion (1993: 175).

4 Interpreters of Mbiti have understood him to mean that Africans in general do not
have a concept of the future in their understanding of time. Because Mbiti's work seems to
convey the view that most of what he wrote is also relevant to many other places in Africa, it
is important to realize that he focused on his own people, the Akamba of Kenya, and that his
conclusions cannot be generalized. I find Mbiti's reference to a short future rather interesting; the fact that there is some hint of a future in *sasa*, though it be short, as Mbiti claims,
demonstrates that even his own people have an understanding of the future.

future. Mbiti argues that because of this lack of a long future in the African societies he studied, history in effect is a backward look.

> History moves backward from the now moment to that period in the past beyond which nothing can go. So the *tene* (past) period is the center of gravity in the Akamba conception of history: people's thinking and understanding of the world are oriented towards this finality ... not to the future but in the past, in the *tene* dimension of time. (1971: 28)

Mbiti argues that the African Inland Mission based its eschatology on a futuristic time frame that also emphasized a world that was coming. This emphasis on the future undermined the central teaching of the New Testament, which Mbiti interprets to be the coming of Christ into history. Mbiti also stresses the importance of the present. Thus for the Akamba, death deprives an individual of participation in that present (1971: 139). There is some affinity with Levinas here because Mbiti also argues that death is violence and not something to be anticipated. Even though Mbiti does not deal with the future because he believes the Akamba have no such concept, his critique of mission eschatology is suggestive. He argues that by preaching an other-worldly, linear understanding of eschatology, missionary Christianity has failed to take seriously other cultures whose view of the present brings together the human and spirit-centered world with the "spiritual" and Christ-centered teaching of the New Testament (139). Missionary eschatology is an abstraction that belongs to the realm of transcendence, which the Akamba reserve for God only (153). Although I find Mbiti's analysis of time wanting, his emphasis on "now" and his rejection of an eschatology that focuses on the future provide an opening for underscoring Levinas's notion of eschatological peace. Levinas calls on us to see the future as that which comes to us as Other. He also claims that, for each person, to undertake the eschatological journey is to be engaged in a concrete historical ethical relation with other people. In that sense, Mbiti's emphasis on the presence of Christ, though derived from a problematic analysis of time, can be amended to emphasize that eschatological peace should not be shifted into the future but should be an ongoing ethical quest by those who search for messianic peace. James Miller argues that the last days are "always here and now and the emergent reality (the future) is always fundamentally new" (18). Although Jürgen Moltmann talks about Christian eschatology from the perspective of future hope, he argues that theology should be centered around eschatology.

> Christian theology must be developed in terms of eschatology.... the traditional doctrine of the rescue of the soul into heaven beyond must become the doctrine of the future of the [reign] of God which renews

heaven and earth. The traditional other-worldly hope must be supplemented by hope for the transformation and renewal of the earth. (23)

I find this view of eschatology, which calls on people to focus on their intersubjective encounters, to be a rich manifestation of the presence of God.[5] One cannot postpone that presence into the future even under the rubric of hope. As Jacques Ellul has pointed out, eschatology grounded on hope is not a terminus toward which we march. "[T]he [reign of] God is bursting violently into our times, into our milieu. It is breaking up the balanced order of march, the timetables and the organizations. It is alive in our midst" (172). In a bold constructive theology centered on the movement of the Spirit, Peter Hodgson argues against an abrupt end, calling it a "literalized and misleading myth."

> God is not merely a chronologically future terminus of world history, but an ever-present one, a terminus that is also a transition, a passing over into eternal historicality of God. We experience this transition both in the fullest moments of our living and in the final moment of our dying. God is always there, always available. This is the dimension of depth, of spirituality, that funds liberation and alters the horizon in which historical praxis is undertaken. (327)

If we return to the apostle Paul, Levinas's position opposes Heidegger's reading because individual ecstatic temporality falls short of what eschatology signifies. Heidegger sees comprehension and understanding of *Dasein*'s authenticity in the world; one could argue instead that reading beyond Heidegger takes the reader to Paul, where temporality does not seek authenticity by facing one's death. "Existing" consists of relations with an Other. Levinas would have us comfort one another not by telling each other to become authentic beings in the face of death but by reaching out to an Other that is destitute. Such an act is an eschatological journey as well as an enactment of eschatological peace.

---

5 Ted Peters (308) argues: "The future actualizes a potential that is already present, just as a cherry tree actualizes the potential that is already in the stone or seed we plant in the ground."

To Love Cain More Than God

Jione Havea
United Theological College, Sydney
and Charles Sturt University

*One's duty regarding the other who makes appeal to one's responsi-
bility is an investing of one's own freedom. In responsibility, which is,
as such, irrecusable and non-transferable, I am instituted as non-
interchangeable: I am chosen as unique and incomparable. My
freedom and my rights, before manifesting themselves in my opposition to the freedom and rights of the other person, will manifest
themselves precisely in the form of responsibility, in human fraternity. An* inexhaustible responsibility: for with the other our
accounts are never settled.
—Emmanuel Levinas (1993b: 125; my emphasis)

... our reading of the Bible will be a militant *reading. The great questions about the word of the Lord arise out of Christian practice. It is
time to reclaim this militant reading of the word of God in faith. It is
time to open the Bible and read it from the perspective of "those who
are persecuted in the cause of right" (Matt. 5:10), from the perspective
of the condemned human beings of this earth—for, after all, theirs is
the kingdom of heaven.*
—Gustavo Gutiérrez (4)

*I am no doubt not the only one who writes in order to have no face.
Do not ask who I am and do not ask me to remain the same: leave it to
our bureaucrats and our police to see that our papers are in order. At
least spare us their morality when we write.*
—Michel Foucault (17)

"*w*-the man knew Eve his wife." So begins Gen 4.

The narrative opens with a *waw*. Events have already happened
and/but/now/so/then/*w* the narrator begins in-between, *inter-esse*, the
beginning and the end of the story (cf. Levinas 1991: 3; 1985: 99–100).

And since words do not always capture a happening story in which characters and events overlap here and there, *inter alia*, the narrator may lose control over his story. The narrator tells the story "in other words,"[1] anchored by a *waw*, in dis\placement.[2] *Inter alia*, stuff happens, and we read the story *inter-esse* (cf. Caputo: 30–31).

1. Obligation to *Alter*-Read

Like the narrator, despite not being tamed by him, we *begin* reading at/from many places (cf. Phillips 1994a).[3] Whether we read Gen 4:1–16 from left to right, right to left, upward, downward, inward, outward, across, or otherwise, we begin *inter-esse, inter alia*. We read toward margins, and away from margins, beginning at a point removed from the beginning, at n+1 (Lacan), marked with a *waw*. To borrow the words of Wiesel, "The place [where we begin reading] is everywhere, anywhere. The time is after the beginning, after creation, after Shabbat" (1976: 38).

Drawn to Levinas's demand for responsibility (response-ability) to the *other*, I invest my freedom as obligation to the marginalized in Gen 4:1–16.[4] *Inter-esse, inter alia*, I read Gen 4:1–16 away from its centers. One of my starting points in this reading is the "underside of history" (Gutiér-rez), the place where the marginalized present their embrace and *Say* something with their silenced bodies.[5] Elusive silences!

---

1 A storyteller embraces fragmentation and risks incoherence. While "our bureaucrats and our police" decide what successful retelling involves (Foucault), I try *inter-esse* to loosen the trap of dialecticism (cf. Levinas 1989b: 65–66). *Inter alia*, I embrace the risk of facelessness (Foucault).

2 Dis\placement is always positional, with *placement* "leaning against" *dis* upon a "\", *as if* displacement is always placement, and vice versa This "\" recalls the leaning walls of the rabbinic study house that will not fall, out of respect for Rabbi Yehoshua, and will not straighten up again, out of respect for Rabbi Eliezer (*b. B. Meṣiʿa* 59a–b).

Dis\placement manifests a double view: it represents both the thoughts that are repressed to the unconscious, the station of ideologies, and lived experiences of displacement, driven by ideologies. The "\" reminds us that consciousness does not always rule in his house (Freud; Lacan) and that readers' desire for polysemy "leans against" the walls of determinacy, as if the "\" extends God's blessing onto the house of reading: Be fertile and multiply … at the risk of subjugation!

3 Gunn (1990) and Jobling (1994) demonstrate that the narrator (a figure in our fantasy) has desires, problematizing his assumed innocence and reliability

4 According to Levinas, a subject's freedom is "immediately limited by its responsibility. This is its great paradox: a free being is already no longer free, because it is responsible for itself" (1987c: 55). The freedom of obligation is *difficile liberté*!

5 West warns against trying to "romanticise and idealise the contribution of the poor" by claiming to "listen to" them (1994: 154). The separation of speaker from listener, of subject from object, is a condition of language and an illusion of the symbolic order (cf. Beal). To

Moreover, I read with presuppositions on the nature of discourse. I presume that words, the texture of voices and the fiber of texts, do awesome things, including doing otherwise than they say (Fewell and Gunn). Words may not capture happening events, but they can still heal and infect, alter and encourage, express and repress. We hear and are moved by words, *more than words*, but we cannot capture voices. We may tune out strange[r] voices, but we cannot deaden them; voices *Say* something in their silences, and silence cannot be silenced. I thus propose to imagine the elusive silences in Gen 4:1–16, to risk hearing the silences.

I also presume that a literary text is a first moment of repression (cf. Levinas 1989b: 103–11).[6] For instance, Gen 4:1–16 *names* Cain as a murderer and settles him under YHWH's "mark" at Nod ("wander") and, being a respected text, it has the power to *fix* (attach, adjust) "his mark" as a cursed wanderer. Readers urge the second moment of repression by announcing the text as *Said:*[7] Cain is the jealous murderer, the first victim of sin (compare Quinones: 87–152); Abel is innocent; YHWH is just, absolutely;[8] and the narrator is impartial and trustworthy.

The Gen 4:1–16 story, however, is not as unambiguous. We are obliged to reread, realizing our freedom as obligation, because we are not neutral *announcers*. We are *Sayers* also. We may, *inter-esse*, rewrite otherwise than *Said*, and we may re- /de-nounce, *inter alia*, as responsibility.[9] In *other* words, we are obliged to *alter*-read.

---

listen only to speakers is to idealize voices/dialogue, which is a privilege of only a few characters, a predilection that limits the freedom of the interpreter.

I am drawn to Irigaray's appeal: "I can't tell you where I am going. Forget me, Mother. Forget you in me, me in you. Let's just forget us. Life continues" (1981: 63). In that regard, *Me voici!* (Levinas). I can only read Otherwise. *Inter-esse*, I am of the poor, one of James Cook's Polynesian "common, low fellows" (cf. Williams: 258).

6 A literary text functions like a work of art: it turns an "I" into a subject by *subjecting* "I" as an object. A text subjectifies and objectifies with the same marks; it represses the event it narrates by leaning its representation against our imagination. Seduced by the illusory nature of language, readers assume that they have captured the "event of the I" (cf. Jameson; Lacan).

7 Bal explores this issue in cultural analysis: "doesn't one repeat the gesture of appropriation and exploitation one seeks to criticize if one reprints as quotations the very material whose use by predecessors is subject to criticism?" (26) To select a point of view is already to take sides, whether one gazes with YHWH, lurks with sin, kills with Cain, or dies with Abel. I read not to commemorate a disaster by re-cord-ing an event, or re-pressing the suppressed, but with Levinas's hint: "It is through reading that references take on reality; through reading, in a way, we come to inhabit a place. The volume of a book can provide the *espace vital!*" (1989b: 192).

8 Concerning the unexplained punishment of Cain, Hendel argues that "Yahweh is *indeed* acting arbitrarily and capriciously" (48, my emphasis; cf. Wiesel 1976).

9 I follow Magonet's lead: "As I will repeatedly suggest, the Bible is a subversive book and demands from its commentators no less self-criticism and self-awareness" (1, cf. 30–31).

And God saw all that he had made and found it very good. (Gen 1:31a)

2. The Stuff of *Alter*-Reading

The obligation to *alter*-read crosses several limits. First, I do not propose to read *about alter* as if *alter* is a being. The *other* of *alter*-read is not an
object to observe, territory to capture, gap to fill, or boundary to level,
but, *inter-esse, events* that allow us to observe, to capture, to fill, and to
level. *Alter* is otherwise than being; it is the *waw*-point, the rupture, be it a
lack or an excess, which is necessary, for instance, before a daughter can
say to her mother, "I would like both of us to be present. So that the one
doesn't disappear in the other, or the other in the one. So that we can
taste each other, feel each other, listen to each other, see each other—
together" (Irigaray 1981: 61). *Alter* is *opening,* where "in" and "out" meet.
In other words, only "in other words," *alter* is fluid while "irrecusable
and non-transferable" (Levinas). To *alter*-read obliges us to reread textual
(in)consistencies as openings, already hetero-interested and always militant (Gutiérrez).

Concerned with opening, *alter*-read traffics in *dis\closure.* Because
we need closure in order to make sense, *closure* "leans against" *dis*, disclosing *inter alia* the vulnerabilities of readers:[10] We are, for instance,
vulnerable to the "we" that I have imagined. My "we" is possible
because there is a "you" (plural) and a "me" who exist separately (cf.
Irigaray 1980: 72); in other words, it exists because of our disunity. My
"we," therefore, is not a *universal we.*[11] In that regard, to *alter*-read is to
resist rigid closure and to dis\close the paradoxes of subjectivity.

Finally, *alter*-read indicates discomfort with the illusion of *sameness*
and two blind spots in systems of signification: the tendency to map
linear chains of signifier-signified, and the unwillingness to let go of
semiotic figures/traces.[12] To *alter*-read is not to be committed to figures

---

10 Dis\closure depends on concealment and elusive absences, and thrives on ambiguities. Irigaray expresses what I call *dis\closure* well: "Your body reveals yesterday in what it
wants today. If you think: yesterday I was, tomorrow I will be, you are thinking: I have died
a little. Be what you are becoming, without clinging to what you could have been, might be.
Never settle. Let's leave definitiveness to the undecided; we don't need it" (1980: 76).

11 My "we" includes communities of struggle and cultures of silence (cf. West 1992)
which are often idealized, unconsciously, as the Cains and Abels of modern history.

12 Reading is a hermeneutics of desire (Jobling 1994; Penchansky). I read the desires of
literary characters, of the narrator, and of readers. When these desires clash I take sides, but
I am not obliged to side with the narrator, nor with the divine voice (cf. Gunn and Fewell:

and traces but to happening events (*il y a*). To *alter*-read is to embrace alterity and dis\placement.

3. *ALTER*-READING "NODY" GENESIS 4:1–16

Jean Calloud offers an interesting and interested reading of Gen 4:1–16,[13] identifying traces of the *figures* of Gen 4:1–16 (e.g., brother, blood) in other parts of the Bible.[14] Calloud's study is interesting in the way it maps the effects of Gen 4:1–16 in the biblical chains of significa-tion, and interested in how it anticipates and discerns the Gen 4:1–16 figures in Scripture, taking the Jesus-event, viewed as the center of Scrip-ture (62), as the final-signified.[15] Interested questions arise: Of what figures is Gen 4:1–16 a trace; in other words, what figures lurk behind this text? What is disfigured in/by this story,[16] or in its readings?[17] What do

---

30–32). To read for desire echoes a popular critique of structuralism and semiotics: the refusal to read *behind* the systems of signification and textual structures (cf. Williams: 6–7). To desire a text is to surrender to it, committing to wrestle with it, like Jacob at Peniel, hoping to limp away with a reading. Because the act of surrendering also involves resist-ance, at least the resistance to other desires, we are always readers in/of texts (cf. Rashkow: 26–27).

[13] *Interesting* and *interested* are West's labels for "deconstruction" (1992). The first signifies its game/play-face, the linguistic turn, and the second its constructive-face, the concern with the poor. Caputo makes a similar distinction, between heteromorphism and heteronomism, in order to clarify that "justice" is the goal of Derridean deconstruction (42–43, 69–70).

[14] Philo's analysis of *types* prefigures Calloud's study. For Philo, Adam signifies the mind and Eve the senses. They produced Cain, "possession," a figure of *self-love* (*Cher.* 40–41). There are various traces of self-love in the Hebrew Bible (cf. *Det.*), one of which is the tower at Babel (Genesis 11), a trace of the city Cain set out to build (*Post.* 49–59; *Conf.* 122–123). Com-pared to Abel, virtue, Cain is vice, and these two types may be traced as far as Augustine's *De civitate Dei.*

Quinones jumps the biblical fence to trace representations of the Cain-Abel *themes* in world literature. With many disguises, such as Abel the preferred of God (*Ama-deus*) and Cain the terrible and executioner, Quinones shows how the Cain-Abel story endures to address breaches in existence and fractures "at the heart of things" (3; see also Gunn and Fewell: 12–33).

[15] Williams's Girardian analysis of mimetic desires and rivalries behind biblical texts of violence and victimization pursues a similar interest. He examines stories of enemy brothers, beginning with the Cain-Abel story, as "master texts" (figure) that anchor the mimetic move-ment toward the "innocent victim" (fulfillment, trace) of the New Testament.

[16] West advances the liberation interests in *disfigured* persons: "biblical studies and other trained readers need 'the other', particularly those 'others' from the margins, in our readings of the Bible. Our readings may be critical, but they are not truly contextual without the presence of ordinary readers" (1995: 191).

[17] The distinction between "text" and "interpretation" is not always clear. A biblical text is always an interpretation, it is already ideological (*pace* Fowl), and it needs reinterpretation.

this story's silences *Say?* I propose to reread in the other direction from Calloud.[18] I begin, again, to *alter*-read.[19]

------

*And Y*HWH *God said, "It is not good. . . . "* (Gen 2:18a)

In spite of the denial of access to the tree of life in Gen 3:22–24, Gen 4:1 picks up the story with the production of new life. At *waw*-point the focus shifts from God, the creative character in the previous episode. *Inter-esse,* a silence: God is not involved in the mode of production (Wiesel 1976: 41). He shows up later, but a rupture is inscribed with a *waw*. The serene narration of the conception and birth of Cain gives the impression that the process was not with pangs and pain, as Gen 3:16 prescribes. Such silences resist *sameness,* dis\closing God's control.

The narrator's opening statement installs gender biases: "the man," whose name is not given, is the *knower,* and his wife, named Eve, is the object he knows, the *knowee.*[20] The account begins from the generalized knower's point of view, but the named knowee is the one who is productive: "Eve conceived and bore Cain." If *name* indicates agency, this knower is a nobody who is simply marked, "X-ed," as "the man," *ha-'adam,* thus blurring the narrative's point of focus.

God returns to the story (in name) upon the voice of the knowee: "I have gained a man [*'ish*] *'et-yhwh.*" Because this story has to do with conception, I imagine a father figure lurking behind Eve's words, in other words, as if she was naming the father of her child. And at the place

-----

On this matter, I appeal to Jameson's concept of *History*: "history is not so much a text, as rather a text-to-be-(re-)constructed. Better still, it is an obligation to do so" (107).

18 Other critics read in other directions. Bassler, for instance, examines how Targum texts reconstruct the words Cain is supposed to have said to Abel before they came to the field (Gen 4:8), the imagined Cain-Abel debate. And West compares two readings from South Africa's context of struggle: Allan A. Boesak's "reading the text" (relating struggles in the text to South African conditions) and Itumeleng J. Mosala's "reading *behind* the text" (relating materialist-historical context behind the text, Gen 4's mode of production, to struggles in the text and in South Africa). These interested modes of reading led West to a metacritical conclusion: "The challenge is to move away from the notion of biblical studies as the pursuit of disinterested truth to something more human and transformative, something which is shaped by a self-critical solidarity with the victims of history" (1990: 318).

19 To *begin again* suggests that earlier attempts may have failed to tame this slippery story. But I do not imagine that I will tame it!

20 The sexual connotation of "to know" dis\closes these labels, *reiterating* (Derrida) the claim that YHWH "knew" Abraham (Gen 18:19) and Israel (Amos 3:2)

where I expect to hear the father's name announced comes God's name, "I have gained a man *'et-yhwh*."

Inter alia the story teases us: Whose birth is announced in Gen 4:1? Is it not curious that, east of the garden, the words of a woman, the speech of a bearer of life and "mother of all the living" (Gen 3:20), bore the name of God?

According to Eve's words, YHWH is involved in-deed. But the extent of his involvement is unclear due to the enigmatic *'et*-particle. The double voice of this monosyllabic word, as an object marker and a preposition, presents readers with two theologically problematic options. Legitimate readings are not always problem free.

The LXX translates *'et* as a preposition, rendering *'et-yhwh* as *dia tou theou*: YHWH is the agent by means of whom Cain is acquired. Westermann finds this legitimate option problematic because *'et* "in the sense of 'with the help of' is never applied to God" (291). Westermann denies YHWH the opportunity to be a helper of a woman, to be a helper of a helper (cf. Gen 2:18–19). To say that YHWH helped Eve in acquiring a child, a process he promised to "make most severe" (Gen 3:16), produces a dilemma for the divine character. It appears that gender and theological biases lurk behind Westermann's reading.

To read *'et* as an object marker is also discomforting, for that suggests that the "man whom Eve acquired *is* YHWH." Behind this reading lurks the events of Gen 3, where Eve caught YHWH's attention. I imagine that when YHWH came calling in Gen 3:9 he gazed upon Eve but called out to the man, like a lover who embraces one but utters the name of another. Did Eve acquire *'et*-YHWH in person in Gen 4, just as she earlier caught his attention in the garden? Who "falls" in Gen 4?

Prior to Gen 4:1, YHWH is portrayed with *'ish*-qualities: He curses his creation in Gen 3:14–15, he condemns and rejects what is different,[21] and he is threatened by ambiguities (cf. Gunn and Fewell: 28–29). The creator who created by differentiation cannot now deal with differences (cf. Rowlett), suggesting that this literary character is not always consistent.

Up to this point, I have taken the word *'ish* to mean "man" but it may also be translated as "husband." Did Eve name her son Cain because she has acquired YHWH as her husband? YHWH played the role of a father in Gen 2, fashioning Eve from the bone he drew from within "the man" (cf.

---

21 I draw the idea that unwillingness to deal with differences is an *'ish*-quality from Gen 2:18–20, in which the man rejects other animals as his helper because they were not "fitting" for him. The woman, on the other hand, was a fitting helper because she was his type. Eve was *'ish*-like.

Fewell and Gunn: 23), and in Gen 4:1 YHWH is presented as a father to Eve's son. Eve has gained a man *'et* YHWH, giving the acquired character (Eve's son) two literary fathers (YHWH and "the knower"). This *alter*-reading, nonetheless, transgresses the constraints that define YHWH as immutable (cf. von Rad: 104–5).

Both translations of *'et* are legitimate, and both are troublesome. I resist the "grab" (cf. Penchansky) of the text in order to make YHWH responsible for Eve's sons (so Rabbi Shimon bar Yocha, cf. Plaut: 15–16), and the ambiguous *'et* accentuates his response-ability.

Elijah approached all the people and said, "How long will you keep hopping between two boughs? If YHWH is God, go after him, w-if Baal, go after him." The people did not answer him a word. (1 Kgs 18:21)

Eve's intention is not stated, and there are different readings of her words. Westermann hears her boasting as a creator who "has brought forth a man in a way that corresponds to the creation of the man by the creator" (290). Westermann avoids an *'ish*-like God figure by replacing it with a God-like *'ishah* (woman). An *'ishah* gives life to an *'ish*, drawing attention to the "coherence between the creation of God and the procreation of woman" (van Wolde: 28).

Van Wolde explains that the relationship between YHWH and Eve is a promise-and-fulfillment situation: "What has been indicated in Genesis 2–3 as an 'ability' or 'capacity' is realized in Gen. 4.1. The ability to bring forth children is transformed into actually bringing forth children.... In the construction *'et-yhwh*, *'et* indicates the sociative, to be translated as 'together with'" (27). YHWH shares the credit for Cain with the knowee. The woman is not a *parallel* creator, in which case she may displace the first creator, but a *sociative* creator alongside the creator-standard (YHWH). Notwithstanding, what Eve desired cannot be fixed. She disappears with Adam until Gen 4:25.[22]

---

22 That Eve may have been an observer to the events of Gen 4:1–16 cannot be ruled out. I imagine Eve looking from a distance, maybe with a smirk on her face, at the events following Gen 4:1, especially the irony of YHWH dealing with her son, a mortal, who challenged his curses. Eve is a woman who was not happy being pushed from the garden, even if leaving the garden was a sign of freedom (Magonet: 111–17). She dares to talk back at YHWH and wills to "shift the blame" (Fewell and Gunn). The chain of curses in Gen 3–4 are announced and renounced, prefiguring the book of Esther, where later edicts challenge but could not reverse earlier ones.

Eve is known once, and she delivers twice. As YHWH earlier made two humans, drawing the second from the first (Gen 2:7–23; cf. Gen 1:27), so Eve produces two humans, drawing the second after the first. The narrator first presents two creation accounts (Gen 1:1–2:24),[23] and now two back-to-back births. He does not identify Abel as the son of Adam/Eve/ YHWH but links him to his brother (Gen 4:2), as if Cain is the "keeper" of Abel's identity; Abel is Cain's figurative trace, "lurking behind the birth door" after Cain.

Prior to Gen 4:4b, YHWH lurks behind the story, but his shadows are visible in the text (cf. Levinas 1989b: 130–43). By association with *hbl* ("breath"), Abel's name echoes YHWH's act of blowing into the nostrils of the earthling in Gen 2:7. In this regard, Abel is doubly stabilized: He is named, and his name signifies life.

The similar situations of "coming into life," of Adam in Gen 2:7 and of Abel in Gen 4:2, binds YHWH to Abel.[24] The association of Adam with Abel begs the issue of placement: The narrator did not refer to Adam by name in Gen 4:1, nor did Eve, and now Abel takes over his role as signifier of life (*hbl*). So far, Adam "the man" has only been useful as a knower. But not many characters know him. *Inter alia*, silences.

Abel's name, however, may be read differently. Westermann suggests that "Gen 3 describes one's state as a creature or a human being as 'dust'; Gen 4 adds another aspect by using the name *hbl*. It looks to a person's contingency and nothingness" (292). Adam is dust; Abel is nothing. As the breath in Gen 2:7 (Adam) is condemned in Gen 3:19, so do I expect for the "breath" (Abel) in Gen 4:2.

Another trace of YHWH appears in the brothers' tasks. The narrator reverses the order of presentation, introducing the task of the second son first. Abel was "shepherding sheep," a task not cursed in Gen 3:14–19 and a creature (sheep) not named prior to Gen 4:2. Abel introduces something new to the story. He acts differently, against *sameness*. Was Abel safe since YHWH did not curse his task? By "keeping an eye on sheep" Abel brings to mind the animals that were named but not accepted as "helper"

---

[23] Most dominant readings of the Genesis creation accounts appeal to the P and J sources but overlook the ideological significance of the textual voices. I embrace the latter.

[24] I imagine that YHWH is involved with, responsive to, and responsible for both brothers. If a conflict develops between them, there will be a corresponding conflict in YHWH's responsibilities: "Indeed, if there were only two of us in the world, I and one other, there would be no problem. The other would be completely my responsibility. But in the real world there are many others. When others enter, each of them external to myself, problems arise. Who is closest to me? Who is the Other? Perhaps something has already occurred between them" (Levinas 1975: 137).

in Gen 2:19–20.[25] The narrator again sets Abel against his father, the one who failed to "keep an eye" on his helpers. The narrator teases our imagination because he who keeps watch will later become the one on whom YHWH gazes (Gen 4:4). In this reading, Abel's task discloses the events lurking behind it and anticipates the introduction of Cain's task.

Cain is "tiller of the soil," recalling not only what was lacking from the creation in Gen 2:5 but also the curse of that task in Gen 3:17 (cf. Jobling 1986: 17–18). Cain is caught between fulfilling God's creation and doing the same task as a curse, caught between thorns and thistles.

By producing "fruit of the soil" (Gen 4:3b) Cain undermines YHWH's curse (Gen 3:18). Cain is a transgressor even before the offering of gifts. I anticipate that he will be ejected like the Gen 3 transgressors, raising critical questions about God's creation: If creation is the act of bringing order to chaos, doesn't God show, by continuing to control it, that the world he created is a chaos? Are we dealing with a creation gone awry (Trible: 72–143) or a messy creation (*pace* Hauser)? A little of both?

Inter-esse, YHWH is *inter alia.* Cain and Abel came to him as if he was a parent (cf. Rosenblatt and Horwitz: 55–56). Their offerings provided YHWH with a dilemma: to accept Cain's offering is to concede that his curse failed, but for YHWH to uphold his curse is to reverse his mandate in Gen 2:5.[26] YHWH could save face by rejecting Cain. According to this *alter-reading*, Cain is a scapegoat (cf. Williams). But the text resists such a constraining reading. Dis\closure.

Cain, the son in whose birth was YHWH named, is in a no-win situation, while Abel, the son named "futility" (*hbl*), is placed, and YHWH curiously lurks behind the story world. When YHWH finally appears, I assume that something is wrong because, thus far, he appears to bring order. Why didn't YHWH just stay away? Why not imagine that things outside of the garden are in good hands (cf. Gen 1:29–31) and observe how his creatures do *good-w-bad* (Gen 2:15–17)? Why not give freedom, for obligation? Why not see how the divine nature of these humans (cf. Gen 3:22) helps them survive? Did YHWH appear because the existence of a man who "has become like one of us" (Gen 3:22) irritated him? Did YHWH show up to show who is in charge? to show off?

---

25 I insert a phonetic pun, taking *rᶜh* ("to shepherd"; Gen 4:2) as an echo of *rʾh* ("to see"; Gen 2:19), the motivation for YHWH's presentation of gifts to Adam.

26 Rabbi Shimon bar Yocha presents a similar dilemma: "Two athletes fight to entertain the king. At the outcome of the contest will the victor be indicted for murder?" (in Wiesel 1976: 54; cf. Plaut).

*And when Moses had finished speaking with them, he put a veil over
his face. Whenever Moses went in before YHWH to speak with him, he
would leave the veil off until he came out.* (Exod 34:33–34a)

YHWH's elusive absence from the story world discloses another
absence: the parents, who are absent until Gen 4:25. "There are gaps in the
text. From the purely human point of view, we cannot but be disturbed
about ... the parents" (Wiesel 1976: 43). Whether they were ignored by the
narrator, displaced by YHWH, or by their sons, the parents' absence is disturbing. And the way they reappear in Gen 4:25, acting as if nothing
wrong occurred in Gen 4:3–16, gives them a sinister depiction. *Inter-esse*,
stuff happens, and to the parents we pose Wiesel's judgment of Abel's
aloofness toward Cain's sorrow when God did not gaze at him and at his
offering: "In the face of suffering one has no right to turn away, not to see.
In the face of injustice, one may not look the other way" (57). Like the
people's answer to Elijah, Adam and Eve answer us not a word; they
respond otherwise than they are obliged. In the case of their children, their
accounts are not settled.[27]

The prelude to YHWH's entry is the presentation of offerings (for traditional readings, see Kugel; Waltke). There is no demand, and no
justification either (cf. Hendel).[28] Stuff happens. Events slowly evolve, as
if things are normal. But with YHWH's entry things rush to a close as if
something needs to be covered up.[29]

A reversal occurs. The order of one moment is reversed in the next.
The firstborn who was mentioned second in the previous story moment

---

27 Those who have experienced the loss (absence) of a parent, or who may be a
single parent due to the loss of a partner, the Levinasian group of "widow" (see Exod
22:20–21 [ET 22:21–22]; compare Fewell and Gunn: 102), would be very troubled with the
parents' absence.

28 Magonet reads Cain's offering within the context of a "test" YHWH gave, which
started in the garden (117–20), the outcome of which is liberation. "I can think of no more
telling proof of the Rabbinic view that far from being a 'fall from grace', the eating of the
fruit and the subsequent expulsion from Eden, was ultimately a great liberation for it gave
the 'children' in Eden the chance to grow up. God cut the strings of the puppets and let them
walk erect upon the earth" (121–22). My reading, on the other hand, finds YHWH's hands still
holding the strings, implying that the difference between *seeking to control* and *out of control*
is not always clear.

29 The sudden acceleration of the momentum portrays YHWH as one who can't handle
the "painful truth." A similar effect may be read in the garden episode when YHWH suddenly appears to pass judgment on Eve. YHWH appears insecure in his interactions with
others, destabilizing the story's divine-human class hegemony.

(announcement of tasks) is now mentioned first. Cain appears as initiator and director of the moment's business, an event that takes place "from end of days" (or "days from the end"). Does this mean that days have passed since the last offering? that it has been days since YHWH cursed the land, so we may expect that the curses have worn off? that after days of tilling Cain produced fruits from the soil *as if* he controls the land? Who is in control? We marvel at the courage of Cain in presenting "fruits from the soil" to YHWH, the one who cursed the soil and told it to yield "thorns and thistles." Did Cain know of YHWH's curse?

To read Cain's "fruits of the soil" with an eye on Gen 3:17–19 reveals shadows lurking behind Gen 4:1–16 (cf. Herion; Spina; Plaut). Though Gen 3:17 allows that man may "eat from the soil" *if he works* (so Gen 3:19), YHWH prescribes in Gen 3:18 that the fruit of man's labor will only be "thorns and thistles" and his food the "grasses of the field" (undermining Gen 1:29). So why should one labor if he will only labor in vain? The soil, on the other hand, did not yield to YHWH's *words* but to Cain's *toil*.[30] This ticked YHWH, who then curses Cain: "If you till the soil, it shall *no longer* yield its strength to you" (Gen 4:12). The soil may have yielded to Cain earlier, but it will no longer do so, even though he is heir to the God-like knowledge of *good-w-bad*.[31]

The event is complicated when Abel for his part "brought the choicest of the firstlings of his flock" (Gen 4:4). Abel fulfills God's direction for humans to "rule ... all the living things that creep on earth" (Gen 1:28), to the excess. Thanks to Abel, the ground knows what blood tastes like. If the offerings were simultaneous, Abel again shadows Cain. At birth and now as offerers, Abel lurks behind Cain. Cain's action was desirable to Abel, who goes forth to capture a firstling, returning our attention to Cain, who is a firstborn himself.

When the story turned eastward we assume that YHWH remained in the garden, where the tree that defines the difference between gods and humans was guarded. When he leaves the garden, maybe because he saw that it is not good for gods to be alone, YHWH enters Cain's space. The guards to the garden cannot confine YHWH because they guard against humans, not gods who wish to exit. If Cain too expected YHWH to remain in the garden, he would have been surprised when YHWH

---

30 At issue is the difference between speech and action, which will resurface in the silenced speech of Gen 4:8.

31 If Cain's success is due to his ability to know *good-w-bad*, then the serpent did not deceive the woman, problematizing the motivation for the curse of the serpent (Gen 3:14–15). Here also we encounter a literary character who is troubled with the possibility of being equaled, preferring to uphold the divine-human divide (cf. Gen 3:22–24).

appears.[32] Time stops as YHWH's (in)action is described: "YHWH gazed on Abel and on his offering. But on Cain and on his offering he did not gaze" (Gen 4:4b–5a).

The text syntactically distinguishes between each offerer and his offering, so a person is gazed upon not because of what he offered (Waltke: 365). YHWH simply gazed (*sh'h*) on Abel but not on Cain. No word is spoken, nor a judgment, only a gaze, an (in)action.

A silent gaze does not indicate valuation, but choosing to gaze on one offerer and not on the other indicates desire, if only as a "delight to the eyes" (cf. Gen 3:6). YHWH remained awfully silent, but his gaze is so penetrating. We are poked with divine comedy: Cain felt *not* being gazed upon, and his face fell. He assumed that he had been rejected.

———

And YHWH said to Ha-Satan, "Have you put your heart against/
to my servant Job, because there is no one like him on the earth,
a blameless and upright man, he fears God and shuns evil?" (Job 1:8)

———

This was not the first time that a gift was not accepted. Earlier, the man looked at the animals, God's gift, but did not find a fitting helper (Gen 2:20). Adam did not declare them "good" but called them names. And to YHWH's second gift he exulted, "At last...." As Adam accepted the second but rejected the first gift, so YHWH gazed at the second but not at the first. No reason is given for Adam's preference, nor for YHWH's gaze (cf. Hendel; Wiesel 1976; Herion; Spina).

I imagine that YHWH's refusal to gaze upon Cain's offering is a countering move, a do-unto-others lesson from an offerer not accepted earlier. If YHWH was intimidated by Cain's offering, I cannot agree that his "flawed character led to his feigned worship" (Waltke: 371; so Josephus). And I refuse the claim that Abel was righteous but Cain was wicked from the very beginning (cf. Krasovec: 12–13). I treat this story as a "Nody" story. It resists taming readings, so it is "naughty," in a very complex manner, so it is "knotty" also.

Van Wolde for her part surrenders to the narrator's desires, explaining that it is "more likely that Cain is envious not because Abel is more successful, but because YHWH looks at a blunderer like Abel while ignoring Cain" (29). I, on the other hand, cannot determine Cain's opinion

---

32 YHWH's sudden appearance in Gen 4:4 is repeated in Gen 4:9, and in both instances Cain is the target. In both instances YHWH also fits the description of one "lurking at the door" and whose "desire" is toward Cain. YHWH lies low, waiting to ambush Cain.

toward Abel before and after Y<small>HWH</small>'s gaze. I expect sibling rivalries (Williams: 25–30, 33–38; Rosenblatt and Horwitz: 53–54), and envy may be a big factor (so Wiesel 1976; Williams), but there is no reason to assume that Cain and Abel were not also each other's good companion. This "Nody" story has room for inconsistencies.

The narrator suggests in Gen 4:5 that Cain was distressed not because of who and what Y<small>HWH</small> did not gaze upon, but because of *what Y<small>HWH</small> did not do.* The problem lies not with Cain, nor Abel, but with Y<small>HWH</small>. Y<small>HWH</small>'s inaction distressed Cain. Abel did not assess Y<small>HWH</small>'s gaze, so we do not know if being gazed upon was *good.* If we read ahead to Abel's murder in the field (Gen 4:8) we may conclude that being gazed upon by Y<small>HWH</small> is really *not good* (from a teleological viewpoint). Job would agree!

Y<small>HWH</small>'s gaze (a deed) made Abel the "keeper" of Cain's identity: Cain is contrasted, differentiated, from Abel. The placement of the brothers' identity shifts. Prior to their arrival in the field Cain is usurped as the keeper of their identity. The narrator's alternating cycle of presenting the brothers since their birth reaches a climax with Cain's displacement under the divine gaze.[33] Was Cain also distressed because of this displacement?

———

Saul said to Samuel, "But I did obey Y<small>HWH</small>! I walked in the way on which Y<small>HWH</small> sent me: I captured King Agag of Amalek, and I proscribed Amalek. The people took from the spoil some sheep and oxen, the first of what had been proscribed, to sacrifice to Y<small>HWH</small> your God at Gilgal."(1 Sam 15:20–21)

———

Like Isaac thinking that he was holding Esau when he was blessing Jacob, Y<small>HWH</small> gazed at Abel and caught a glimpse of Cain. Seeing that "his face fell," Y<small>HWH</small> responds with a rebuke: "Surely, *if you do good, there is uplift.* But if you do not do good, sin lurks at the opening; its urge is toward you, but you can rule it" (Gen 4:7). Y<small>HWH</small> seems troubled with something Cain did, which did not cause what Y<small>HWH</small> takes to be good.

———

33 Note the disruption of the pattern, with Y<small>HWH</small> taking Abel's place in the final rotation:

Gen 4:1	Birth: Cain is born first, then Abel.
Gen 4:2	Task: Abel's task is introduced first, then Cain's.
Gen 4:3–4a	Offering: Cain makes an offering first, then Abel.
Gen 4:4b–5a	Gaze: Y<small>HWH</small> gazes on Abel, but not on Cain.
Gen 4:5	Reaction to gaze: Cain is distressed; Y<small>HWH</small> interrupts in Gen 4:6.

In the face-off between Cain and Abel, Y<small>HWH</small> takes Abel's place.

What YHWH meant by *good*, however, is ambiguous.[34] To "till the soil" is *good* (Gen 2:5; 3:23), but to succeed in it seems not good (Gen 3:17b–18). Is Cain's ability to produce fruits from the soil his *sin*, the indication that he did not cause good? By saying that Cain can rule sin (Gen 4:7b), YHWH shifts our attention from the action that did not cause good to what Cain must now do—rule sin. Like a parent waving a rattle before a crying child to distract her, YHWH distracts Cain and seeks to control our reading. This divine character grabs, as a good deontologist!

YHWH *names* "sin," subjectifying it as that which lurks behind the door and which desires Cain (Gen 4:7).[35] The relation between "desire" (*tshwqh*) and YHWH's command "to dominate [*mshl*] sin" deserves a closer look. To assume that *tshwqh* is the only condition for *mshl* (cf. Bledstein) is to overlook the sense of insecurity that breeds the desire to *mshl*. YHWH's command is thus thorny. While seeking *to dominate* may or may not eliminate sin, it will surely confirm that Cain is attracted to, and insecure because of, sin. Cain is vulnerable to something that objectifies him, and he cannot ignore it because of what YHWH just explained. He is in double jeopardy, with choices that lead to the same effect—"damned if you do and damned if you don't." "To dominate" or "not to dominate" is not the question. Rather, it has to do with existing between "thorns and thistles." A "Nody" story, in-deed!

I digress to *alter*-read *tshwqh* (desire) as a quality, rather than synonym, of *kht't* (sin). There is more to *kht't* than *tshwqh*, but in Gen 4:7 and 3:16 *kht't* may be identified through *tshwqh*. The "sin at the door" is identified by its desire for Cain, so it is separate from Cain, otherwise it cannot lurk and have desire for him.[36] I suggested earlier that Abel

---

34 Because what God considers *good* is a value judgment, it is helpful to distinguish *good in being* from *good in perception*, and we should not rule out the possibility that God may misjudge. In other words, when God declares the creation "very good" (Gen 1:31), it does not necessarily mean that it was "very good in being." We read (across sources) that the creation was not *good in being* when God declares that "it was *not good* for man to be alone." But this does not mean that the creation was evil. What *good* means to God is obscure, and I wonder if in Gen 4:7–8 he did not misjudge a *nongood in being* for a *good*, or a *good in being* for a *nongood*.

35 The lexical similarities between Gen 4:7 and Gen 3:16 leads many readers to associate sin with the woman, projecting 4:7 onto 3:16; hence the husband should rule his wife just as sin ruled Cain (cf. Bledstein). These readers overlook that sin, the one who desires in 4:7, is the one who rules. As such the woman, the one who desires in 3:16, should rule in order for their projection to stick (cf. Busenitz: 206–7).

36 This reading differs from van Wolde's identification of sin with *rbts* ("to lurk," "to lie in wait"): "at the door is sin, the sin of lying in wait. *Rbts* [my transliteration] specifies the contents of *kht't*: we are not concerned with a sinful deed in general, but with the specific, well-defined sin of 'prowling' or 'lying in ambush for'" (31). For van Wolde, sin is an

expresses desires toward Cain at birth and during the presentation of offerings: he lurks "at the door" behind Cain. Moreover, Abel's offering provided the difference between "being gazed upon" and "not being gazed upon," which defined "doing good," for which Cain is rebuked. If Abel is the "sin lurking at the door," Cain carries out YHWH's command in Gen 4:8b: To "dominate sin" is to kill Abel. Here, as Saul was told, murder signifies obedience.[37] Did Cain kill Abel on account of YHWH's demand and/or on behalf of Abel's victim? For the narrator, however, Cain is disorderly. Constraints break: A brother does not care for another, and the protector of sheep cannot protect himself.

Where was YHWH when Cain killed Abel? Assume that YHWH was in the field and that Cain felt his presence: Why would he still kill Abel?

Perhaps he wanted to remain alone: an only child and, after his parents' death, the only man. Alone like God and perhaps alone in place of God. Like God, he thought to offer himself a human sacrifice in holocaust. He wanted to be cruel like Him, a stranger like Him, an avenger like Him. And like Him, present and absent at the same time, absent by his presence, present *in* his absence. Cain killed to become God. To kill God (Wiesel 1976: 58).

Cain's motivation is eclipsed by the ellipsis ("opening") in Gen 4:8, which suggests that a "murder is never justified, even when committed to ensure a better future" (Wiesel 1976: 63).

Violence builds up from Cain's transgression of YHWH's curse to two brothers exiting to the open field. Dead-men walking! In Gen 4:4 Abel captures a firstborn, but in Gen 4:8 a firstborn disAbels a character on whom YHWH gazed. The divine gaze does not always protect. Job would agree! Does this event signify that "Cain has not ruled but has been ruled, overcome by the lust that lies in ambush" (Brueggemann: 60)? Who rules whom? Who is in (out of?) control?

Cain speaks just before the two brothers arrive at the field, but what he said is not heard (Gen 4:8). Most readers fill this gap, to smoothen a troubling story, surrendering to the narrator's drive to condemn Cain. "This 'empty' speaking would then suggest, or testify to, the negation of the existence of the other as an equal, as a brother, and it can be seen as pointing ahead to the actual elimination of the other" (van Wolde: 35).

---

internal attitude that one may control. Gen 4:7, on the other hand, indicates that *kht't* is distinct from *rbts* and *tshwqh*.

37 Since no code against murder was given prior to Gen 4:8, how was Cain to know that murder was wrong? God's command to subjugate is ambiguous: "The desire to subjugate is an ethically ambiguous one, for it may mean the desire to subjugate good (where subjugation is evil) or to subjugate evil (where subjugation is good)" (Fewell and Gunn: 25).

Like a dental filling over a cavity, van Wolde's reading highlights the gap under erasure. The ellipsis in Gen 4:8, a silence, problematizes her attempt to *name* the victim.

YHWH had just spoken to Cain (Gen 4:6–7), and we expect to hear his response next. We do hear Cain, but he was speaking to Abel (as if he was responding to YHWH). But Cain's *speech* is forgotten as the narrator tells his *deed*. He is silenced, and we are to judge him according to his action. The narrator grabs our reading, but silences (ellipsis) *Say* from behind the text.

But Samuel said: "Does YHWH delight in burnt offerings and sacrifices as much as in obedience to YHWH's command? Surely, obedience is better than sacrifice, compliance than the fat of rams. For rebellion is like the sin of divination, defiance like the iniquity of teraphim. Because you rejected YHWH's command, he has rejected you as king." (1 Sam 15:22–23)

Thus far Abel has yet to speak: he was born, spoken of, he acted, was gazed at, and now spoken with. During Abel's narrative life, only Cain related to him as a subject worthy of speech. A *good* deed? But the narrator will not allow Abel to hear anything because the silencing of Cain makes Abel deaf. He denies Abel the ability to respond (responsibility), as if he died before Cain killed him, doubly murdered, by the narrator and by Cain, and *inter alia* by readers. Eve replaces Abel with Seth (Gen 4:25), and Gen 5 dehistorizes Cain and Abel by excluding them from Adam's genealogy.[38] When Abel finally got to *Say* anything, when he was finally heard, he was already dead and it was his "blood" that cried to YHWH (Gen 4:10). Abel finally had a place, in displacement.

Abel's voice, his blood, comes to haunt YHWH and Cain. The replacement of speech with deed, disruption of dialogue, and shuffling of addressee and speaker destabilize attempts to firmly fill the gap. Few characters speak, and fewer are heard: Who is disfigured in/by this

----

38 Williams argues that this replacement is part of P's "vision of a nonviolent society" (29). But by showing that nonviolence is confirmed by exclusion (textual re-pression), Williams testifies to the ideological nature of P's text. Williams's preference for P dis\closes a blind spot: to define categories according to a notion of *violence* (Girard) suggests orientation to *force*. In communities of struggle where power is not always in the form of force, on the other hand, to be excluded is already violent and resistance is not always with brute force. Silence is also a form of resistance.

story? Abel? Cain? YHWH? narrator? readers? To whom did the blood of Abel's offering cry? These silences make this story difficult to nip in the bud. A "Nody" story, in deed!

Following the silenced speech comes a dialogue, and we anticipate resolutions. In Gen 4:9 YHWH suddenly becomes talkative, as if he was guilty of something. He responds to Cain's deed with a question ("Where is your brother Abel?"), which presumes that Cain knew of Abel's whereabouts.[39] Cain responds with his own question ("Am I my brother's keeper?"), shifting our attention to YHWH and his response-ability. These questions recall figures identified earlier: at birth, Cain was the "keeper" of Abel's identity while YHWH was the "keeper" of Cain's identity. Connecting these two identifying marks make YHWH the keeper of Abel's identity. Cain's question therefore shifts the blame to YHWH, their narrative (grand)father and identity keeper.

If a brother's keeper is "one who faithfully cares for his brother in his need" (Riemann: 482), then YHWH's gaze, which stabilized this "futile breath," presents YHWH as a good keeper (!). YHWH continues to be Abel's keeper by showing concern for the voice of his blood and when he later punishes Cain for killing Abel. Before and after Abel's murder, YHWH acts as Abel's keeper. Cain's question becomes taunting, as if he is asking, Why ask me, Lord?

But who was Abel's brother? Van Wolde insists that "Cain is not a brother and does not behave as a brother. In his speaking, YHWH urges Cain to accept Abel as his brother and to behave as a brother himself" (33). Abel was a brother, but he did not have a brother because Cain did not *look* upon him as one.[40] What about YHWH? Recall YHWH's ambiguous role in Eve's *'et*, according to which he qualifies as helper, father, husband, man, and child of Eve. The last possibility makes YHWH Abel's brother. And since he looked at Abel, if we follow van Wolde's line of argument, YHWH is a better brother than Cain. Where then did YHWH look when "Cain set upon *his* [YHWH's? Cain's?] brother

---

39 YHWH's question echoes his earlier question in the garden, "Where are you?" Like a reader, YHWH is curious to know what is not obvious. And like YHWH, we raise questions in order to trap the text.

40 Instead of *looking* ("the supreme form of expression for a good relationship"; van Wolde: 32) at Abel, Cain "lies in ambush" for him as his enemy. Cain is the brother who is not a brother. Van Wolde's reading is influenced by "YHWH's gaze," in which "looking" is a *good* act. She overlooks the outcome of YHWH's "looking," Abel's murder, and that Cain was the only one who spoke with Abel. To "look at" implies distance and objectification, but to "speak with" implies involvement. Whether one form of expression is better than the other is a matter of judgment (bear in mind that speech is also means for cursing, while sight is sometimes blind[ing]).

Abel and killed him" (Gen 4:8)? If one who *does not look* is not a brother, how responsible, in terms of Levinas's idea of human frater-nity (1993b: 125), was YHWH in the field? Cain did not *act* as Abel's brother, nor did YHWH (cf. Plaut).

Cain is Abel's *keeper* if by *shmr* we understand a "watcher," someone who "imprisons," who "rules over." In that sense Cain's question has a submissive tone, "Oh no. Have I become my brother's keeper?" (cf. Wiesel 1976: 59). YHWH could have affirmed Cain, "In-deed, you are his keeper!" But YHWH appears threatened, and he fixes the blame on Cain with a harsh sentence. Assuming that the judgment is on behalf of the victim and an indication of the judge's jurisdiction, YHWH also brings blame upon himself. To accuse and punish is to assume responsibility for the victim and victimizer both. YHWH cares, but a bit too late. He reacts. A *good* deed?

YHWH's reaction acknowledges that Abel's blood *is* his responsibility.[41] But why wait to re-act, rather then prevent? Is this story not *alter* enough so that *we* may account for Abel? How may we account for a silenced charac-ter whose subjectivity is denied? for a dead literary character? Is not the rewriting of a murder case a critique of the injustice performed? The char-acters who speak can shift the blame, and the narrator fixes their desires. Or the narrator may unfix if she desires, and readers may dis\close and resist. We may *alter*-read.

———

Hannah answered, she said, "No, my lord! I am a woman sorely troubled. I have drunk no wine or strong drink, but I have been pouring out my life to the face of YHWH. Do not take your maidservant for a worthless woman because I have thus far only been speaking out of my great anxiety and distress." (1 Sam 1:15–16)

———

YHWH for his part chose to place a curse, a constraint, upon Cain. His curse is total: more cursed than the ground, which will no longer

---

41 Westermann perceives in Gen 4:10 an element that dramatizes this story: "Cain wanted to be done with Abel. But he is not to be done with; the life that has been stilled cries out" to God *qua* "blood avenger" who hears and confronts the killer (305). This portrayal of YHWH as avenger is problematic. First, there is no indication that Cain's curse was for the purpose of avenging Abel's blood. How is someone avenged in the curse of another? Abel, after all, remains dead. Second, the modification of Cain's curse in Gen 4:15 begs the ques-tion of whether the avenging of Abel's blood was also modified. Can YHWH modify the curse without modifying the deliverance?

yield to him, and Cain will wander ceaselessly, unable to settle.
Ha'adamah (ground) and *ha'adam* (man) are placed at odds; the one is
condemned not to submit to the other. But neither one may be conceived without the other, so they are linked ("\"-ed). Cain is condemned
to wander, an activity for which Abram was called (Gen 12) and Israel
freed (Exodus–Numbers). Cain's "curse" later signifies election and liberation. The curse is quite "Nody": to wander is to be free (to go), to be
free is to be displaced (the exodus generation was an exiled generation),
and to be displaced is discomforting (unless it is normalized, "in other
words," *good;* cf. Williams).

In Gen 3:19 YHWH determined that human destiny is *ha'adamah,* but
in Gen 4:14 Cain laments that YHWH has banished him "from upon the
face of *ha'adamah.*" Was Cain banished from the task of tilling
ha'adamah or from death? If Cain's lament is heeded, it will reverse the
curse of Gen 3:19 (return to dust) but endorse the condition of Gen 3:23
(to till the soil, which requires that he settles) by providing what was
lacking in Gen 2:5 (man to till earth). Was Cain trying to be accountable
for *ha'adamah?* Was he trying to show YHWH what it means to be
obliged to the creation? how to act between thorns and thistles? how
freedom is obligation?

When YHWH marks Cain (Gen 4:15), I assume that Cain is protected. Or was YHWH marking Cain for himself? Cain's mark (*'wt*) is a
point of dis\closure: if we insert, in a linguistic event, the narrator's *w*
into Eve's *'t* we name YHWH's *'wt. Inter-esse,* double voices. The mark
does not eliminate the initial curse nor provide protection for Cain.
Rather, it reveals what YHWH will do if (i.e., *after*) anyone kills Cain.
The mark allows YHWH to be late, later!

Cain departs from YHWH's presence, but he does not become a cease-
less wanderer. He transgresses YHWH's constraints by settling in a land,
Nod. But he also fulfills the curse by *settling* at Nod, a land named
"Wander." In Other words, YHWH sentences Cain to be "Nody."[42]

Cain is free, yet bound. Fulfillment and transgression overlap. At the
end of Gen 4, which is not the end of the story, Cain escapes the story
world to settle in Nod; he is dis\placed, to lurk behind this reading
where liberation and exile overlap. This *alter*-reading blurs the story's dis-
tinctions, out of love to Cain.

---

42 Görg argues that the Hebrew "land of Nod" is borrowed from an Egyptian phrase
that means "land of God" (8). This makes Cain's punishment more ironic: he is *marked* to
be with God!

4. ALTERING LOVE, IN OTHER WORDS, LOVE TO CAIN

I retraced the disfiguring process back to the garden, *alter*-reading silences and absences, selectively,[43] and discovered that the difference between the *order* in the garden and the *alienation* outside of it is very slight. In this *altering*-reading I dis\closed a "Nody" story. At *w*-point two characters live in displacement, and at YHWH's *'wt* a character is marked because he murdered his brother. The one who enters the story in Gen 4:1 is pushed out in Gen 4:16, and he leaves behind the presence of he who was "conceived and born" by the words of a knowee, a woman-mother.

This *alter*-reading muddies the subjectification game, disclosing that victim and victimizer exist not in isolation from one another. Our Abel is not fully innocent, and our Cain has a chance to interact, to mess, with the lord of the story world. I do not deny Arturo Graf: "No matter what you say, you Cain have killed your brother" (in Quinones: 8). That factual statement, however, cannot silence the silences of this story.

What about the Cains and Abels at the underside of modern history, the repressed people at communities of struggle and cultures of silence? What do we *Say* with them?

If this *alter*-reading encourages the Cains and Abels of history to confront the lords of history, of texts, and of faith with the voice of blood, presence of silence, or only with taunting questions, then we have taken a step toward rewriting a repressing story (cf. West 1995: 186). In other words, by means of *alter*-reading, may we rewrite the wrongs of our stories even if it involves loving Cain more than God.[44]

To love Cain demands more loving than is needed for loving God, and it is not in the place of loving God. Nor in the place of loving Abel. Love to Cain is difficult love. It involves Hannah-like courage to *alter*-read for lost figures, and for disfigures, in such places as the stories of non-Israelite firstborns not passed over at Egypt, of the exodus generation who died in wandering,[45] of the "dwellers of the land" lurked (Num 13) and displaced in Joshua-Judges, of Ezra-Nehemiah's "people of the

---

43 So I am vulnerable to our bureaucrats and police, the ones who write up overreading tickets (cf. Foucault). *Inter alia*, I dis\close their silences by naming our selectivism!

44 This call echoes Levinas's love for the Torah more than for God: "Man will love Him in spite of all that God may attempt in order to discourage man's love.... It is necessary that God unveil His face; it is necessary that justice and power be rejoined. There must be just institutions on this earth. But only the man who has recognized God obscured can demand this unveiling" (1979b: 219–20; cf. 1990c: 16).

45 The distinction between "murderer" and "manslayer" in Num 35:16–28, with cities of refuge designated in Deut 4:41–43 for manslayers, suggests that Cain would have a more sympathetic reading by the wilderness wanderers.

land," and in the cries in/of the stories of the Cains and Abels of history. This *alter*-reading therefore ends not at fulfillment, but *inter-esse:* "At no time can one say: I have done all my duty. Except the hypocrite" (Levinas 1985: 105–6).

I hope to have given the Cains and Abels of the Bible and of history, and the lords, the courage to rewrite their, and our, misrecognitions. I have rewritten an old story, "in other words." In this *alter* version lords do not always rule, figures drift and slip, silences and absences dis\figure, and texts interfere with other texts.

Through this *alter*-reading I discovered that to constrain is to set free, to set free is to constrain: freedom and obligation, story and text, *Saying* and *Said*, voices and deeds, silences and absences, are so "Nody." *Inter-esse* stuff happens: dis\closure, obligation, freedom, and so, as an alternative reading, I *Say* that *alter* is always already native.

One last task of alter-reading remains, necessary for dis\closure: *w*-I let my reading go.[46]

---

[46] This article is a revision of a presentation to the "Reading, Rhetoric, and Hebrew Bible" and the "Semiotics and Exegesis" sections (1995 AAR-SBL meeting, Philadelphia).

My adviser Danna N. Fewell, who is too present to be quoted, shares the responsibility for making this reading an event in rereading! Gary Phillips's encouraging "go to it!" turned my freedom into obligation, and David M. Gunn, Elaine Robinson, and Joerg Rieger offered critical readings. I trust that I did not meet all of "our" expectations, for I saddle at Nod!

DAMAGES DUE TO FIRE:
LEVINAS, THE BIBLE, AND THE HOLOCAUST

Tod Linafelt
Georgetown University

> *At the time of his execution, they wrapped Rabbi Hanina in a Torah scroll and set fire to him and to the Torah scroll, while his daughter, throwing herself at his feet, screamed: "Is this the Torah, and this its reward?" "My daughter," he said to her, ... "if it is for the Torah scroll that you are weeping, lo, the Torah is fire, and fire cannot consume fire. Behold, the letters are flying into the air, and only the parchment itself is burning.*
>
> —Tractate "Mourning"

> *We received the Torah at Sinai*
> *And in Lublin we gave it back.*
> *The dead don't praise God.*
> *The Torah was written for the living.*
>
> —Jacob Glatstein

How to articulate the meeting of the black and white fire of the Torah with the fires of Auschwitz? Can we still take the first of these epigraphs at face value, imagining that the Torah has survived the all-burning of the Holocaust? Are we able to read the Hebrew Bible in the same manner as we did before the Shoah, its essence untouched by the flames even as the letters that Rabbi Hanina saw floating away from the parchment? Or is the second epigraph closer to the truth, imagining the Torah murdered in the death camps along with the six million, though the deed has yet to reach our ears? How is it possible to read the Hebrew Bible *at all* in light of the Shoah?

Questions such as these have been largely ignored in the field of biblical studies.[1] And while the responses represented by the above

---

1 This holds true even in books where one would logically expect the questions to be addressed, e.g., Brooks and Collins. While there is a section in Schüssler Fiorenza and Tracy

epigraphs have a certain legitimacy in specific contexts, neither offers a mode by which to engage further any questions of how the Bible might be read differently from a post-Holocaust perspective. They represent two poles of nonengagement, diametrically opposed in ideology, yet functionally the same. To solicit a genuine engagement, one that will affect, perhaps, both how we read the Bible and how we view the Holocaust, we must attempt to tread the dangerous middle ground between these two poles. Taking Emmanuel Levinas as our guide—and writing in constant conversation with both his talmudic reading, "Damages Due to Fire," and with Lev 10, a text that knows much about such damages—we may begin to explore the damages to the Bible due to the fires of the Holocaust.

1. READING WITH LEVINAS

Levinas offers, first of all, a warning. In his essay, "To Love the Torah More Than God," where he reflects on the fictive memoirs of a survivor of the Warsaw ghetto, Levinas writes the following about the Holocaust:

> We are not going to recount all of it, even though the world has learned nothing and forgotten everything. We refuse to make an exhibition of the Passion of Passions or to extract any petty vanity as the author or producer of these inhuman cries. They echo and resound inextinguishably throughout eternities. Let us listen only to the thought which is articulated in them. (1979b: 217)

So the middle ground we tread immediately demands another middle ground, or better, a constant alternation ("an alternation of alternations" [Levinas 1994c: 115]): an alternation between the demand not to co-opt and the demand not to ignore. The first demand guards against the temptation to reduce the Shoah to a rhetorical maneuver that lends an easy emotional aspect to one's work. The second demand guards against an insulation by which the discipline of biblical studies ignores its post-Holocaust interpretive context. The tension between these two demands must be maintained if we are to fashion an ethically responsible approach to reading the Bible after the Holocaust.

---

devoted to "Biblical Studies," it contains only one article on New Testament anti-Judaism and, inexplicably, one on church history. The few people who have done explicit post-Holocaust readings of biblical texts are significantly not primarily known as biblical scholars. See, e.g., Blumenthal, Fackenheim, Néher, and Wiesel's collections of midrashic legends on biblical characters (1976; 1981; 1991). I have treated these works more fully in Linafelt 1994 and have addressed some of these issues in Linafelt 1995a.

Levinas offers us other guidelines for reading. While recognizing the independent "status" of Scripture, that "its word comes from elsewhere, from outside," he recognizes that Scripture "at the same time, lives within the person receiving it" (1989c: 194). Indeed, Levinas celebrates the richness of a plurality of interpretations: "The multiplicity of people, each one of them indispensable, is necessary to produce all the dimensions of meaning" (195). So to read with Levinas means to honor both the otherness of the text and our present readerly horizon. But Levinas adds one other guideline: we must not imagine simply two poles of reader and text, for there is always on the horizon the long history of interpretation. "Tradition, running through history, does not impose its conclusions upon us, but it does demand that we make contact with what it sweeps before it" (197). It is this tradition of reading, more than any "objective" reality of the text itself, to which one is responsible and by which the "subjective" reality of the interpreter is balanced. So whatever the extent of the rupture in history represented by the Shoah, we may not glibly dismiss previous readings as no longer relevant, and we may in fact find in them unsuspected allies.

An approach to reading the Bible with Levinas *after the Holocaust*, then, requires constant attention to (1) the text itself, its contours and coherence as well as its gaps and lacks; (2) the present post-Holocaust readerly horizon, which brings its own gaps and lacks; and (3) the history of interpretation, which often attempts to fill the gaps it finds in the texts but which just as often widens these gaps even more. It is, of course, somewhat artificial to produce a list of requirements for a "Levinasian approach" to reading Scripture, for Levinas himself has written little explicitly on the act of reading, preferring instead to *take up the task* of reading Scripture, as evidenced in his many talmudic readings. In these readings one can observe Levinas modeling the above approach in his vigilance toward the details and the rhetorical flow of the text under consideration, the constant circumspection with regard to his own role as interpreter, and the respect he gives to previous interpreters, whether or not he finally agrees with them. In Levinas's treatment of a passage from the talmudic tractate *Baba Kama* concerning the restitution for damages due to fire, for example, he takes great care to guide the reader through the structure of the text and repeatedly defers not only to the *amoraim* represented in the *gemara* but also to later thinkers such as the Maharsha, Haim of Volozhin, Maimonides, and even Leibniz. But as if to unsettle any easy continuity with tradition, Levinas allows the Shoah to irrupt into his reading, as it seems it inevitably must in any discussion today of destruction by fire: "Do we not smell here, more strongly than a while back, beyond all violence which still submits to will and reason, the odor of the camps" (1990c: 190). Levinas has elsewhere described interpretation as a way of extracting a "secret scent" (1990c: 55) otherwise unavailable. The scent is not always pleasant, yet it cannot be ignored. In my own reading of Lev 10—which elicits the odor of the camps no less than Levinas's talmudic text—I have likewise allowed the Shoah to enter a discourse to which it seems alien. Yet once the odor is acknowledged, we find it to be not nearly so alien as we may wish.

2. A READING OF LEVITICUS 10:1–5

Into the well-ordered and ritualized chapters of Leviticus irrupts the strange story of Nadab and Abihu.

> [1] The sons of Aaron, Nadab and Abihu, each took his pan and kindled a fire in it. They placed incense on it, and they brought near before YHWH "strange fire,"[2] which he had not commanded them. [2] And fire came forth from before YHWH and it consumed them, and they died before YHWH. [3] Then Moses said to Aaron, "This is what YHWH meant when he said,
>   'Through my near-ones[3] I shall be holy,
>   and before all the people I shall gain glory.' "[4]
> But Aaron was silent. [4] Moses called to Mishael and Elzaphan—the sons of Uzziel the uncle of Aaron—and he said to them, "Come near, carry your brothers away from before the holy place[5] to outside the

---

2 The phrase *'esh zarah* (LXX *pyr allotrion*) has spawned a wide variety of translations. I find the traditional English phrase "strange fire" (KJV; old JPS) still the most compelling rendering. *Zur* certainly at times has the sense of "foreign," which lends support to NJPS's "alien fire." Such a narrowing of meaning is unwarranted, however, given *zur*'s broader meaning of "to be a stranger." I find both the NRSV's "unholy" and Milgrom's "unauthorized" (1991: 598) to be without support. Milgrom's rendering is an extension of his earlier argument that *zar* in Priestly use means "a person who is unauthorized to perform the cultic act in question" (1970: 8). I would agree with Kirschner (381) and Greenstein (58) that *zar* does not necessarily carry the same force in reference to *'esh*.

3 I follow Greenstein in using the phrase "my near-ones" rather than the ubiquitous "those who are near to me" (NRSV, JPS, passim), primarily because its conciseness is more faithful to the single word of the Hebrew. It also carries the connotation of a specific group of people—i.e., the priests (Ezek 42:13)—who have access to YHWH rather than simply any one who happens to be near.

4 This niphal of *kbd* is variously rendered as "I will be glorified" (NRSV), "I will glorify myself" (Milgrom 1991: 603), "I must be honored" (Wenham: 152), and "I shall be honored" (Greenstein: 56). I have followed the JPS translation, "I shall gain glory," which agrees with the similar usage in Ezek 28:22, where YHWH gains glory over Sidon.

5 The phrase "holy place" (*haqqodesh*) is retained here in part to preserve the allusion to *qdsh* in 10:3 and in part because I am not convinced that a specific location of the burning can be identified. Most English translations simply render it "sanctuary," but Milgrom (1991: 606) takes it to mean the entire tabernacle court. And he notes that rabbinic interpreters generally saw it as the tent of meeting itself.

camp." [5] So they came near and carried them outside the camp in their tunics, as Moses said. (Author's translation)

While the book of Job is often cited as the closest thing to a post-Holocaust parable in the canon of the Hebrew Bible, the story of Nadab and Abihu is perhaps even more disturbingly appropriate.[6]

> We are entering the realm of total disorder, of sheer Element, no longer in the service of any thought. (Levinas 1990c: 187)

In what follows I put this realm of sheer Element in conversation with images and themes from our present post-Holocaust horizon as well as more traditional writings, without attempting to read the biblical text in the service of any thought that might explain or comprehend or even respond to it.

A. The Image of Fire

There is, first of all, the image of fire: fire haunts this text. Fire—the sign of God's blessing in earlier chapters of Leviticus—destroys the young priests named Nadab and Abihu, and it leaves in its wake only ash, with which the survivors must deal. Fire is an image that also haunts those who survived the attempt at systematic destruction of European Jewry in the 1930s and 1940s.

> All the names, all the
> names burnt up
> with the rest. So much
> ash to bless. (Celan: 141)

The image of fire summons to the imagination not only the ovens of Auschwitz but the very term "Holocaust." Overused, co-opted, nearly devoid of meaning, the term derives from the "burnt offering," *ha-'olah* (or *holocaustos* in the Greek), found throughout the book of Leviticus. Indeed, the fire that came forth to devour the sons of Aaron is the same fire that came forth to devour the *'olah* in 11:22–24.

> Fire, an elementary force to which other elementary forces will add themselves, multiplying damages beyond any rational conjecture! (Levinas 1990c: 185)

---

6 The present article continues a long-term interest in how to interpret Lev 10. For a much different approach to the same text, see Beal and Linafelt 1995.

In this sense, Damrosch is correct in writing that "the officiants themselves go the way of the burnt offering just made by their father" (70).
Nadab and Abihu essentially become human burnt offerings, or "holo-
causts." Attributed to God in this text, the word "holocaust" momentarily
regains its power to jar us, even as we recognize its inappropriateness to
describe what Wiesel has taken to calling simply "the Event." And so we
are jolted into the twentieth century and forced to consider yet another
Holocaust that is no less horrendous than the story in Lev 10.

> From heaven to the heaven of heavens to the heaven of night long con-
> voys of smoke. (Pagis: 31)

It is difficult to imagine even the most pious of interpreters not being
troubled by the outlandishly severe punishment of Nadab and Abihu.
Leviticus Rabbah comments:

> Even Titus, wicked as he was, could venture into the Holy of Holies,
> slash both veils, and go forth in peace. But Aaron's sons, who came into
> the Tabernacle to present an offering, were taken out burnt. (20:5)

Reading this passage as "a punishment in search of a crime" (Greenstein:
56), interpreters have gone to great lengths to "explain" the burning of
the two young priests. A dozen different rabbinic justifications are identified by Avigdor Shinan (cited in Visotzky: 175–80), ranging from
drinking wine before approaching to presuming to decide the law in the
presence of Moses. Unable to admit with Levinas "the tragic priority of
the righteous" within the "arbitrariness of extermination" (1990c: 187),
modern interpreters have shown no less imagination than the rabbis in
their quest to identify the unspecified crime. Many interpretations center
on the meaning of *'esh zarah* as the key, variously taking it to represent
"pagan incense," fire kindled by "human means," a private incense offering, fire from outside the altar area, and Zoroastrian cultic practices.[7]
    The upshot of all these attempts to identify the cultic malpractice of
Nadab and Abihu is that it places the blame for their incineration on the
priests themselves. These explanations are all "theodicies" in the sense
that they justify God's actions in the narrative at the expense of the two
priests. Even those who admit that the offense of Nadab and Abihu is
obscure beyond recovery do not hesitate to assure us that "plainly they
were guilty of folly and irreverence" (Micklem: 49).

---

7 Respectively, Clements (29); Morgenstern (6); Milgrom (1991: 631); Haran (115); and
Laughlin (564).

It is, of course, not "plain" that they were guilty of anything, and the reader who wishes to resist such settlements by theodicy is in fact aided by the text's own stubborn resistance to easy explanation. What Levinas writes of his talmudic text is equally true with our text. The referent of *'esh zarah* is notoriously indeterminate. Moreover, despite mention of *'esh zarah* in Num 3:4 and 26:61, it is not at all clear that the meaning of this phrase is in fact the key to unlocking the mystery of the passage. For example, in Lev 16 *'esh zarah* is not mentioned at all, and one gets the impression that their "coming near" is what prompted the incident.

Reading this story through a post-Holocaust hermeneutic encourages one to capitalize on this resistance of the text to identify the "sin" of Nadab and Abihu. More than that, it requires that one question the very paradigm of punishment on account of sin, for in the death of the six million the paradigm is shown to be bankrupt. As Greenberg (34) writes:

> Tell the children in the pits they are burning for their sins. An honest man—better, a decent man—would spit at such a god rather than accept this rationale if it were true.

After the Shoah we can no longer read this text—as Bamberger (804) tells us the rabbis did—under the assumption that "God never acts unjustly."

B. Yhwh's Near-Ones

Moses himself offers what amounts to a theodicy in 10:3 to explain the burning. Like virtually all theodicies, this cryptic utterance is painfully inadequate to explain the tragedy it addresses. How, for example, are we to understand YHWH's holiness as contingent on YHWH's near-ones? Do we follow Rashbam and Ramban (in Milgrom 1991: 601), who interpret this statement to mean "I shall be *treated* as holy"? If so, does the failure of Nadab and Abihu to treat YHWH as holy—if indeed they failed—justify their incineration? Or does the death of the two priests somehow serve to actually sanctify YHWH, as suggested by Milgrom (1991: 602)? And in what way are we to understand YHWH as gaining glory from the incident? Is it through bullying the witnesses? David Noel Freedman (in Milgrom 1991: 603) sums up this line of reasoning when he writes that "by a single action, YHWH affirms his total sanctity ... and also establishes his glory among the onlookers."

Despite Freedman's surety of tone, YHWH's justice is not so easily salvaged. "It is necessary that justice and power be rejoined" (Levinas 1979b: 220). The power to incinerate priests and terrify onlookers does not translate so easily into justice and total sanctity.

> Holiness serves no purpose, then. It is completely useless, completely
> gratuitous; gratuitous for those who die as a result of it, certainly; but
> gratuitous for the world whose sin this death was to atone for. Useless
> sacrifice! (Levinas 1990c: 188)

No, the cryptic oracle attributed to YHWH cannot dispel the questions of a
post-Holocaust reader.

Philo offers a different sort of theodicy, one that does not attempt to
blame Nadab and Abihu but sees in their sacrificial deaths a positive,
nearly mystical experience.

> They were not seized by a savage, evil beast, but were taken up by a
> rush of fire unquenchable, by an undying splendor, since in sincerity
> they cast aside sloth and delay, and consecrated their zeal, hot and fiery,
> flesh-consuming and swiftly moving, to piety, a zeal which was alien to
> creation, but akin to God. (*Somn.* 2.67)

While Philo thus preserves the righteousness of the two priests, he overlooks the tragedy of their priority as YHWH's near-ones. If this is what it
means to be a near-one of YHWH's—to be somehow akin to God or
"chosen"—then we can begin to understand the sentiment expressed in
Kadia Molodowsky's poem "God of Mercy" (in Roskies: 570):

> O God of Mercy
> For the time being
> Choose another people,
> We are tired of death,
> tired of corpses.

The text seems to subvert its own tendencies toward explanation by
presenting the "theodicy" as a previous quote of YHWH's. As countless
commentators have noticed, however, the quote is not to be found in the
canon of the Hebrew Scriptures. The structure of the text begins to
unravel. The rules are not as clear as Lev 1–8 would have us believe; the
duties of the priests are not as secure, the theodicy of Moses not as convincing. For the post-Holocaust reader, perhaps no theodicy would be
convincing but would be rather "indecent, as all theodicy probably is"
(Levinas 1990c: 187).

In his play, *The Trial of God*, Elie Wiesel takes this idea one step further. In a trial staged by the few survivors of a seventeenth-century
pogrom, only one character is willing to defend "the honor and kindness
of God" (1979b: 159). The character does so eloquently, using arguments
that are not unfamiliar to the modem reader. In the final scene, however,
the purveyor of theodicy is revealed to be none other than Satan. Wiesel's

message is a powerful challenge: theodicies in a post-Holocaust world are not just unconvincing; they are themselves evil.

C. The Silence of Aaron

Aaron's response to the theodicy offered by Moses is one of muteness. The text tells us no more than that "Aaron was silent." Subsequent interpreters tell us that this silence indicates a stoic acceptance of the death of his sons. Bamberger's representative treatment says only that "he refrained from weeping and from complaints against God" (801). Levine would have us believe that "Aaron accepted God's harsh judgment and did not cry out or complain at his painful loss" (60).

Yet might not the silence itself be a form of complaint against YHWH? Wiesel recounts the following story of Rabbi Levi-Yitzhak of Berditchev:

> Once he remained standing in his pulpit from morning till night without moving his lips. Earlier he had issued a warning to God: "If you refuse to answer our prayers, I shall refuse to go on saying them."

A post-Holocaust reading of Lev 10 suggests a similar understanding of Aaron's silence in 10:3. Instead of stoic acceptance, it signals anger and unwillingness to acknowledge the decree of Moses.

Or perhaps Aaron, like the Holocaust survivors of the twentieth century, is simply struck dumb by the horrific magnitude of the event.

> How is one to say, how is one to communicate that which by its very nature defies language? How is one to tell without betraying the dead, without betraying oneself. (Wiesel 1978: 235)

So writes Wiesel, who himself went through a self-imposed ten-year period of silence concerning the Shoah, before finally writing the book *Night*. Wiesel certainly was not modeling a "stoic acceptance" of the murder of his family and the obliteration of the world he knew.

To apprehend Aaron's response at all, perhaps we must employ an "aesthetics of shock, an anesthetics" (Lyotard: 31). The phrase is used by Lyotard in an effort to describe the feeling of the sublime, as articulated by Immanuel Kant in his *Third Critique*. The feeling of the sublime "bears witness to the fact that an 'excess' has 'touched' the mind, more than it is able to handle" (Lyotard: 32). The sublime is "violent to the imagination" (Kant 1987: 99), evoking "a rapid alternation of repulsion from and attraction to, one and the same object" (115). ("The turning upside down of order through the intervention of the elemental and uncontrollable?" [Levinas 1990c: 186]) The result, for one who encounters the sublime, is a stupor. Read thus, the attraction to the power and magnitude of YHWH's presence clashes with revulsion at the horrible consequences, paralyzing the hapless Aaron. An aesthetics of shock reveals neither beauty nor justice, but perhaps an experience of the sublime.

D. Cleaning Up the Scene of the "Crime"

Moses, the story tells us, is concerned to remove the bodies of the incinerated priests to outside the camp. There is little doubt that at one level the standard explanations of "impurity resulting from contact with corpses" motivate Moses' concern. Yet the emphasis given to their removal—it is mentioned in the direct speech of Moses and the report of Mishael and Elzaphan carrying it out—preserves a desire to eradicate the evidence. The trace of this "cultic homicide" (Roskies: 72) is to be banished outside the borders of the camp.

The report of Mishael and Elzaphan, were it preserved, might read like that of Simon Srebnik, survivor of Chelmno, who told the following story in the film *Shoah* (Lanzmann: 15):

> There was a concrete platform some distance away, and the bones that hadn't burned we took. We carried the bones there, where others had to crush them. It was very fine, that powdered bone. Then it was put into sacks, and when there were enough sacks, we went to a bridge on the Narew River, and dumped the powder. The current carried it off. It drifted downstream.

This effort to do away with the remains of murdered individual Jews mirrors the attempt of National Socialism to remove Jews from Europe altogether. SS leader Heinrich Himmler described the so-called "Final Solution" as "an unwritten and never-to-be-written page of glory" in Germany's history (in Roth and Berenbaum: 8). The attempt of the Nazis to eradicate all trace of the victims of the Holocaust, of course, was not successful. About the failure of such totalizing tendencies, Jean-François Lyotard (23) writes:

> One converts the Jews in the Middle Ages, they resist by mental restriction. One expels them during the classical age, they return. One integrates them in the modem era, they persist in their difference. One exterminates them in the twentieth century. But this slaughter pretends to be without memory, without trace, and through this testifies again to what it slaughters.

The attempt to eliminate the trace of Nadab and Abihu has likewise failed. As Levinas remarks concerning his talmudic text on fire damage: "The very fact of a discussion about the liabilities a destructive fire implies challenges the fatality of destruction" (Levinas 1990c: 182). Likewise, our biblical text itself stands (however inadequately) as a gravemarker, as a challenge to the final erasing of the burning.

> In this sentence, I see the tomb of a tomb, the monument of an impossible tomb—forbidden, like the memory of a cenotaph, deprived of the patience of mourning. (Derrida 1991b: 53)

"Forbidden" to remain in the camp, "deprived of the mourning" of their father and their brothers (see 10:6), Nadab and Abihu nonetheless resist obliteration by means of the "cenotaph" ("a tomb or monument erected in honor of a person or group of persons whose remains are elsewhere" [Webster, 9th ed.]) of this story. Another "never-to-be-written page," written for all to read?

E. Gainsaying YHWH's Glory

In the end, of course, I have come no closer to settling "the" meaning of Lev 10 than the numerous interpreters before me. This strange story, like the strange fire of Nadab and Abihu, continues to resist easy explanations. Reading in light of the implications of the Holocaust, however, has given us new questions and new perspectives on the text.

Emil Fackenheim (32) has written, in reference to another passage, that in some interpretive situations we have no choice but "to take sides with the mothers of the children, against the narrator, against Moses and, if necessary, against God Himself." A post-Holocaust hermeneutic encourages such a stance in relation to Lev 10. Perhaps we are required here to take sides *against* the narrator, Moses, and even God; and to side instead *with* the mothers of those consumed by the fires of the Holocaust.

It is too much to imagine an ending to this story in Leviticus similar to the ending of Levinas's talmudic text:

> Thus, the one who set the fire has to pay. The Holy One, Blessed be He, said: It is incumbent on me to make restitution for the fire which I have set. (Cited in Levinas 1990c: 181)

It is too much to imagine. It is just barely enough to demand.

Of course, a post-Holocaust reading need not always end in taking sides against God. We can imagine reading texts of joy and texts of hope as well, not against God, but with God and against the kingdom of night. But—"singed with the fires of reality" (Néher: 216)—they will at best be the joy of an almost, and the hope of a perhaps.

> ... almost a glimmer, perhaps of morning? (Jabès: 67)

CONSTITUTION AND AGENCY IN LIGHT OF SOME PASSAGES FROM EZEKIEL 1–4: A RE-READING OF LEVINAS

Martin C. Srajek
The Infant-Parent Institute

INTRODUCTION

The work of Emmanuel Levinas has the following distinct features: (1) it is a polemic against philosophical ontologies and proposes strategies that work around the use of ontology in philosophical discourse; (2) it is antidialectical because the Hegelian model of philosophical dialectics is founded on the notion of identity and therefore not adequately equipped to conceive of otherness; (3) it proposes a notion of responsibility as absolute submission to the other for whom we are responsible. The implication of the prophet Ezekiel into the text of Levinas's philosophy modifies these three features and to some degree reverses them. Beginning with point 3, and working our way backwards through 2 and 1, we will see that Ezekiel's responsibility is characterized by the partial *refusal to* submit to God, which results in a *dialectic* of resistance and surrender, which in turn necessitates an *ontological account* precisely to overcome ontology. I am suggesting that this apparent contradiction orients us to the issue of constitution and agency in Levinas whereby constitution implies the ontological dimension and agency the dialectic dimension. As a consequence, I am arguing that Levinas's decision to bring Ezekiel into his own text reflects his attempt to counter a common misunderstanding about ethical responsibility. Contrary to this misunderstanding of Levinas's work, which assumes that responsibility can only be explained through absolute submission, I argue that, even in Levinas, it can occur only if—like Ezekiel—we resist and thereby acknowledge the significance of the otherness of God and our neighbor. In other words, in order to understand what follows, we have to be able to come to terms with a hesitation, namely, the use of the term "ontological" to designate some of Levinas's work. I want to apply this term in order to get a better grasp of the scope of Levinas's texts, as well as their limitations.

Much of Levinas's work is and remains ontological, despite his serious attempt to critique and break with the philosophy of ontology that reaches from Plato to Heidegger. This means, by his own definition, that his texts, like those of traditional philosophy, are susceptible to an "attachment of being [and] thus remain a movement of knowledge and truth, an adventure of experience between the clear and the obscure" (1989a: 169). Levinas's texts cohere and form a theme in the same way that "being is manifested with a theme" (1987b: 109). This process of thematizing is due to language, which "can be interpreted as the manifestation of truth, as the way being takes to show itself" (ibid.). Any text will eventually be interpreted as such a "manifestation of truth" precisely because it is linguistic. Levinas's texts by themselves do not achieve the break from the ontological sphere that they propose to be necessary. Rather, they manifest the grip of the ontological over reality. The only two ways in which this grip could be loosened and the thematic stagnation lifted are either to ensure that interpretation as a challenge to established themes will not cease or to juxtapose one text with another in such a way that one always causes thematic disturbances in the other and hence prevents the other text from coming to something like a thematic rest.

Levinas's references to the prophet Ezekiel work in both ways and, in my opinion, produce an opening through which ontology can indeed be transcended. In doing so, they shed light on the meaning of ethical responsibility. The references provide us with a hermeneutics of reading and interpretation, and they also show the juxtaposition of two texts—biblical and philosophical. Especially with respect to the latter, it will be the task of this essay to draw out the consequences of such a reading and to show how a dialectical reading of Levinas's text and that of Ezekiel allows for the transcending of ontological stagnation toward a sphere of dynamic responsibility.

In order to understand how he creates this opening, we need to understand Levinas's choice of the prophet Ezekiel as an exemplary model in two key places in his writing. The argument that I will make is that this choice indicates a certain departure from one of the most known and important Levinasian paradigms, namely, that of the other commanding me absolutely. This paradigm has had a double function for Levinas. On the one hand, it indicates a break with ontology by designating the other as that which can no longer be comprehended ontologically. On the other hand, the other stands for the fundamental situation of the ethical par excellence, in which I owe my service to the other absolutely.

My departure from this paradigm is really not a rejection of his earlier thought, but it is an answer to the question: What is the meaning of absolute otherness (and therefore the meaning of responsibility), and how can it be understood in a living context? Through this departure, I want to indicate that Levinas's approach remains problematic if it is seen as merely philosophical. For, in that case, it cannot successfully separate itself from a language that is itself ontological. The language of philosophy is the language of being and therefore remains inadequate to describe absolute otherness.

The significance of those few passages from Ezekiel that can be found in Levinas's work can, in my estimation, not be overemphasized. For they indicate that Levinas's intent is a description not only of who we are but also of how we fare, given who we are. While the former remains within the framework of ontology despite its antiontological rhetoric (really only a tad removed from Heidegger's claim in "A Letter on Humanism" [1993] that fundamental ontology is ethics), the latter—through the figure of the prophet/priest Ezekiel—achieves a look at otherness in two dynamic situations. I hope to show that, after thinking through some of the characteristics of the book of Ezekiel (based on passages quoted by Levinas himself), we will have to adopt an amended notion of the relationship with the other and allow for a richer understanding of his philosophy of the other. Mostly, this amended notion will create a platform from which responsibility will attain a dynamic and active ethical dimension (a product of constitution and agency) rather than just being a variation of Heidegger's notion of *Geworfenheit* shot through with passivity. Looking at Ezekiel will allow us to see that—though passivity is an important foundational criterion for Levinas—responsibility is predicated on acts of interpretation and resistance. Levinas's use of Ezekiel enriches his notion of the face-to-face encounter with the other by allowing one to go beyond an understanding of this encounter, which conceives of it as mere slavery and obsession, toward one that, indeed, asks for responsibility.

I will first introduce the places in Levinas's work where references to Ezekiel occur and then illuminate the quotes from the perspective of the texts in which Levinas uses them. Having achieved that, I will give an account of the calling of Ezekiel as a prophet by drawing on some categories that are genuine to Levinas's work but also by bringing in some other material worked out by André Néher. I will end by showing that Levinas's choice of Ezekiel as a model for his understanding of responsibility implies a conception of ethics that, rather than emphasizing responsibility as absolute dependence and obsession, is conceived as an ethics of responsibility through the dialectic of resistance and surrender.

To my knowledge, only two explicit references to the prophet Ezekiel can be found in Levinas's work. These references are found in places where they either highlight certain qualities of Levinas's text or even summarize it as a whole; they thus obtain an undeniable importance for Levinas's texts. The first reference I would like to discuss can be found in the essay "Revelation in the Jewish Tradition," where Levinas reflects extensively on the meaning and significance of the claim that the Jews are the "people of the Book" (1989c: 192).

> If Israel is the "people of the Book" by virtue of its land, an extension of its in-folio manuscripts and scrolls, it also earns this title in another way: it is books that have nourished Israel, almost in the physical sense of the term, like the prophet who swallows the scroll in chapter 3 of Ezekiel. A strange diet, indeed, of celestial foods! (1989c: 199)

The second reference is from his 1974 opus *Otherwise Than Being or Beyond Essence.* It consists of two separate quotes that precede the whole text of the book and thus serve as an intonation of how Levinas wants his own text to be understood.

> Or if a righteous man turn from his righteousness and do what is wrong, and I make that the occasion for bringing about this downfall, he shall die; because you did not warn him, he shall die for his sin, and the righteous deeds which he has done shall not be remembered, but his blood will I require at your hand. (Ezek 3:20)

> Then he ... said to him, "Pass through the city—through Jerusalem—and set a mark upon the foreheads of the men who sigh and cry for all the abominations that are done in the midst of it." And to the others he said in my hearing, "Pass through the city after him, and slay without mercy or pity. Old men, young men and maidens, little children and women—strike them all dead! But touch no one on whom is the mark. And begin at my sanctuary." (Ezek 9:4–6)

I believe that these two references set the tone quite adequately for the questions that have to be raised when it comes to the issue of Levinas's relation to the Bible. While the first one is an answer to the question "How are we constituted?" and therefore answers an ontological question, the second quote answers the question "How should we act?" and thus highlights the dialectical nature of agency. We have to ask whether the introduction of the biblical prophet/priest Ezekiel in any way modifies the direction of Levinas's philosophical analysis. We had noted earlier that Levinas's references to the book of Ezekiel suggest reassessment of his conception of the relationship with the other. Having looked at the two references to Ezekiel, we are now better equipped to anticipate how the argument will unfold. We will examine Levinas's concept of the relationship with the other in two steps. First, we will look at the general relationship that the Jew has with the world. This, in Levinas's work, translates into the question of reading and interpreting Scripture and, in my reading, also is an answer to the question of an ontological constitution. Second, we will look at particular relationships with an other—first with God, then with other human beings—as they are laid out in the book of Ezekiel. This emphasizes the problem of agency and highlights the dialectical qualities of ethical agency in Levinas. Both of these steps focus on bringing out the meaning of responsibility. In the section that follows this analysis, I will attempt a narrative summary of some important aspects of the book of Ezekiel, centering especially on the developing concept of responsibility through Ezekiel's interaction with God, Scripture, and humans. In the end, it will be our task to analyze both steps in comparison with the Ezekiel narrative and to show how the book of Ezekiel serves as a paradigm for the thought of Levinas.

Constitution

In Levinas's view, the reading and interpretation of Scripture are two literally vital activities for the Jewish community. The desire for exegesis and interpretation is not only an intellectual project, but it also creates *espace vitale* for the Jews. Reading and interpretation produce space in which one can live. The space that Levinas has in mind carries with it all connotations that space can have. It is a physical space, a social space, a legal space, an emotional space, and, of course, also a space for revelation. Scripture, in other words, is the parameter of Jewish existence. In it and through it happens everything that could be considered Jewish. For the Jews, then, the scriptural texts are not only an *object* that could be either dealt with or ignored, but they are also inextricably bound up with the meaning of Jewish existence. They partake of the subjectivity, that is, the agency, of Jewish life. The texts of Scripture are the subject of Jewish life. Thus, as indicated above, Levinas asserts that an analysis of the relationship with the world will, for the Jewish reader, necessarily have to be an analysis of the relationship with Scripture.

The problem that inheres in the scope of such an analysis lies with the status of Scripture itself. Is Scripture simply a historical account of historic events (exiles, wars, prophets, revelations) as they happened to the Jews, or is it a text that *still* contains the possibility of revelation? For Levinas, the question becomes how it is possible to understand the historicity of these texts without losing their ahistorical revelatory content.

His thesis is that, over and beyond the agency of Jewish life, which is enhanced, and in some way produced, by the texts of Scripture, these historical texts also form the relational medium between God and the people. They are, at the same time, sites of interpretation *and* of revelation. When Levinas speaks of interpretation, he has in mind the curious inquiry into the possibility of meaning. When he speaks of revelation, he is thinking of a giving of meaning from inside these texts. Through them God reveals Godself and through them a closeness with God is established and guaranteed. In Levinas's understanding, then, this closeness cannot be described only in terms of a hermeneutics of truthful interpretation but must also be understood in the context of divine revelation. Every time one begins to read and/or interpret a scriptural text, one also initiates a relationship with God as an act of God's revelation. For this to be possible, we have to imagine these texts as fragmented, open-ended, and unfinished pieces of writing that—by virtue of their unfinishedness—give room to interpretation as well as to revelation. From this perspective, the texts are an infinite source of revelatory meaning and significance only waiting to be tapped by the act of human interpretation.

The significance of the prophet Ezekiel for Levinas in this context lies in the extent to which Scripture is not only the object to be interpreted but is understood as the condition of interpretation. Ezekiel's eating of the scrolls of the Torah indicates his becoming Scripture. Every cell of his body, every act as well as every thought, will henceforth breathe Scripture and thus form the hermeneutical framework out of which the priest understands his world. In this way the fragmentation of Scripture, its resulting openness for interpretation, and its revelatory potential become part of the human constitution. Phenomenologically speaking, fragmentation is present for the Jews in the form of a desire to interpret. This desire betrays the absence of full meaning and thus a certain fragmentation with respect to the question of how one is to lead a full and fulfilled life. The point of the story of Ezekiel is to show that this desire is instilled in us through Scripture itself. The consumption of Scripture is, paradoxically, an ontological indicator for Levinas. It explains our constitutional fragmentation and thus *undermines* (*with* ontological means) the imperviousness of the ontological in favor of the openness of the ethical. It is possible to make a similar distinction for God. Theosophically speaking, God's revelation is indicative of a fragmentation that appears as the desire to give. Theologically speaking, this revelation is an indication that God is constitutionally dependent on humanity for recognition. The openness of the text makes possible a relationship with God as interpretation while, at the same time, making space for the emergence of revelation. In other words, the existence of the text itself is not only dependent on being revealed by God, but it is also dependent on being interpreted by humanity. As a whole, the text enhances the proliferation of the community, both in the form of a community with God and in the form of a community with each other.

The move of ontology against ontological imperviousness is replicated through Levinas's insistence on the historical interpretation of Scripture. Truth as a totality is dependent on a multiplicity of people working on it. As revelation contained in Scripture, truth requires history and a hermeneutics of infinite human uniqueness in order to come forth entirely. In their function as interpreters of Scripture, humans are "the irruption of God within Being, or the bursting out of Being towards God" (1989c: 202). "[T]he human mind is *inherently* open to inspiration and … man is *inherently* able to become a prophet" (204; my emphasis); "man is the site of transcendence" (205).

This triangular relation between God, humans, and Scripture could be understood as a way to overcome the situation of fragmentation. However, although an "overcoming" is certainly at the horizon (both for the desire to interpret as well as for the desire to reveal), it must not be understood literally. While it can be said that, for Levinas, overcoming is present in the act of communication in general and, therefore, also in the acts of interpretation and revelation, it must be emphasized that for him the word (in particular the spoken word) constitutes a form of surrender. For when I speak I surrender my words to the other without having further control over how they might be perceived. It is more fitting, then, to say that this surrender increases the fragmentation rather than reducing it. The situation between God and humans remains, according to Levinas, nonreciprocal and without a trace of symmetry. The only possible way to understand the act of reading and revelation is to look at it as an asymptotic situation in which oneness is both infinite possibility and finite impossibility. Reading and revelation bring both God and humans infinitely close to this oneness; however, neither side will reach it fully. This perpetuates the process of interpretation and revelation *ad infinitum*, and that is precisely Levinas's point.

For Levinas, this surrender is synonymous with "responsibility." Interpretation is not only a sign of a desire for truth and wholeness, but it also betrays the infinite desire to respond to the other. We are so much drawn in by this desire to respond to the other that Levinas describes responsibility in terms of being held hostage or being obsessed by the other. In the act of interpretation as surrender, however, responsibility goes beyond the act of interpretation itself and becomes a complete giving-over of oneself to the other. In the words *me voici* (in Hebrew *hinneni*), "Here I am!" my surrender turns from a responsible act in which I am the subject or agent into an accusation in which I am the object or accused. While the former takes place in the mode of activity, the latter reveals me as utterly passive.

So much for the question of how Levinas envisions the *act* of reading and its concomitant hermeneutic situation. Let us now turn to the *effect* that the reading of Scripture has on the reader. For this we need to turn to the second set of quotes and the book that is preceded by them: *Otherwise Than Being or Beyond Essence.*

Agency

The question for Levinas is whether the Bible speaks the language of responsibility and obsession that he has introduced to describe the primary ethical relationship. Does the Bible support the type of counter-ontological reading that Levinas has introduced into the discourse of philosophy? We will see that the book of Ezekiel represents for Levinas, first of all, a certain prototypical pattern for our relationship with God from which then, secondly, is derived a behavioral prototype that concerns the ethical relationship with my fellow human beings.

The ethical relationship with the other, that is, with the other human being next to me, begins for Levinas with an openness and desire for God, the ultimate other. In his essay "God and Philosophy," Levinas lays out, while borrowing heavily from Descartes, how it is that as finite human beings we can have a sense of the infinite God. Levinas's main contention is that the infinite is not just the privation of the finite, but it is in-finite, that is, it dwells in the finite. However, this inclusion of the idea of the infinite in the finite is problematic in so far as it seems to suggest that the thought of God is comparable to that of things finite. Is thinking God, or perceiving God, then, the same as is thinking or perceiving an object? Levinas rejects that thought vehemently.

> The idea of God is in me, but God already breaking up the conscious-
> ness which aims at ideas, and unlike any content.... There is a putting
> of the Infinite into thought, but this is wholly different from what is
> structured as a comprehension of a *cogitatum* by a *cogitatio.* (1989a: 174)

It is, in other words, as if the thought of the infinite, that is, the thought of God, causes a sort of fragmentation of consciousness that is both disabling and enabling at the same time. It is disabling because it breaks up the ontological quietness of consciousness for which every thought is a theme, that is, a holding together and stratifying of the world and the things that are in it. It is enabling because it is precisely this fragmentation that causes the openness toward God that Levinas has in mind as the fundamental constellation of the ethical. God, in other words, has always already insinuated Godself into every thought and idea that I could possibly have, thus breaking it up and making it receptive to the command of the other.

In Levinas's thinking, divine fragmentation of the finite subject—first visible as my desire for the holy—translates into an altruistic fragmentation, a being hollowed out of the finite subject—visible as my desire for the other to command me as neighbor. The finite and infinite are woven in with each other and form a unique structure of agency and obedience vis-à-vis the other. Recognizing God not just as an external force, but as the infinite in ourselves, results in obeying God's command to love our neighbor. Only a radical monotheism that emphasizes both God's absolute difference and the apodictic nature of God's commandment can have this effect of agency and obedience. Hence theology always translates into ethics.

The parallel with Ezekiel lies in the fact that the language of insinuation, fragmentation, and of breaking up resembles that of resistance and surrender found in the book of Ezekiel. Levinas explicates this resemblance when he says that

> the figure of the Infinite put in me, and, according to Descartes, contemporaneous with my creation, would mean that the not being able to comprehend the Infinite by thought is somehow a positive relationship with this thought—but with this thought as passive, as a *cogitatio* as though *dumbfounded* and no longer, or not yet, commanding the *cogitatum*. (1989a: 175; my emphasis)

The choice of the word "dumbfounded" is clearly not an accident. The implication of Ezek 3:25–26 into Levinas's counterontological conception of the ethical suggests that Levinas understands Ezekiel as the *prototypical* ethical agent: fragmented, bound and gagged, and made ready, though never actively ready, for the work he is commanded to do. The further study of Ezekiel will show that Levinas's ethics, despite his rather open-minded approach to the interpretation of the Bible, is predicated on a notion of absolute power that rests with God. It will further show, however, that while God is powerful enough to command, God is not powerful enough to ensure that a commandment given will be obeyed. "God," as Levinas reminds us, "is an authority without power" (Wright, Hughes, and Ainley: 169).

The book *Otherwise Than Being or Beyond Essence* is a book about the possibility of transcendence and—connected to this primary possibility—the possibility of ethics. For Levinas, ethics can only occur in a realm in which the other can appear as the other unmediated by the mental agencies and metaphysical systems created by the "I." The subjectivism of the "I" that—in Levinas's view—is also the basis for all traditional ontological thought is, ultimately, a solipsism inadequate to serve the other in the way that ethics would require. Only if transcendence is possible, and if we can understand the possibility of transcendence, will we be able to understand ethics.

The meaning of transcendence is that of "passing over to being's other" (1981: 3). This passing over has been achieved fully only if we can look at it without detecting a connection with being. "Otherwise than being" is Levinas's expression for this situation, and it is markedly different from "being otherwise." The force of this distinction derives from the explicit way in which Levinas disallows its understanding as a mere playing with language. Surely, the expressions "otherwise than being" and "being otherwise" are both instances of language and as such connected to a linguistic ontological structure centered around the predicate "to be." Saying one rather than the other does not rescue the project in any sensible way. What does rescue it, however, is the fact that Levinas introduces a distinction between two different linguistic phases, one of which functions as a signifier for an ethical transcendence that is unrecuperable and outside the linguistic structures of essence. The distinction is that between the saying and the said. While the saying implies transcendence, the said implies immanence.

It is important to understand the necessity of the term "imply" in this context. Naturally, the saying is just as much a part of language as the said, and the two are equally embedded in the structures of essence. What makes the crucial difference is the implication of a dynamics that precedes the saying and shows me in utter submission to the other on whose willingness to listen my saying depends. It is a flicker, a momentary occurrence, that cannot be extracted from the whole situation. But even though what I will say might be dominating the other, it is at this very moment of saying that I am absolutely bound to the other. Without the other, what I have to say will not be heard, will be in vain, and—in the long run—saying will end.

Levinas calls this relationship with the other "responsibility." But what he means by it is not so much the moral task to respond as the ability to respond. My ability to say is conditioned by the other; in this condition I find the basis of my subjectivity, that is, my ability to be a subject. The passage from Ezek 3 that Levinas quotes at the beginning of his book expresses precisely this form of conditioning that leaves us helpless, bound, and silenced vis-à-vis the other. It is a state of utter responsibility *in potentiam*, waiting to become prophecy *in actualis*. God makes Ezekiel a sentry, a guard, and thus puts him into the impossible situation of being accountable to God and his fellow people at the same time. The meaning of being a prophet is to be absolutely commissioned by God to speak, while simultaneously being reduced to a state of absolute dependence on one's fellow beings for the possibility of speaking. Responsibility, in other words, emerges when one is stretched out between the transcendence of God and that of the other.

By way of a short summary, the following can be said about Levinas's texts and their relationship to the book of Ezekiel: Ezekiel represents on the one hand a model for how the individual person should relate to the world and God through the medium of Scripture. This medium is not arbitrarily chosen but really is an integral part of how we are constituted as human beings. Paradoxically, the semiontological language of constitution here undermines ontology itself because of the interpretive incompleteness of the scriptural medium. On the other hand, Ezekiel the priest stands paradigmatically for the relationship with the other that Levinas conceives as an obsession. Ezekiel's passivity, first part of his resistance, then prescribed by God, has all the characteristics of the absolute dependence of the self on the other. Both references to Ezekiel also highlight a different kind of ability. Whereas the former thinks of responsibility as my interpretive response to the texts of Scripture (and hence my participation in the shaping of *espace vitale*), the latter thinks of responsibility as a moral quality, namely, as protecting my fellow humans from wrongdoings and the subsequent wrath of God. We are now ready to move to a reading of the first few chapters of Ezekiel.

Dialectic of Resistance and Surrender in Ezekiel

The book of Ezekiel is a text about responsibility that comes in a twofold way: as the *act of responding to* and as *being responsible for*. The book puts under serious scrutiny the ways in which God responds to the people of Israel and to the priest Ezekiel. It looks at how Ezekiel and the Israelites respond to God and seeks to elicit a theological response from the reader. However, the book also urges a sense of being responsible for each other that is predicated upon the act of responding to each other. This is particularly true for Ezekiel himself. A superficial reading of the book, as yet another text about yet another prophet, will not reveal the different levels of responsibility through which we are guided as readers. A prophet—whether it is Ezekiel, Isaiah, Jeremiah, or Amos—is not a particularly responsible person, but somebody who is unfortunate enough to have been chosen by God as a vehicle for God's word (for since the time of the kings, God no longer speaks to the Israelites directly but only through a human mouthpiece). In other words, a prophet is a person beset by God, forced to say things that he or she would never have thought of on his or her own. For this reason it would be absurd to call the priest Ezekiel responsible when he ends up doing exactly as God instructs him to do. It would be cynical to glorify the sense of oppression and sheer slavery that inheres in the part of the story dealing with the call of the prophet. Ezekiel has no choice; he is a helpless hostage, and as such he can only hope that God will release him and not kill him. Consequently, there is an acute absence of action on his part. Even to say that Ezekiel acts, in so far as he is ready to accept God's orders, would be to overstate the situation. For such readiness would presuppose a moment of agreement, of active decision making (possibly a *hinneni*) on the part of the priest. An agreement, however, is missing from the text absolutely.

Yet the oppression through which Ezekiel is made into a prophet is not "pure." Between God and Ezekiel a dialectic of forces is at work through which a responsibility beyond the act of responding can emerge. Néher describes this emergence of responsibility under the heading "Prophets Who Mislay the Key to Themselves" (152). For as soon as we accept the premise that all prophecy presupposes that the prophet submit himself absolutely to God (i.e., to an existence of utter passivity), we notice that Ezekiel breaks with the ideal of submission required of him. The "vocal relationship" that usually exists between a prophet and God is "broken off" because Ezekiel "refuse[s] to express [himself] in words, [he becomes] an illegible page" (ibid.). Significant portions of the book of Ezekiel are actually spent describing the length to which God goes to force Ezekiel to be his prophet. It is a veritable performance of power and might that is played out before Ezekiel's eyes, an awesome spectacle cleverly chosen by God as an intimidation and shaming strategy, to force the priest into becoming a prophet to the exiles in Babylon. The most frightening aspect of this performance is its presentation of familiar things combined in an utterly unfamiliar way. Ezekiel's call vision is a collage of human and animal parts, as well as inanimate objects, of wings and wheels, of light and dark, and of silence and thunder. It is a disturbing juxtaposition that spells chaos while evoking God's power as creator. It suggests that, if God willed it, creation could be made to fall apart and be put together in any way conceivable. This is the kind of power that Ezekiel has to confront.

Yet Ezekiel shows no external signs of shame, intimidation, or fear of chaos. Instead, he keeps silent and "increases and internalizes [his] refractoriness ... which obliges the Adversary to reckon with silence instead of sweeping it aside" (Néher: 158). Néher points out that the task that God settles on for Ezekiel "is of an exceptional simplicity. It consists of proclaiming four Hebrew words; *koh amar adonai ha-shem....* Thus saith the Lord God (Ezek 2:4)" (160). But to Ezekiel God's strategy is transparent: "A word from Moses, a cry from Jeremiah was sufficient for God to see into them.... Ezekiel was [not] to betray himself, for silence rendered [him] impenetrable" (152). Certainly, "God's hand was on him" (1:3), and he was so overwhelmed by what he saw and had to go through that he fell on his face (1:28) and was "stunned for seven days" (3:15). Yet, despite those reactions, Ezekiel does not argue with God but instead remains silent for large parts of the book. God first interprets this silence as fear (2:6). Néher suggests that the eating of the Torah scrolls is meant to allay Ezekiel's fear and to equip him for his task as a prophet (162). However, I would like to go along with Néher and suggest that fear is far too "banal" (160) a cause to account for Ezekiel's silence. This silence must be interpreted as resistance (cf. on this point Néher: 160). Ezekiel is silently scrutinizing what he is hearing. The eventual feelings of "bitterness" and "heat of the spirit" (3:14) that he senses are not caused by God's performance but by the actual confrontation with the hardness and rebelliousness of his own people. Still, Ezekiel keeps quiet and does not show to God any obvious sign of agreement. This triggers the impatient warning God gives to Ezekiel (which is also quoted by Levinas):

> Mortal, I have made you a sentinel for the house of Israel; whenever you hear a word from my mouth, you shall give them warning from me. If I say to the wicked, "You shall surely die," and you give them no warning, or speak to warn the wicked from their wicked way, in order to save their life, those wicked persons shall die for their iniquity; but their blood I will require at your hand. But if you warn the wicked, and they do not turn from their wickedness, or from their wicked way, they shall die for their iniquity; but you will have saved your life. Again, if the righteous turn from their righteousness and commit iniquity, and I lay a stumbling block before them, they shall die; because you have not warned them, they shall die for their sin, and their righteous deeds that they have done shall not be remembered; but their blood I will require at your hand. If, however, you warn the righteous not to sin, and they do not sin, they shall surely live, because they took warning; and you will have saved your life. (3:17–21 NRSV)

How else could one read this passage but as God's invocation of Ezekiel's responsibility? But Ezekiel's response to this warning is still not servile agreement, but again silence. The priest, again, falls on his face, forcing God to recognize this silence. He will continue to refuse to go where God tells him to go and to say what God tells him to say.

God's response to Ezekiel is stunning. For rather than trying to break Ezekiel's refractoriness, God makes the priest's very silence a part of his prophecy:

> As for you, mortal, cords shall be placed on you, and you shall be bound with them, so that you cannot go out among the people; and I will make

> your tongue cling to the roof of your mouth, so that you shall be speech-
> less and unable to reprove them. (3:25–26)

In other words, God seizes upon the only inroad that is left to make Ezekiel a prophet. By accepting the priest's silence as the word that will carry God's word, Ezekiel now becomes the prophet of God's silence. In the event that God indeed wants Ezekiel to prophesy, God will have to coerce him with the words "mortal, hear what I have to say...," thus conjuring up an image, not of a person who is ready to say whatever God tells him to say, but of somebody who is grabbed by the collar, pulled up and set on his feet, and confronted with yet another task, not to mention the ridicule that echoes in the address "mortal," which invokes Ezekiel's finiteness and insignificance (as opposed to God's infinity and significance) every time the priest is addressed. Compared to God, Ezekiel is a flea, a nobody unfortunate enough to have been chosen by God for this project. The difference between God and him seems to be the difference between activity and passivity. Ezekiel is utterly passive while God takes him, sets him, relocates him, gags him, and silences him. Ezekiel is precisely what Levinas would call "being obsessed" with God. He is held hostage and, as such, is forced to bear God's every whim.

Yet there is a kind of agency in the absolute passivity of the priest. Ezekiel's passivity is not modeled after the Stoic denial of suffering and emotions. Rather, Ezekiel's passivity is a willful passivity. Every time he prophesies, it will be because God has overcome him again. Ezekiel has to become a prophet again and again. In other words, despite the vision of the "merkabah," despite the Torah scrolls that Ezekiel is forced to eat, despite, also, the warning that God gives to him, and, finally, despite Ezekiel's binding ... this prophet is not easy to get ... not even to do the work of God. Why is that?

On the one hand, it is easy to see how the likelihood of Ezekiel's highly sophisticated theological training makes the extent of God's demonstration of power necessary. Someone of Ezekiel's caliber will not easily trust a vision or dream but will rather seek for theological reasons either to dismiss the vision or to accept it. That this might have been Ezekiel's reaction is corroborated by the tirades that—in the name of God—he hurls against the false prophets (Ezek 13), who pretended to have had a revelation even though what they were saying was nothing more than their own imagination. Moreover, as a priest, it is likely that Ezekiel felt rather suspicious toward prophecy in general, because it tended to take place outside of the institutional structures of the Jewish religion. It is, furthermore, interesting to note that Ezekiel's only reported verbal objection to his new role as a prophet is of a theological nature.

When God tells him how to prepare a certain kind of bread that he is to eat for a certain length of time, Ezekiel complains about the uncleanness of the whole process, and God appeases his theological misgivings by slightly changing the instructions (4:14–15). The function of the book of Ezekiel, then, is clearly to emphasize Ezekiel's responsibility as the theological responsibility to decide between prophecy and cult. His unwillingness to give in to the prophetic calling reflects his understanding of the necessity of theological institutions and structures that will provide the people with a solid foundation for their faith.

On the other hand, it becomes clear that, through Ezekiel, a new dimension of self-confidence emerges without which the theme of responsibility could not be understood adequately. Ezekiel is a critical thinker, and it is through the process of critical appropriation of God's revelation that the book turns into a document of ethical awareness and responsibility. If Ezekiel didn't show any resistance to God, then God would certainly get to speak, but it would be difficult to imagine how things might continue afterwards. Ezekiel's resistance indicates active reception and thus opens up the possibility of a responsibility that goes beyond the time when God will have stopped speaking through the prophet. In other words, lasting change as an effect of God's word is the more likely the more it has been critically examined.

Thus, it might be said that, between Ezekiel and God, *being responsible for* is a product of a dialectic of power, that is, of resistance and surrender in which both share. This dialectic is embedded in the dialogical structure of *responding to* and entails *being responsible for*. In other words, the dialogos (the logos that comes to us directly *through* the middle of the struggle between Ezekiel and God) is that of *being responsible for*. Although the forms of responsibility that we encounter throughout the book are laced with imperfection, although they are skewed, imbalanced, asymmetrical, and although they leave one with the sense that responsibility, in most cases, is not much more than—literally—the ability to respond or not to respond, it is precisely this last point that makes this book so very interesting. For it is Ezekiel's silence, his apparent lack of responsibility, his surrender to God, one might say, that is significant.

Indeed, given that Ezekiel is quiet almost throughout the whole book, wouldn't it be more appropriate to look at this book as Ezekiel's refusal or inability to be responsible, rather than as his agreement to become the prophet or sentinel God wants him to be? To answer this question we must take a look at how the book of Ezekiel is composed. It is Ezekiel himself who narrates these events as they happened to him. There is a superior kind of responsibility, that of a moral agent as well as that of a theological scholar, in the fact that Ezekiel the priest takes it upon himself to impart to future generations the things that happened to him by writing them down. Ezekiel becomes a more responsible human being because of the struggle with God through which he was forced to go. Without this struggle he might have been a prophet, but he would not have been a responsible priest. For what follows the event of the actual prophecy is the event of narration. Whereas the former shows the priest as bound and gagged, the latter shows him as an autonomous writer recalling his encounter with God.

It is only through Ezekiel's retrospective narration of these events that his supreme responsibility becomes a fact. We can say that, in the structure of the book, it is the nominative perspective that Ezekiel takes toward his encounters with God that turns the book from yet another prophetic book into a book about responsibility. Ezekiel says "I" and thus turns from a mere puppet into a responsible agent. His narration of his own calling as a prophet bears the double *signum* of the responsible human being and of the approving priest. In it Ezekiel acknowledges the reality of the revelation as well as the scrutiny that he applied to it before he acknowledged it as real.

Aside from these considerations about the person of Ezekiel himself, this book, as a narrative, becomes a reflection on theological principles that thematize the connections between God and humanity, and between God and one human being, as well as between one human being and humanity. In sum, these principles are: God's holy name; the untenability of a fate-action connection (which allows no statute of limitations on punishment for sins committed and thus carries responsibility for them from one generation to the next until punishment has taken place); the paradoxical problem that God cannot punish without profaning God's name; and the issue of God's mercy (the reviving of the dried bones and the rebuilding of the temple).[1] Aside, then, from the different levels of

---

[1] God's response to the sin of the Israelites comes with an almost mind-numbing rage hurled against the Israelites as well as other nations by Ezekiel in the name of God. Much of this rage is precisely over that name of God. It has been profaned by the people, and God wants them to repent. Yet there is a clear sense of God's impotence, in that any action of God might profane God's name. In essence, God is saying "I cannot take action against you for that might profane my name. The only thing that I can do is make you a new offer and hope that this time you will be able and willing to follow the guidelines that I am giving you."

However, this is connected to the expectation, woven into the text of the book, of a response in the form of shame. Though the book is about the possibility of God's mercy, it predicates this mercy on shame, i.e., the recognition of one's own sinfulness and wrongdoing. Shame as recognition, combined with God's mercy, will enable the Israelites to return to their homes and to rebuild the temple.

All this is cast in a new context into which the book sets the question of responsibility. Whereas before, fair retribution for one's actions was not limited to the individual and

responsibility that are connected to the role of the priest Ezekiel, the book also connects responsibility with the need for theological reflection and theological institutions. God's insistence on Ezekiel's function as the sentinel of the people of Israel not only jibes well with how the priest saw himself in the role of the priest, but must also have struck him as the most constructive way for God to intervene at all. Without responsibility, none of the things that are wrong in God's eyes will change (if they change they will soon revert back to the old condition). That God spends all this time on convincing Ezekiel indicates the import that Ezekiel's theological approval of this prophecy will have. Ezekiel will be the beginning of an institution of theological deliberation and care that four centuries later is picked up again by the Pharisees.

Constitution "and" Agency

How does all this relate to the thought of Levinas? It seems from what was said above that a person such as the priest Ezekiel does not easily fit into the scheme of an absolute responsibility. As already indicated, responsibility from Levinas's viewpoint consists in the complete surrender of oneself, characterized in the phrase *me voici*. Ezekiel's resistance, despite the rich theological harvest it yields, appears to be quite distant from the attitude that Levinas has in mind. Would it not be more appropriate to talk about two different kinds of responsibility in Levinas and Ezekiel? The answer to this question must be no, for, as we will see shortly, Ezekiel's resistance to God prepares for an ethical responsibility on a practical level that truly reaches beyond essence, that is, that transcends ontology and thus is intended by Levinas.

I mentioned in the beginning that the goal of this essay was to show that the ontological nature of Levinas's own text could be transcended only if it is possible to find a model that can cause "thematic disturbances" in his texts, decenter them, and thereby allow for a moment of otherness to flow through his work. The two quotes from Ezekiel at which we have looked in this essay exemplify—when held next to each

---

could be inherited by later generations, here God lets the Israelites know that every individual will be held responsible for his or her own wrongdoings. This is good news and bad news. It is good news because it will no longer be necessary to worry about the sins of previous generations. They have either been atoned for or else passed unrecognized, but clearly they will not be causing more harm to later generations. It is bad news, for every individual must understand that they will have to answer personally for their own wrongdoings. There is no chance that this could be conveniently handed over to one's children and grand-children in hopes that, perhaps some day, a statute of limitations will have been reached and nobody will be held accountable anymore.

other—how this can work. While Levinas, with the help of the first passage, tries to give an answer to the ontological question (i.e., what in our constitution enables us to interpret and understand the revelation?), the second passage is clearly set out to answer the question of how we should act. The problem is that, although theoretically the answer to the second question should follow from the answer to the first, it does not. In the example of Ezekiel we see that despite his being fed the scrolls he continues to resist and defy God's commands. There is, in other words, not only a struggle going on between God and Ezekiel; there is also already an incongruence between the first account of Ezekiel having been fed the scrolls and, allegedly, been made ready to prophesy, and the second account in which further force is necessary to make him conform to God's will. While the first focuses on what Ezekiel *is* (ontological), the second focuses on what he must *do* (dialectical). The competition between the two is relentless.

With respect to agency, we can summarize as follows: Ezekiel matters to Levinas in his function as a sentinel of the Israelites and the other nations. However, he is a strange sentinel, dumbfounded and bound and in no way able to warn the people unless God permits it. Ezekiel, in other words, is the most passive guard one can imagine. Still, Ezekiel is not just God's mouthpiece, like so many other prophets. Levinas, I would submit, takes this into consideration and, precisely for that reason, chooses Ezekiel as the entrance-way into *Otherwise Than Being*. Ezekiel's theological resistance to God moves the question of responsibility to a level of practical concern that permits the previously mentioned breaking away from ontology. For all theorizing about the other remains an ontologizing of the other. In this sense the philosophy of the other is no different from the philosophy of the same. It is only when we move into the dialectic of the same and the other that ontology is effectively transcended. But a dialectic is a struggle. The text of Ezekiel emphasizes that God struggles to convince the priest to become a prophet. Ezekiel resists and chooses to remain silent through the course of the first two and a half chapters. God confronts him with awesome visions; the sight of the "chariot" is only one of many ways God tries to persuade the priest to open his mouth so that God can speak through him. Ezekiel is aware that the slightest reaction to God's attempts would destroy his defense. He is, therefore, not willing even to utter a sign of awe or terror. In the end, of course, God wins. But the circumstances of that victory are thought-provoking: rather than voiding Ezekiel's prior resistance, it instead emphasizes his own deliberate action. Ezekiel is now more silent and resilient than he could have ever been on his own.

For Levinas, Ezek 3:16–21 is meant as a hermeneutic indicator; it instructs us to read the philosophy of the other dialectically, that is, to be bound by it and hence to be utterly passive while still being responsible and hence active. But along with this passage comes Ezekiel's silence, his deliberate refusal to be God's prophet for theological reasons.

With respect to constitution we can distinguish between three different interpretations of the first passage and summarize these positions in the following way.

First, it is possible to override much of what has been adduced above about the instances of Ezekiel's resistance and continue to read these passages as corroborating biblical evidence used by Levinas to highlight certain characteristics of his philosophy. In this case the eating of the scrolls would have to be understood as the exchange of my own physical substance with the substance of Scripture as the other. By eating it, Ezekiel has become the other, that is, Scripture. The reference to Ezek 3:16–21 would then highlight Ezekiel's awesome responsibility toward his fellow human beings as well as his absolute dependence on God.

Second, it is possible to read both references as hermeneutic indicators. They suggest ways of reading Scripture and of reading Scripture into other texts. Scripture, then, becomes its own other (Scripture interpreting Scripture), and it becomes the other to which nonscriptural texts have to respond as well. This has the advantage of giving us a clear picture of some possible methodological considerations that might have moved Levinas to include these references in his texts. But it has the disadvantage of ignoring completely what the impact of the content of these references on Levinas's text might be.

Third, we can read these references as challenging the text of Levinas. The description of the eating of the scroll turns into a question about God's methods when calling a prophet, and the ensuing struggle through which Ezekiel goes with God demonstrates aptly that it is up to humans to say, as Néher puts it, "God, You've made a mistake" (153).

I would like to suggest that it is possible and necessary to put all three interpretations together, for only together can they prevent the possibility of ontological stagnation most effectively. To begin with the second point, it is clearly one of Levinas's goals to provide us with a text that avoids the monolithic qualities of a purely philosophical or a purely biblical text. Doing philosophy on biblical grounds as well as doing biblical exegesis on philosophical grounds makes this possible and thus circumvents the pitfalls of either biblical or philosophical thematization. Given that this interaction of philosophical and biblical material works, the first and third points allow us to establish a dialectical reading between the impression of God's awesome power, on the one hand, and of Ezekiel's resistance, on the other. The emerging synthesis of such a reading is Ezekiel's responsibility for his fellow human beings. This synthesis, however, presents a challenge to a philosophy of the other read as pure obsession and instead substitutes an approach of ethical responsibility gained through a continual process of resistance and surrender.

Constitution and agency in the philosophy of Levinas stand in a dialectical relationship with each other. They produce a movement whose product is ethical respons-ability. An adequate understanding of Levinas's approach cannot mean avoiding both ontology and dialectics, but it necessitates a move in which we bring ontology and dialectics so close that their competing claims about the nature of human existence and responsibility begin to generate a form of responsibility that constantly renews itself through its ontological as well as its dialectical source.

LOVE YOUR NEIGHBOR AS AN OTHER: REFLECTIONS ON LEVINAS'S ETHICS AND THE HEBREW BIBLE[1]

Tamara Cohn Eskenazi
Hebrew Union College-Jewish Institute of Religion, Los Angeles

This paper is an ethical, personal, intellectual attempt to resolve a conundrum that Levinas's work presents to me. The question that concerns me is how to account for the fact that Levinas can articulate some of the most profound ethical insights of the Hebrew Bible and of feminist ethics of self and yet make certain, startling statements about woman and the feminine? How is it, for example, that Levinas can be so eloquent about the importance of facing "the widow, the orphan, and the stranger" yet always speak of the stranger as a "he"? In pursuing this question I hope to shed some light on larger questions concerning Levinas, the Bible, and feminist views.

The paper proceeds in three stages: (1) a summary of the connections between Levinas's key ideas and the Hebrew Bible, especially concerning the neighbor as other; (2) an examination of feminist issues in Levinas; and, finally, (3) some tentative conclusions toward understanding the conundrum.

1

As I have shown in the introduction to this volume, Levinas has put his finger, in both obvious and subtle ways, on a pulse that runs through the Tanak/Hebrew Bible. As I suggested there, his philosophy provides categories that illumine both form and content of the Hebrew Bible: one

---

1 This essay in many ways reflects an actual and imagined dialogue with two extraordinary conversation partners: Rachel Adler and Annette Aronowicz, whose voices in person and through their writings (Adler on Jewish feminist theology and Aronowicz on Levinas) stimulated me to press questions further than I would have otherwise. I am most grateful for these conversations. This essay was presented originally as a paper at the "Semiotics and Exegesis Section" of the Society of Biblical Literature Annual Meeting, Chicago, November 1994.

recognizes the prevalence of the face and its potential significance; the very use of genealogies emerges as an expression of Levinas's infinity; the characterizations not only of Abraham, whom Levinas himself presents as paradigm, but even more of Moses, who truly reflects a commitment to a future in which he has no part, reveal their affinity with Levinas's notion of infinity (pp. 8–9 in this volume).

In this essay I want to focus on Levinas's notion of neighbor and its implications in order to explore continuity and tension between Levinas and the Bible on this very point.

Levinas develops the notion of neighbor in *Otherwise Than Being:*

> The neighbor concerns me before all assumption.... I am bound to him.... He orders me before being recognized. Here there is a relation of kinship outside of all biology, "against all logic." It is not because the neighbor would be recognized as belonging to the same genus as me that he concerns me. He is precisely *other*. The community with him begins in my obligation to him. (*OTB:* 87; his emphasis)

"The way of the neighbor is a face. The face of a neighbor signifies for me an unexceptionable responsibility, preceding every consent, every pact, every contract" (*OTB:* 88).

For Levinas, the language of neighbor is invitation to face what is in proximity and thus can be faced (rather than abstracted or generalized). "The order that orders me to the other does not show itself to me, save through the trace of its reclusion, as a face of a neighbor" (*OTB:* 140).

For Levinas it is the proximity—a reformulation of the face-to-face—that matters, not any other characteristic of the neighbor. The neighbor is the one most directly, most immediately, "face"; the neighbor is the least abstract "other." "The neighbor qua other ... concerns me for the first time (even if he is an old acquaintance, an old friend, an old love, long caught up in the fabric of my social relations) in a contingency that excludes the a priori." "The neighbor concerns me with his exclusive singularity" with his "exclusive alterity" (*OTB:* 86).

For Levinas the language of neighbor is a summons to face the one who is in proximity. The reason for focusing on the neighbor is contiguous with the one for responding to the face: one must begin where one stands, not project commitments into abstractions or convert them into ideology. The neighbor and the face of the other are proximities: they are the nearest.[2] The neighbor is one who is near, as the face that meets us.

---

2 Levinas seems to be drawing here upon Franz Rosenzweig. I thank Annette Aronowicz for reminding me of Rosenzweig's address at the opening of the Frankfurt's Jüdisches Lehrhaus, which emphasizes the importance of starting with what is nearest and from where one stands. See Rosenzweig, "On Jewish Learning" (231).

Although at first blush Levinas's notion of facing the other recalls Buber's "I and Thou," in fact Buber and Levinas part company on this very subject. In particular, Levinas criticizes Buber for the informality of the "You" (Gibbs: 189). Gibbs sums up their differences:

> Buber, according to Levinas, was guilty of viewing the "I-you" as a spir-
> itual friendship [Levinas 1976: 40]. Levinas insists on the height and
> poverty of the other and on feeding the poor.... Levinas prefers the
> absence of intimacy.... There is no focus on the relation that obtains
> between the other and me for Levinas; the disrelation, the gap and sepa-
> ration, is the key. This approach of the other does not involve my
> responsibility only in order that we may enter into a rich relation. Lev-
> inas emphasizes that I encounter a stranger who may never get to be my
> friend, who may always stand as one who commands me. Such asym-
> metry and absence of reciprocity of the "I-you" characterizes Levinas'
> interpretation of responsibility for the other. (Gibbs: 189)

In later works, Levinas himself describes his difference from Buber as follows: "Intersubjectivity thus appears in Buber's work as a reciprocal responsibility." Elsewhere he writes: "In my analyses, the approach to other is not originally in my speaking out to the other, but in my respon-sibility for him or her. That is the original ethical relation. That responsibility is elicited, brought about by the face to face of the other person" ("Martin Buber, Gabriel Marcel and Philosophy" [1993b: 35]).

> Responsibility for the other person, a responsibility neither condi-
> tioned nor measured by any free acts of which it would be the
> consequence. Gratuitous responsibility resembling that of a hostage ...
> without requiring reciprocity.... Here, then, contrary to Buber's I-
> Thou, there is no initial equality (Is the use of the familiar I-Thou
> justified?). Ethical inequality: subordination to the other, original dia-
> cony. (1993b: 44)

In many ways Levinas reflects and refracts biblical understanding of self vis-à-vis the other who remains other—be it the stranger or God—cultivating a relationship that is not bound by presumption.

With Levinas's categories as backdrop it is possible to discern with new eyes the extent to which the Hebrew Bible, especially in the Torah, reflects an ethics that seeks to safeguard against assimilating or domi-nating the other. We see that the I-Thou encounter in the Hebrew Bible is relatively rare. The biblical insistence on cultivating the relationship with a God who remains other and uniconic echoes Levinas's insights about the necessity, not merely possibility, of such a relation. The defini-tion of holy as separate yet relational (in covenant), coupled with the command to be holy for God is holy (see esp. Lev 19) further expresses

Levinas-type relation; so too does the legal material that addresses the "you" as the powerful one who must conduct himself[3] in self-limiting ways for the benefit of others. Biblical teachings such as these correspond to the boundary setting in responsibility that Levinas expresses with his concern for the otherness of the neighbor who commands me with his face. Levinas helps also illumine the love commandments in the Hebrew Bible; in particular, he illumines the relationship between the two such commandments in Lev 19. In an interesting way, Levinas's description of the neighbor implicitly links Lev 19:18 (love your neighbor) with Lev 19:34 (love the stranger). Rabbinic sages have done the same, but with an important difference. The rabbis assimilated the love of stranger (*ger*) to the love of neighbor, thereby interpreting the *ger*/stranger as a proselyte, diminishing his status of other. Levinas goes in the opposite direction. He seems to assimilate the neighbor into the stranger, claiming their equality as *others* to be faced in responsibility.

It is Levinas's elaborations on the irremissible responsibility to the other as other that help us also understand the function of stories such as those about Hagar in which the reader is compelled to sympathize with the other, the one who is not "us": the woman, the slave, the one from the "other side of the tracks," other group, other "religion," other class; Hagar, the paradigmatic "Other" (note the pun on the name: Hagar/ *ger*/stranger).[4]

2

Emmanuel Levinas's work reorients and redefines categories by which philosophical discourse is conducted. From a feminist perspective, he has also constructed a self that replaces the logos-centered, separatist self with a relational self based on connectivity that values difference, revolutionizing thereby the philosophical tradition the devalued woman as the paradigmatic other.

In constructing an ethical, relational self that preserves the integrity of the other and does not presume to either dominate or assimilate such other, Levinas also articulates models of self that resemble those proposed by significant feminist analyses (see, e.g., Keller; Benjamin). If his views are in some ways biblical, then they also thereby allow us to see the potential in the Hebrew Bible for such a model of the self as well and to reclaim the Bible for a feminist vision of self.

---

3 I deliberately retain the masculine pronoun of the Decalogue.

4 For a brilliant reading of the role of a paradigmatic Other in the Gospel of John, see Phillips 1994b. This reading invites a comparable analysis of Hagar in Genesis.

Like several important feminists, Levinas reconstitutes the subject, exploring how we best understand the subject without succumbing to essentialism or constructing the other on the basis of the same and in antagonism toward it. Since woman in Western religion and philosophy has been, as de Beauvoir has shown, the paradigmatic other, the revaluation of the Other in Levinas invites feminist appreciation and appropriation. It is therefore not surprising that several feminists acknowledge their indebtedness to Levinas.

After all, Levinas dethrones logocentrism in philosophical discourse and replaces it with relation. He constitutes a subject—a self—on the model of connectivity, rather than the dominant patriarchal, separatist object/subject self. He opposes the fusing self of normative Western traditions with one that does not merge/assimilate the other into oneself or recast the other in the categories of the same but remains, instead, in relation of responsibility. He reclaims the body and resists abstractions. He emphasizes the particular who is not to be universalized. He constructs and valorizes alterity without essentialism.

Levinas's various formulations are attempts to highlight these categories of self in relation, categories that many feminists share. Indeed, several important feminists, especially French feminists, rely on Levinas's philosophy and ethics. "The originality of the Levinasian ethics does not lie in a new categorization of alterity, but rather in its obstinate refusal to think the other" (Ziarek: 64; to think the other would be to avoid facing her or him). This refusal does not result in a rejection of philosophy or ethics but, on the contrary, in their repositioning and reorientation. "What interests me in Levinas's philosophy," writes Ziarek, "is precisely his attempt to delineate a signification of the other without, or beyond, the mediation of a third term, that is, without subordinating alterity to a conceptual or linguistic system."[5]

As Elizabeth Grosz notes (esp. chs. 4 and 5), it is Levinas who provides Irigaray with a ground for conceiving the relation between self and the other and a critique of (Western) thinking that understands the other as a variation of the same. As Irigaray explores female subjectivity, it is Levinas who provides the theoretical categories. Thus Grosz, who analyzes Irigaray's work, asks: "What kind of alterity would a feminine subject presume?" She answers that, for Irigaray, this

is the fundamental question of ethics, a consequence of the self's necessary condition of subjectivity. The other makes possible the subject's

---

[5] Ziarek: 63. Nevertheless, as her essay shows, it is Levinas who helps Ziarek "solicit" an important interpretation of feminist possibilities in Kristeva.

relation to others in a social world; ethics is the result of the need to
negotiate between one existence and another. Ethics is thus framed by
and in its turn frames the subject's confrontation with the other.

The otherness of the other cannot be understood on the model of
the self: the other is irreducibly other, different, independent. Yet ethics
has hitherto recognized only one sort of subject, the male, formulating
its principles on the presumption of the singularity and primacy of this
subject. In seeking an ethics based on the recognition of alterity rather
than modelled on the self-same, one of Irigaray's most influential
sources is the Judaic scholar, phenomenologist and theorist of ethics,
Emmanuel Levinas. (Grosz: 141)

It is here, Grosz continues, that Irigaray finds a rare exception to the
phallocentric reduction of women to subhuman or pre-ethical status
(146). Levinas's "conception of the other's priority over the subject, and
the establishment of the domain of ethics as a consequence of this confrontation with otherness" provides "one of Irigaray's major themes in
her project of an ethics of sexual difference" (ibid.).

> Levinas' work is especially relevant to Irigaray's current preoccupations,
> given his refusal to conceive of either the subject or the other as disem-
> bodied beings. For him, they are corporeal subjects, sexual subjects,
> capable of touching, seeing, engaging and negotiating with the other's
> materiality. (Grosz: 143)

In this description, Grosz does not merely sum up Levinas's contribution
to Irigaray's feminist project but sums up a distinctly biblical perception of
persons. Her description likewise articulates the place and mode of the
ethical discourse in the Bible, especially the Torah, namely, the concreteness of the engagement in material as the expression of the "spiritual."

Yet Irigaray and Levinas also part company, and their differences are
tantalizing. To cast their difference in terms pertinent to this paper's
focus, one can say that Irigaray charges that Levinas fails to see woman as
neighbor. For Irigaray, gender constitutes the fundamental difference that
Levinas evades. From Irigaray's perspective (as Grosz puts it), if

> ethics is constituted out of the confrontation with another who is funda-
> mentally different, then the relations between the sexes constitutes the
> ethical question.... An ethics of sexual difference would have to rethink
> the encounter between the self-same subject and an irreducibly sexually
> different other, an exchange between two beings who must be presumed
> to be different. (146)

Irigaray accepts Levinas's emphasis on maternity but objects to his
devaluing of the erotic as an ethical stance and as a manifestation of the

divine. Levinas's feminine is not a recognition of the other as female but a male construct based on modification and at times mere reversal of the same. Furthermore, Levinas evades the ethical and religious significance of the sexual union.[6]

In Levinas, according to Irigaray, "the male subject ... makes use of the support of the feminine in the intentionality of pleasure for its own becoming. In this transformation of the flesh of the other into his own temporality, it is clear that the masculine subject loses the feminine as other" (110).

Other possibilities elude Levinas for two reasons, says Irigaray. First, Levinas maintains distance with the other in the experience of love (1991: 110–11).[7] Second, "Levinas ... substitutes the son for the feminine" (111). His emphasis on paternity is a deracination of the irreducible difference of the other (112).[8]

From Irigaray's point of view, "this gesture fails to achieve the relation to the other, and doubly so: it does not recognize the feminine other and the self as other in relation to her; it does not leave the child to his own generation. It seems to me pertinent to add that it does not recognize God in love.... Who is the other, if sexual difference is not recognized or known?" (111–12).

Irigaray is further concerned to locate ethics in the natural universe, not merely in social and political (113), a universe that does not seem to figure, she observes, in Levinas's work. For Irigaray, "who is the other if it is not rooted and situated in the natural universe?" (ibid.). She concludes: "After having been so far—or so close—in the approach to the other sex, in my view to the other, to the mystery of the other, Levinas clings on once more to this rock of patriarchy in the very place of carnal love" (ibid.).

> Although he takes pleasure in caressing, he abandons the feminine other.... The feminine other is left without her own specific face. On this

---

6 Irigaray 1991: 110. Since Irigaray bases her critique of Levinas on his *Time and the Other* (orig. 1947), one could read passages in *Otherwise Than Being* (orig. 1974) as an attempt to respond to such a critique. But Levinas still does not go far enough.

7 Irigaray continues: "This autistic, egological, solitary love does not correspond to the shared outpouring, to the loss of boundaries which take place for both lovers when they cross the boundary of skin into the mucous membranes of the body, leaving the circle which encloses my solitude to meet in a shared space, a shared breath" (1991: 111). "In this relation, we are at least three, each of which is irreducible to any of the others: you, me, and our work (oeuvre), that ecstasy of ourselves in us (*de nous en nous*) ... prior to any child" (ibid.).

8 See my remarks on paternity and fecundity in Levinas in the introduction to this volume (8–9).

point, his philosophy falls radically short of ethics.... To go beyond the face of metaphysics would mean precisely to leave the woman her face, and even to assist her to discover it and to keep it.[9]

Although Levinas reformulates and modifies his statements on woman and the feminine in writings subsequent to *Time and the Other* (which is the focus of Irigaray's critique), possibly as a deliberate response to Irigaray, fundamental differences remain, differences (I suggest) that have much to do with the Bible.

In *Ethics and Infinity* (1985; orig. 1982), Levinas seems to echo Irigaray's views: "The feminine is other for a masculine being not only because of a different nature but also inasmuch as alterity is in some way its nature. In the erotic relation it is not a matter of another attribute in the Other, but of an attribute of alterity in the Other" (*EI*: 65).

> the feminine is described as the *of itself other*, as the origin of the very concept of alterity. What importance the ultimate pertinence of these views and the important correctives they demand have! They permit grasping in what sense, irreducible to that of numerical difference or a difference in nature, one can think the alterity which commands the erotic relation. Nothing in this relationship reduces the alterity that is exalted in it. (Ibid.)

Here Levinas recognize the Other as feminine and valorizes the feminine as other. But as Tina Chanter observes, contradictions in Levinas on the subject of the feminine make it risky to draw hasty conclusions. "Not only between earlier and later texts but even within the same texts, Levinas at times appears to affirm the priority of the ethical, and at other times the priority of the feminine."[10] Chanter concludes that despite some

---

9 Ibid., 113–14. Irigaray adds: "The caress sinks into despair, the fall, for Levinas too. He certainly aspires to something else and to the Other (*Autrui*). But the other, woman, he does not notice her existence. And what other or Other (*Autre*) is possible outside of this realization?" (116).

10 Chanter 1991: 134. She continues: "While in *Time and the Other*, the transcendent, which, one assumes, includes the ethical, is seen as a mode of the feminine [1979a: 15; 1987c: 36], and in *Existence and Existents* the feminine is said to be the other par excellence [1947: 145; 1978a: 85], the status of the erotic relation becomes ambiguous in *Totality and Infinity*. Levinas says there, 'In love transcendence goes both further and less far than language' [1961: 232; TI: 254]. That is, it is both more and less transcendent than the face in the ethical relation. The ambiguity is compounded when, having read in the section 'The Dwelling' that Martin Buber's I-Thou relation is a relation with feminine alterity [1961: 129; *TI*: 155], one then reads in the section called 'Phenomenology of Eros' that the movement of love does not share the structure of the I-Thou relation [1961: 238; *TI*: 261 and 1961: 242; *TI*: 264]."

equivocations Levinas's "use of terms such as 'femininity' and 'maternity' is sexually specific."[11]

Behind the cotton wool of Levinas's eloquent and elastic formulations one can discern certain patterns on the subject of the feminine and ethics. It is, as I will show, interesting to compare these patterns with aspects of the Hebrew Bible.

Levinas fundamentally refuses to grant sexual/gender differences an *ethical* priority. Perhaps the clearest exposition of this view is his commentary on the talmudic passage that explores the creation of humanity. In his essay, "And God Created Woman," Levinas writes: "The feminine does not derive from the masculine; rather, the division into feminine and masculine—the dichotomy—derives from what is human" (1990c: 167–68).[12]

> The social governs the erotic.... It is not woman who is secondary, it is the relationship with woman which is secondary, it is the relationship with woman as woman that does not belong to what is fundamentally human. Fundamental are the tasks that man accomplishes as a human being and that woman accomplishes as a human being. They have other things to do besides cooing, and, moreover, something else to do and more, than to limit themselves to the relations that are established because of the differences in sex.... Man and woman, when authentically human, work together as responsible beings. The sexual is only an accessory of the human. (1990c: 168–70)

Against Freud, Levinas (speaking through the rabbis), maintains that the libido does not explain the soul.[13]

---

11 Chanter 1991: 134. Chalier (127) for different reasons, also makes a similar observation. She counters Levinas's reduction of woman to either the sexual or maternal by offering a Levinas-type reading of Gen 24, the story of Rebekah, in which she points out that Rebekah's treatment of the servant Eliezer represents a model of hospitality superior to Abraham's (who is paradigmatic for Levinas as for other commentators). "Rebecca [*sic*] is aware of the helplessness of the face of the Other.... She gives proof of her responsibility for the Other who, in spite of all his wealth, is but a stranger. 'My position as I consists in being able to respond to the essential destitution of the Other, finding resources for myself. The Other who dominates me in his transcendence is thus the stranger, the widow and the Orphan to whom I am obligated' [1961: 190; *TI*: 215]." Note the masculine language even when Levinas describes the widow!

12 It is always somewhat risky in examining a commentary to conclude with certainty where a commentator voices his or her opinion and where such commentator merely speaks for the text under scrutiny. Nevertheless, despite his evasive caveat, Levinas's own position seems to be represented here.

13 "It is that which is human that would explain the acuteness of conflicts knotted into Freudian complexes. It is not the acuteness of libidinous desire that, in itself, would explain

Equally fundamental to Levinas is the opposition to merger, even in the intimacy of the erotic union. For him, "alterity and duality do not disappear in the loving relationship. The idea of a love that would be a confusion between two beings is a false romantic idea. The pathos of the erotic relationship is the fact of being two, and that the other is absolutely other" (*EI:* 66). Thus Levinas reaffirms in *Ethics and Infinity* the passages in the earlier *Time and the Other* to which Irigaray objects (yet note, too, how at the same time he echoes the concern with complementarities that one finds also in Benjamin):

> The difference of sex is not the duality of two complementary terms. For two complementary terms presuppose a pre-existing whole. Now to say the sexual duality presupposes a whole is to posit in advance love as fusion. The pathos of love consists to the contrary in an insurmountable duality of beings; ... The relationship does not ipso facto neutralize alterity but conserves it. ... The other as other here is not an object which becomes ours or which becomes us, to the contrary, it withdraws into its mystery.[14]

3

It is time to bring the several threads together by making the following observations. First, I suggest that Levinas's fundamental understanding of self as constituted by an ethical relation to the other expresses, on the one hand, a biblical perception of self and, on the other hand, a feminist perception of a self. Levinas thereby provides a "missing link," as it were, that enables us to see a specific feminist potential in the Hebrew Bible.

Second, not surprisingly, given what I just said, there is a striking parallel between feminist critiques of Levinas and certain feminist critiques of the Hebrew Bible. For example, Levinas is consistent with the biblical text of Gen 1:26–27 that states how humans were created. The shift between the singular *adam* ("and God created the *adam;* in the image

---

the soul. As I see it, this is what my text shows. I am not taking sides; today, I am commenting" (1990c: 170). One notes with displeasure Levinas's evasion at this point. His basic agreement with the rabbis on this point, however, emerges clearly as the essay progresses.

14 1979a: 78–79, quoted in *EI:* 67. Levinas further writes, "It is only by showing in what way eros differs from possession and power that we can acknowledge a communication in eros. It is neither a struggle, nor a fusion, nor a knowledge. One must recognize its exceptional place among relations. It is the relationship with alterity, with mystery, that is, with the future, with what in the world where there is everything, is never there" (1979a: 81, quoted in *EI:* 68).

of God created he him/it") and the plural ("male and female created he them") can be read as a statement that gender is derivative from the human, as Levinas maintains in "And God Created Woman." Derrida's critique of Levinas on the issue of gender applies equally, then, to Gen 1 and 2. In Levinas, "sexual difference is not conceived as a difference between the masculine and the feminine but only as the feminine speci-ficity, as the relation to 'woman qua woman,' this difference marks only the feminine subject.... In other words, we risk a hypothesis that only femininity is sexed and gendered while the masculine remains sexually unmarked" (Zierak: 68, summing up Derrida 1991a).

Third, it seems to me that Levinas's points of resistance parallel bib-lical ones: where Levinas holds the line and refuses to budge resembles where the Hebrew Bible refuses to budge vis-à-vis its own cultural milieu, that is, granting divinity to human relations, valorizing merger, valorizing nature (as does Irigaray; see above). *His equivocation replicates the inconsistencies we find in the Hebrew Bible on ethics and gender or self and the feminine.*

While Irigaray attributes Levinas's recalcitrance to a patriarchal incli-nation, other possibilities also exist and deserve serious attention. Levinas has gone a long way in attempting to accommodate, unsuccessfully at the end, the feminine. His project can help us understand something about Levinas's overriding concerns and, likewise, help us, in turn, also to comprehend something about plausible biblical agenda. The parallels between his formulations and reformulations can also help us under-stand some important things about the phenomenon in biblical and Levinasian models of ethics and gender. While it may be true as Irigaray implies (and as critics of the Hebrew Bible imply in relation to it) that Levinas's limitations from a feminist perspective can be explained as a vestige of unshakeable patriarchal leanings (or bias), such an explanation is, in my opinion, too simple and misleading. In understanding the ground of Levinas's prevarications on the subject of the connection of the feminine, the ethical, the erotic, the divine we may get closer also to understanding such prevarications in the biblical text.

As in antiquity, so for Levinas, certain things are at stake. To protect them he constructs a network of teachings that have certain repercus-sions for a feminist perspective, presenting both positive potential and pitfalls. Levinas's motives are explicit. His attempts to respond and accommodate the feminine and the female are genuine. His failure to do so satisfactorily is rooted less in blindness and more in perception of cer-tain irreconcilable positions.

Levinas takes a stand against the perennial drive for unity that per-sists in early encounters between the ethos of the Hebrew Bible and other cultural forces. This tension between the drive to unicity (as Boyarin calls it) was not limited only to Israel's ancient, biblical period but marks the basic divergence, according to Boyarin, also between Judaism and Christianity (esp. 1–10). For Levinas, this kind of opposition represents also the tension between totality and infinity.

Levinas therefore refuses to acknowledge a straight line, a continuous development from the erotic to the ethical, not because such a line cannot exist but because such a line has fed the culture of totality, of ecstasy, of domination and assimilation, in a word, the celebratory Nietzschian vision (on this point, see Caputo, esp. his chapter on "Dionysus vs. the Rabbi"). He refuses to cross the line between the divine and the human either in the face-to-face with the neighbor or in the union of love. His first priority is to protect otherness by explaining and valorizing it. Different types of relations exist. But, in his view, they pose a danger that he seeks to eschew.

Irigaray rightly connects the limits of Levinas's ethics with what she considers the flaws of monotheism. Here again the parallels between a critique of Levinas has much in common with feminist critique of the Hebrew Bible in general. It therefore may elucidate comprehension of biblical dynamics. Levinas and the Hebrew Bible emphasize boundary maintenance between self and other in the face of a cultural tendency toward merging—both in terms of the sexes and the divine/human relation. Thus, love for Irigaray "can become spiritual and divine" (1991: 115). Her questions to Levinas about the divinity of love echo a Canaanite challenge to Israel's religions, say, in eighth or sixth century B.C.E.

Indeed, Irigaray's questions to Levinas become at the end of her article explicit questions to the Torah and to the God of the Hebrew Bible:

> [God] does not share, [117] he dictates (*il impose*). He separates himself, when he gives Moses the inscription of the law.... The law creates invisibility, so that God (in his glory?) cannot be looked upon. What happens to seeing, to flesh, in this disappearance of God? Where can one's eye alight if the divine is no longer to be seen? and if it does not continue to dwell in the flesh of the other in order to illuminate it, to offer up to the look the other's flesh as divine, as the locus of a divine to be shared? (116–17)

My point is that Levinas does not simply reiterate the biblical position on gender and the ethics of the other but attempts, like the Bible, to create an alternate vision in conflict with certain familiar cultural impulses. His relation to the Mosaic austerity is not so much derivative from the Torah but a product of similar, initial concern with resisting the charismatic, the ecstatic, the drive to unity. With rare exception, the paradigmatic relation for Levinas is that with the other whose face commands. Levinas recognizes the relation with the same and even the relation with the other who is not a stranger but an intimate (*tu*). But both play only a limited role as he presses to cultivate alterity and responsibility. A relation with the same is the danger to avoid; the intimate relation is at best the fuel that makes us able to face the other "outside" the circle of intimacy in the realm that matters, that of the ethical (the goal: live in a tent hospitably, like Abraham, with flaps open on all sides).

Let me conclude by quoting Zierak, with whom I agree on the following point. She writes: "Although I claim that Levinasian philosophy can be very productive for feminist ethics, at the same time I raise questions about the role of femininity in his own texts.... Levinas asserts the primacy of the ethical encounter with the other but is then unable to articulate sexual difference in terms of this encounter" (63, and see above, note 5).

Such inability, in Levinas and in the Hebrew Bible, cannot be reduced to blindness (or malice) but must be acknowledged as a response to the difficulty in constructing an ethical system in which the fragility of our commitment to the other as other can be protected in the face of the engulfing attraction to the same. Surmounting such difficulty remains still the task, in theory as in practice.

"AND GOD CREATED WOMAN": READING THE BIBLE OTHERWISE

Susan E. Shapiro
University of Massachusetts, Amherst

1. METHODOLOGICAL PRELUDE

The name Emmanuel Levinas has become associated with the "face," "the Other person," "alterity," and "ethics," among other terms. These terms and figures appear not only in his "properly" philosophical writings, such as *Totality and Infinity* and *Otherwise Than Being or Beyond Essence*, but in his so-called "Jewish writings" as well. While some interpreters read these two bodies of texts as unrelated,[1] others emphasize their important proximity, even their intersection.[2]

---

[1] It is also the case that many of those interested in Levinas as a philosopher do not read his "Jewish writings" at all. As will become clear in this essay, a reading only of Levinas's philosophical writings may not be sufficient for an understanding of what Levinas terms "Greek" and, thus, even for an understanding of his philosophical texts and their import.

[2] There is a similar debate in the contemporary reception of the writings of Moses Maimonides. Some—most notably Leo Strauss—read his philosophical writing, especially his *Guide of the Perplexed*, as addressed to a different (philosophically trained) audience than his talmudic writings, for example his *Mishneh Torah*, which they read as addressed to another (nonphilosophical, Jewish) audience. Others—prominently, Isadore Twersky (see esp. 1980)—read Maimonides' talmudic writings as containing philosophical insights compatible with those found in the *Guide*. Twersky emphasizes the role of aggadah in both the *Guide* and *Mishneh Torah*, and he also tends to regard Maimonides' position on halakah as more consistent between these works than do others. Although there are, thus, analogies between the reception of Maimonides' and Levinas's hybrid writings, especially in the context of the modern or Enlightenment antinomy between reason and religion, there are significant differences between them in how the relations and differences between philosophical and talmudic discourses are drawn.

While the nub of the debate in the reception of Maimonides' writings has much (although, by no means, all) to do with the ultimate status of halakic authority in relation to philosophy, Levinas repeatedly limits his readings of talmudic texts as a turn to aggadah, not halakah. In this way, he emphasizes the continuities between aggadah and philosophy

Levinas's philosophical writings make ethics first philosophy by
opening up its discourse to the Other. Levinas emphasizes both the exterior other (especially in his *Totality and Infinity*) and the otherness (that
is, nonidentity) already residing within both writing and the self (especially in his *Otherwise Than Being or Beyond Essence*). The traces of this
later other residing within and, in a way, anterior to the self (especially
as figured through "maternality"), re-turn one to the claims of exteriority, in what Levinas calls a "reversal of ontology," to the beyond or
otherwise than being.[3]

---

and not the potential conflicts between philosophy and (particular) halakot, although he
does reflect on the importance and status of the law in Judaism. Levinas is interested in the
relation between what he terms "Greek" and "Hebrew," a relation of asymmetrical supple-
mentation. I will treat this theme in the body of this article, especially as regards Levinas's
thinking about the relation between particular and universal. In both cases, that of Maimonides and that of Levinas, some of the split readings of their respective corpora may be
accounted for as the difficulty both within Judaism and the West—following Leo Strauss's
and, ultimately, Pascal's language—of thinking "Athens and Jerusalem" as not necessarily
opposed terms. As Levinas will suggest, this difficulty has much to do with the very problems he addresses: regard for the neighbor, the Other, and the ambiguities of assimilation in
the West. Thinking the relation between Levinas's philosophical and talmudic essays will,
thus, be implicated within the question of the relations between "Greek" and "Hebrew" and
the ethical demands of the Other, the neighbor, in his thought. As Annette Aronowicz notes
in her introduction to *Nine Talmudic Readings*: "In a sense, Levinas's own life during this
period best illustrates the contents of these essays, for while he was heading a Jewish school,
writing essays on the Jewish tradition, and, from 1960, giving Talmudic commentaries at the
yearly colloquia of Jewish intellectuals in Paris, he was also writing his great philosophical
works, the works that speak to all human beings in 'Greek,' *Totalité et infini* (1961) and
Autrement qu'être ou au-delà de l'essence (1974), to mention the two generally recognized as his
major contributions to the philosophical tradition. The Jewish subjects were fed by the philosophical work, and the philosophical work was fed by the contact with Jewish sources. The
Jew and the 'Greek' were in constant relation" (in Levinas 1990c: xiv–xv).

   3 While Levinas's thought resonates with Jacques Derrida's emphasis on difference and
the supplement, his turn to the beyond or otherwise than being and, especially, to exteriority differs markedly from Derrida's location of undecidable difference both within and
beyond the Same and his view of the other within, upon which the self is dependent, which
dependence it effaces. Derrida's reading of Levinas is critical on these points, especially in
his earlier essay, "Violence and Metaphysics" (1978). This essay is a response primarily to
Levinas's *Totality and Infinity*. Levinas's *Otherwise Than Being or Beyond Essence* is (only) in
part responsive to Derrida's critique in "Violence and Metaphysics." This critique includes
the following points: (1) that Levinas is no longer writing philosophy if he begins with exteriority, and (2) that despite Levinas's attempts to think beyond identity and otherwise than
being, his thought remains trapped within a logocentric grammar, thus making ontology and
not ethics first philosophy. Levinas's development of the distinction between the *saying* and
the *said* in *Otherwise Than Being* is (in part) a response to Derrida's critique (although this distinction already is employed in Levinas's *Totality and Infinity*). It also resembles in certain
respects Derrida's own turn to rhetoric over logic. As regards the feminine, Derrida suggests

This is the strange ontological structure presupposed by this responsibility whereby one person assumes the destiny and the very existence of another, and is answerable for this other in a way, however, that is not characteristic of him. (1994a: 107)

This reversal of/in ontology is both a putting the other first and a casting of ethics as first philosophy. In being for another, the self is put at the disposal of the other person and undergoes a trauma and a revolution in orientation.[4] This reversal of ontology is such that the self no longer is

---

in "Violence and Metaphysics" that "*Totality and Infinity* pushes the respect for dissymmetry so far that it seems impossible, essentially impossible, that it could have been written by a woman. Its philosophical subject is man (*vir*).... Is not this principled impossibility for a book to have been written by a woman unique in the history of metaphysics? Levinas acknowledges elsewhere that femininity is an 'ontological category.' Should this remark be placed in relation to the essential virility of metaphysical language? But perhaps metaphysical desire is essentially virile, even in what is called women" (1978: 320 n. 92).

In Derrida's later writing on Levinas, most notably "At This Very Moment in This Work Here I Am" (1991a), Derrida seems more focused on the importance of the claims of ethics and alterity in Levinas's writing and of Levinas's treatment of the feminine in this regard. Here, especially, see Derrida's reading of "Song of Songs" into what he considers a lacuna in Levinas's text(s). In Derrida's most recent writing on Levinas and the feminine, he locates a double approach in or another reading (than in Derrida 1991a) of Levinas's "definition" of "the hospitable one" in *Totality and Infinity* as "before every inhabitant, the welcoming one par excellence, welcoming in itself—the feminine being." Derrida writes as follows: "One approach would be to acknowledge, so as then to question, ... the traditional and androcentric attribution of certain characteristics to woman.... But another reading of these lines might be attempted, one that would not oppose in a polemical or dialectical fashion either this first reading or this interpretation of Levinas.... The other approach to this description would no longer raise concerns about a classical androcentrism. It might even, on the contrary, make of this text a sort of feminist manifesto.... Need one choose here between two incompatible readings, between an androcentric hyperbole and a feminist one? Is there any place for such a choice in ethics? And in politics? Nothing is less certain" (1999: 44-45). I will later address the problem of this polarized nonchoice between "classical androcentrism" and a "feminist manifesto." The contradiction that Derrida describes and places in an *epochē*, I wager here can be treated both more critically and more productively in other terms.

4 This trauma of the self is figured by Levinas both as a rupture coming from the outside, the relation to the other, and as an excess within the self that cannot be contained and that spills over toward the other. The first figure resembles that of a wound, a tear, a fissure. It seems to figure this "trauma" of/in the self as like that of a crisis, a harm, even the effects of a catastrophic event. The second figure, on the other hand, resembles that of the experience of excess in/of Love for the other. Both of these figures may coincide in some kabbalistic (as in Lurianic Kabbalah) figurations of the relation between God and humankind in a creation figured through entangled tropes of both love and catastrophe. Levinas brings these two tropes of love and catastrophe together in my obligation to remember that I was a slave in Egypt as a form of love for the other person, as follows: "The trauma I experience as a slave in the land of Egypt constitutes my humanity itself. This immediately

moved simply by the desire to persist in being, the Same, but becomes ethical to the extent that the self puts acting on behalf of the other person(s) before its own desire to persist. This opening of philosophy to the Other is revolutionary; the reversal of ontology that puts ethics and the other person(s) first also opens (what Levinas terms) the "Greek" to the "Hebrew."[5] This shifting and reversal of terms within philosophy, for Levinas, opens it to the otherwise than being and, thus, to the Bible.

> The Torah demands, in opposition to the natural perseverance of each being in his or her own being (a fundamental ontological law), care for the stranger, the widow and the orphan, a preoccupation with the other person. A reversal of the order of things! We do not have as much awe as we should at this *reversal of ontology into ethics,* and in a sense, the dependency within it of being on the disinterestment of justice. The word [*parole*] of reversal, whose mood is imperative, the *precept,* and thus precisely the writing of the Torah, a book that dominates the consciousness that follows the affairs and laws of the earth and deciphers the eternity of its present—a prophetic book of alterity and the future.[6]

---

brings me closer to all problems of the damned on earth, of all those who are persecuted, as if in my suffering as a slave I prayed in a prayer that was not yet oration, and as if this love of the stranger were already the reply given to me through my heart of flesh" (1994a: 142).

5 On Levinas's use of the terms *Greek* and *Hebrew,* see Gibbs (156–75). Gibbs draws out three distinct senses of the term *Greek* in Levinas's talmudic essays: "First, 'Greek' is the rule of the universal, the power of a political state. Second, it is the love of knowledge, the desire to know in an an-ethical way, the 'Western Odyssey' of consciousness, the return of all knowing to self-knowledge. Third, 'Greek' is the language of rhetoric, at which point 'Greek' wisdom is re-evaluated" (158). According to Gibbs, "Levinas characterizes 'Hebrew' language much less fully. It is, most of all, the language of the Bible—and here, too, language means a way of thought. Levinas often refers to it simply as 'Biblical Thought.' 'Hebrew' is not the grammarians' Biblical Hebrew; rather, it is the Sages' mode of thought. The texts of Midrash and Talmud are written in it, and students argue in it when reading those texts. 'Hebrew' is essentially social, spoken in conversations over texts, and its manner of conceiving is concrete, practical, and above all, always ethical" (157).

6 "Contempt for the Torah As Idolatry" (1994b: 61–62; my emphasis). In a kindred passage, Levinas writes: "The Bible: and ontological inversion? The original perseverance of realities in their being ... is inverted in the man announced to humanity in Israel. Thus, for being that is dedicated to being, for being that has no other purpose than to be, the human self might also signify the possibility of answering for the other, who 'is none of my business,' who is nothing to me. 'Thou shalt not kill,' that is to say, 'Thou shalt love thy neighbor.' This is an odd recommendation for an existence summoned to live at all costs.... There is this possibility of a responsibility for the alterity of the other person, for the stranger without domicile or words with which to converse, for the material conditions of one who is hungry or thirsty, for the nakedness of the defenseless mortal.... The other, the one separated from me, outside the community: the face of the person who asks, a face that is already the community: the face of the person who asks, a face that is already a request, but also the face of one recognized in love as irreplaceable, unique.... And from that moment forth, in

This openness to "Hebrew" and the Bible is not, however, without qualification and is not a mere reversal of terms. The "Greek" is neither effaced by nor subsumed under "Hebrew." Ontology does not disappear, for, according to Levinas, not only does "Greek" have to learn from "Hebrew" that which it tends to forget—that is, the irreducible importance of the particular—but "Hebrew" must be reminded by "Greek" of that of which it may lose sight, that is, the universal.

For example, in describing the responsibility of one for the other, Levinas introduces the concept of the "third party," the one who is not the first other to come along and, thus, to make a claim on me, but another other for whom "I" am responsible as well. It is for the sake of "my" responsibility to this "third party"—already articulated within the Bible, but capable of being forgotten in the excessiveness of "my" responsibility to "the first person to come along"—that the "Greek" reminds the "Hebrew" of this continued obligation to the other other(s), the universal.

> It is ... an enactment of the revelation in the responsibility for the first person to come our way...: a responsibility exceeding the demand heard by myself in the face of the other.... But "the first person to come along" for myself and the other person would also constitute the third party, who joins us or always accompanied us. The third party is also my other, also my neighbor. Who would be the first to speak? Where does the priority lie? A decision must be made. The Bible requires justice and deliberation! From the heart of love, from the heart of mercy. One must judge, one must reach a conclusion. There must be knowledge, verification, objective science, system. There must be judgments, the state, political authority. The unique beings recognized by love, which are extrinsic to all genera, must be brought into the community, the world. One must bring oneself into the world. Hence the first violence within mercy! For love of the unique, the one and only must be given up. The humanity of the human must be set back within the horizon of the universal. Oh, welcome messages from Greece! To become educated among the Greeks, to learn their language and their wisdom. Greek ... recommended by the Bible itself. (1994b: 134)

According to Levinas, "Greek" serves to remind "Hebrew" of the universal within its own discourse, an excessive obligation that it may, however, forget in its obsession with its obligation to the uniqueness of the other person. "Greek" offers this corrective, this reminder to "Hebrew," because it is a discourse of generalization, of inclusion. This

---

this self persevering in being, there emerges mercy and the overturning of being's tautology of pure 'being qua being'" (1994b: 133).

is so even if there is a certain "necessary" violence enacted thereby within mercy, that is, in relation to the unique otherness of the other, in order to attain this universality. Levinas describes "Greek" as follows:

> Greek is the term I use to designate, above and beyond the vocabulary, grammar and wisdom with which it originated in Hellas, the manner in which the universality of the West is expressed, or tries to express itself—rising above the local particularism of the quaint, traditional, poetic or religious. It is a language without prejudice, a way of speaking that bites reality without leaving any marks—capable, in attempting to articulate the truth, of obliterating any traces left by it—capable of unsaying, of resaying. (1994b: 134–35)

However, as I have mentioned, the danger is that Greek, because it effaces the traces of the particular within its saying, can become sheerly formal and abstract, leaving the claims of the unique, that is, the other person(s), utterly behind.

> [T]here is an obsession with an order to be established on universal but abstract rules—i.e., political rules, while underestimating or forgetting the uniqueness of the other person, whose right is, after all, at the origin of rights, yet always a new calling.... The ... temptation of an ideological rationalism, and of experiments carried out through the rigor of deduction, administration and violence. A philosophy of history, a dialectic leading to peace among men—is such a thing possible after the Gulag and Auschwitz? ... [One] sees hope only in the goodness of one person toward another, the "little kindness" I have called mercy, the *rahamim* of the Bible.... A spirituality whose future is unknown. (1994b: 135)

Levinas returns thus to the Bible, a Bible, however, supplemented by both "Greek" and the rabbis. For the Bible is not to be read without commentaries. In fact, for Levinas, the reading of the Tanakh is to be mediated through the Talmud. It is the rabbinic reading of the Bible that Levinas recovers for the West, even as that reading is to be perpetually made contemporary. "Hebrew," thus, signifies not only the Bible. Nor does it refer only to the rabbis. Rather, "Hebrew," for Levinas, is a term that, juxtaposed to "Greek," perpetually returns thought to engagement with the particular, with the example,[7] with that which he terms—in an

---

7 In "Contempt for the Torah As Idolatry," Levinas connects talmudic reasoning and the example as follows: "The Talmudic life and destiny of the Torah, which is also an endless return, in its interpretation of several degrees, to particular cases, to the concreteness of reality, to analyses that never lose themselves in generalities but return to the examples—

allusion to Jacob—"the struggle with the angel."[8] For this re-turn to the particular is a regarding of the face of the other person(s). It is the "constant struggle within us between our two adherences; to the spirit and to what is known as the letter" (1989b: 220).

This struggle occurs, therefore, not only between "Hebrew" and "Greek" but within the talmudic readings of the Bible itself.

> Jacob's struggle with the Angel has the same meaning: the overcoming, in the existence of Israel, of the angelism or other-worldliness of pure interiority. Look at the effort with which this victory is won! But is it really won? There is no victor. And when the Angel's clasp is released it is Jacob's religion which remains, a little bruised. It is an unending struggle. (1989b: 220)

---

resisting invariable conceptual entities. An analysis whose free discussion is ever current" (1994b: 58). In his "On the Jewish Reading of Scripture," Levinas further articulates the importance of the example in the ethical reasoning of the Talmud as follows: "Without fading before their concepts, things denoted in a concrete fashion are yet enriched with meanings by the multiplicity of their concrete aspects. This is what we call the paradigmatic modality of Talmudic reflection: notions remain constantly in contact with the examples or refer back to them, whereas they should have been content as springboards to rise to the level of generalization, or they clarify the thought which scrutinizes by the secret light of hidden or isolated worlds from which it bursts forth; and simultaneously this world inserted or lost in signs is illuminated by the thought which comes to it from outside or from the other end of the canon, revealing its possibilities which were awaiting the exegesis, immobilized, in some way, in the letters" (1994a: 103; repr. in this volume; see p. 19).

8 Annette Aronowicz describes the stakes of this struggle for the "Hebrew" and its relation to the universal through (but not leaving behind) particulars, as follows: "Levinas once characterized the perpetual tension between the universal and the specific, a movement which finds no resting point, as the struggle with the angel, referring to the famous story of Jacob in Genesis 32. An angel is that which has no body. It is pure spirit or pure interiority. The genius of the Jewish tradition, Levinas says, is its awareness of the danger of such disembodied truths.

> The great power of Talmudic casuistry is to be the special discipline which seeks in the particular the precise moment in which the general principle runs the risk of becoming its own opposite, which watches over the general from the basis of the particular. This preserves us from ideology. Ideology is the generosity and clarity of a principle which did not take into account the inversion stalking this generous principle when it is applied or, to come back to the image mentioned a moment ago: The Talmud is the struggle with the Angel. (1982[a]: 98–99, trans. Annette Aronowicz)

The universality that Levinas has in mind, then, is not a homogenous unity but a respect for each particular, a particular from which a universal must be wrested or in which a universal must be embedded, each time anew" (Aronowicz in Levinas 1990c: xxx). For other translations of the above passage from "The Pact," see that of Gary D. Mole in Levinas 1994a: 79 and that of Seán Hand (which emphasizes the importance of a vigilance over the moment in which the general principle "is at risk of turning into its opposite; it surveys the general from the standpoint of the particular") in Levinas 1989b: 220.

The problem is that the angel, which is a purely spiritual being, "does not participate in that condition which the Torah considers to be inseparable from life.... He is a principle of generosity, but no more than a principle." Thus, vigilance of the principle is required from "below," from the vantage point of the particular, the example, the flesh-and-blood person(s). This vigilance is important because from the vantage point of pure spirit (the angel)—that is, the principle itself—there is no regard for the consequences of its application. Indeed,

> it is the special discipline [of talmudic casuistry] which studies the particular case in order to identify the precise moment within it when the general principle is at risk of turning into its opposite; it surveys the general from the standpoint of the particular.... This is why the adherence to the particular law is an irreducible dimension of any allegiance. (Ibid.)

There is, thus, a temptation not only within "Greek," but within "Hebrew" itself, to embrace the principle of generosity and, thereby, to leave the letter and the law behind. This is why talmudic dialectic is "concerned with the passage from the general principle embodied in the Law to its possible execution, its concrete effects" (ibid.) For there is a "betrayal which lies in wait for this general principle at the moment of its application" (ibid.). Thus, just as there is a danger within "Hebrew" that it may forget the universal, so there is the corresponding danger within "Hebrew," and not only "Greek," that it may adhere only to pure principle(s) if it identifies with, and does not struggle with, the Angel.

The "Angel" signifies not only the leaving behind or surpassing of the law—a danger Levinas ascribes within Judaism to Hassidism—but also a sheerly allegorical reading of the Bible. The struggle is unresolved and ongoing. It is not simply a choice between the letter and the spirit but a struggle in reading the Bible with and between both. The universal erupts through the reading of the letter, to which, however, interpretation must always return, just as, for Levinas, "the adherence to the particular law [and not only its general principle] is an irreducible dimension" (ibid.).

While both temptations, of exclusive adherence either to the spirit or to the letter, are, thus, present in "Hebrew," Levinas stresses the difference between "Greek" and "Hebrew" as one in which "Greek" supplements "Hebrew" by reminding it of the universal. And "Hebrew" is usually characterized by Levinas as reminding "Greek" of the face of the other person(s), the particular, the example. It is the resistance to the reduction in philosophical discourse ("Greek") of the different to the Same, the other to the self, and ethics to ontology. For, as I have noted, Levinas finds within philosophy's apparently generous or inclusive gesture (of subsuming the particular under the universal and the instance under the concept) a violence that effaces the alterity of the other person(s). In contrast,

> The Talmudic life and destiny of the Torah, which is also an endless return, in its interpretation of several degrees, to particular cases, to the concreteness of reality, to analyses that never lose themselves in generalities but return to the examples—resisting invariable conceptual entities. An analysis whose free discussion is ever current. ("Contempt for the Torah As Idolatry"; 1994b: 58)

However, as I have noted, in focusing only on the particular, "Hebrew" may forget the other others, the universal.[9] "Greek" and "Hebrew" must supplement one another. This is why ethics requires a reversal in, and not the abolition of, ontology. It is also why the Bible must be supplemented and mediated through reading(s) of the rabbis on the Tanakh.[10]

In this essay, I will focus on Levinas's talmudic reading of one biblical text. My interests, however, are not only in an exegesis of a particular biblical text but also in an examination of Levinas's hermeneutical assumptions as tested through this one example. For, as Levinas has argued, the status of the example is paramount in talmudic reasoning and in "Hebrew." However, as the example I have chosen is, perhaps, Levinas's least generous reading—and, in that sense, atypical of his reading practices—I will ask why this is so and what alternative interpretation(s) may be possible, that is, whether the rabbis may be read otherwise. In other words, I will perform just what Levinas calls for: a contemporary reading of Levinas's reading of the rabbis' reading the Tanakh—in particular, Gen 2:4–25. The talmudic essay that directly treats this biblical text is his "And God Created Woman" (1990a: 161–77; this essay was published in French in Levinas 1977). In reading this essay, I will also address aspects of several other of his essays, including "Desacralization and Disenchantment" (1990c: 136–60; also

---

9 The importance of remembering the universal while regarding the particular is related to Levinas's critique of Martin Buber's emphasis on the dyad, the "I-Thou" relation, to the exclusion of the Third, the others who are not at this moment before me but who look at me (as well), according to Levinas, in the other's regard. The role of the Third and the "third party" in Levinas's philosophical thought is an often-neglected matter. Levinas consistently reads the rabbis as emphasizing this kind of responsibility to the others beyond the other(s) before me. The so called "Love Commandment" emphasized in Levinas's thought repeatedly returns in different forms to this question, to this obligation.

10 Levinas points out that just as the Hebrew Bible is read in Judaism through the Talmud (and midrashim), so the Old Testament is read in Christianity through the New Testament (and parables). Christianity is understood by Levinas to be comprised of both "Greek" and "Hebrew."

published in French in Levinas 1977), "Judaism and the Feminine" (1990b: 30–38), and "Judaism and Kenosis" (1994b: 114–32), among others. I will employ the terms *feminine* and *Woman* in accord with their usage in these texts.[11]

Following Levinas's example, I will read his interpretations of biblical texts for both "Hebrew" and "Greek" and their relation. Thus, while I focus on Levinas's "Jewish writings," I will read these essays both with and against some of Levinas's philosophical texts on Woman, the feminine, and gender. Indeed, I will begin by turning to some of Levinas's "Greek" writings on these topics. In concluding, I will wonder after the differences and similarities between these "Greek" and "Hebrew" views and their import for Levinas's larger project of reading and thinking otherwise than being. In this regard, I address Levinas's treatment of rhetoric and idolatry in both sets of his writings, especially in how they bear on both his understanding of "sexual difference" and "Hebrew" and "Greek." Indeed, I worry that his characterization of rhetoric and idolatry serves to reinscribe within his writing the very gender hierarchy and subordination of female to male and Woman to Man that Levinas apparently would undo. I call for a reconfiguring of the gendering of the relations between rhetoric and philosophy, and I consider, as well, resources within Levinas's "Hebrew" writings for reading the Tanakh through the rabbis otherwise.

2. The Problem: Thinking "Sexual Difference" Otherwise

Oppositional gender difference and the subordination of the feminine to the masculine are ancient philosophical *topoi*. Indeed, Levinas traces this subordination back to Parmenides and the "Eleatic" notion of being.[12] In *Time and the Other*, Levinas suggests that the very otherness of the other person cannot be recognized when difference is mapped spatially and when matter is utterly subordinated to form. Without an irreducible and impassible difference between self and other, for Levinas, ethics is impossible. In order to locate such an alterity, he calls for a thinking otherwise of "sexual difference."[13] Critiquing the subordination

---

11 This use is patently heteronormative. Both Chanter (1988) and Ansley attempt to soften the exclusivity of this orientation in Levinas's thought, alas, I believe, unsuccessfully.

12 However, one must also consider the sources of this subordination as evidenced in Levinas's thought in the stories of the creation of Man and Woman in Genesis.

13 He writes: "Sex is not some specific difference. It is situated beside the logical division into genera and species. This division certainly never manages to reunite an empirical content. But it is not in this sense that it does not permit one to account for the difference

in spatial terms of the feminine as matter to the masculine as form, Levinas instead turns to time as the locus of thinking "sexual differ- ence." He seeks a way, thereby, to locate a difference that will not always already return it to the economy of the Same. Thinking "sexual difference" otherwise, for Levinas, becomes a condition of the very pos- sibility of ethics itself.

> Human alterity is not thought starting with the purely formal alterity by which some terms are distinguished from others in every multiplicity (where each one is already other as the bearer of different attributes or, in a multiplicity of equal terms, where each one is other than the other through its individuation). The notion of a transcendent alterity—one that opens time—is at first sought starting with an *alterity-content*—that is, starting with femininity. Femininity—and one would have to see in what sense this can be said of masculinity or of virility; that is, of the dif- ferences between the sexes in general—appeared to me as a difference contrasting strongly with other differences, not merely as a quality dif- ferent from all others, but as the very quality of difference. (1987c: 36)

The "feminine" is a trope running throughout Levinas's work. In his "Greek" articulation of the ontological problem of thinking "sexual dif- ference," Levinas examines the "Eleatic notion of being."[14] The founding question of this metaphysical tradition was whether the world is irre- ducibly multiple and changing or, on the other hand, ultimately One and static. In reducing the many to the One, this style of philosophizing femi- nizes matter as intrinsically plural, passive, and changing and, then, utterly subsumes and subordinates it—without a trace—to the unity of form. Levinas claims that this mode of philosophizing leaves no room in which to think difference or alterity. Nor, he claims, does what he terms

---

between the sexes. The difference between the sexes is a formal structure, but one that carves up reality in another sense and conditions the very possibility of reality as multiple, against the unity of being proclaimed by Parmenides." (1987c: 85).

14 "The Eleatic notion of being dominates Plato's philosophy, where multiplicity was subordinated to the one, and where the role of the feminine was thought within the cate- gories of passivity and activity, and was reduced to matter. Plato did not grasp the feminine in its specifically erotic notion. In his philosophy of love he left to the feminine no other role than that of furnishing an example of the Idea, which alone can be the object of love.... Beginning with Plato, the social ideal will be sought for in an ideal of fusion. It will be thought that, in its relationship with the other, by being swallowed up in a collective repre- sentation, a common ideal.... Set against the cosmos that is Plato's world, is the world of the spirit [*l'esprit*] where the implications of eros are not reduced to the logic of genus, and where the ego takes the place of the same and the Other takes the place of the other" (Lev- inas 1987c: 92–94).

"neutered" or nongendered philosophical thinking (such as Heidegger's) offer a way in which to locate irreducible otherness. Thinking sexual difference otherwise thus is a necessary precondition of making space—or rather, for Levinas, making time—for the Other. Ethics in Levinas's thought, thus, becomes intrinsically related to the task of thinking "sexual difference" in terms of temporality.

This task persists throughout Levinas's writings. In his "Philosophy, Justice, and Love," Levinas remarks as follows:

> I used to think that otherness began in the feminine. That is, in fact, a very strange otherness: woman is neither the contradictory nor the opposite of man, nor like other differences. It is not like the opposition between light and darkness. It is a distinction that is not contingent, and whose place must be sought in relation to love.... Before Eros there was the Face; Eros itself is possible only between Faces. The problem of Eros is philosophical and concerns otherness. Thirty years ago I wrote a book called Le temps et l'autre [Time and the Other]—in which I thought that the feminine was otherness itself, and I do not retract that.[15]

3. "Sexual Difference" in "And God Created Woman"

If thinking "sexual difference" otherwise is not only part of what distinguishes Levinas's work but also that which significantly makes possible his Other-oriented ethics, how can we account for the persistent subordination of the feminine and, especially, of the category "Woman" in his thought?

With this question in mind, I turn now to Levinas's essay "And God Created Woman," his commentary on b. Berakhot 61a. In this text we find both the promise and the problems of Levinas's attempts to think sexual difference otherwise. In this essay, Levinas explicitly turns away from Greek accounts—such as that of Aristophanes in Plato's Symposium—of the origin and relation of male and female.[16] In their place, he turns to

---

15 1998: 113. Derrida (1999: 139 n. 37) cites yet another time at which "Levinas will return to the logic of these propositions" (in "remarks recorded in February 1985, in the Zurich weekly Construire by L. Adert and J.-Ch. Aeschlimann"): "At the time of my little book entitled Time and the Other, I thought that femininity was a modality of alterity—this 'other genre,' this 'other gender'—and that sexuality and eroticism were this non-indifference to the other, irreducible to the formal alterity of the terms taken together as a whole. I today think that it is necessary to go back even further and that the exposure, the nakedness, and the 'imperative request' of the face of the Other constitute a modality that the feminine already presupposes: the proximity of the neighbor is non-formal alterity."

16 Here I read the matter differently than does Tina Chanter, who focuses her interpretation on Levinas's Totality and Infinity. She suggests that "Levinas's account of eros and

rabbinic arguments about how to interpret God's creation and, thus, the relation of man and woman as told in Genesis. One may wonder, however, at Levinas's choice in particular of *Berakhot* 61a as a text through which to raise these issues, for it is one of the most misogynistic rabbinic readings of the creation stories. Indeed, as I will show, the argument in *Berakhot* 61a constrains Levinas's interpretation of the creation, character, and relation of man and woman in ways that seem opposed to his attempts to think "sexual difference" otherwise. For example, in "And God Created Woman," Levinas treats Woman as the "accessory" to Man, made out of his "tail," not his "Face." Also, as I will demonstrate, the fact that Eve is in this biblical account created second is important for Levinas in that she does not, then, interfere with the primordial intimacy of the relationship between God and Man. She comes "after the event," that is, after the creation of Adam. Indeed, Levinas finds in this mode of temporality—this coming after—Woman's very feminine difference from Man. Does Levinas consider his essay "And God Created Woman" a thinking otherwise about "sexual difference"? I will repeatedly raise this question in different ways throughout my exposition of this text.

For Levinas, it is important that Eve is like Man because she is created out of him. Woman, thus, is primarily understood as a part of the human in as much as she is like Man. But "Woman as Woman," that is, in her sexuality, is regarded by Levinas as the eroticized Other. As such, she is less than human. It is Man who has greater proximity both to the Universal and to the Divine. Woman may someday catch up with Man and join him on this universal plane made possible, according to Levinas, by the priority of the masculine. The feminine, then, is not only "after the event," but Woman lags behind and always follows Man. Indeed, Levinas thinks that Woman may be just "two centuries" behind Man.

In this way, Levinas can have it both ways. He can set up a prior masculine universality in which Woman can take her place to the extent to which she becomes capable of putting aside her feminine sexuality. Woman thus bears within herself erotic otherness, in all of its ambiguity. Woman's exclusive bearing of eros thereby leaves undisrupted Man's

---

desire draws so heavily upon Plato's *Symposium* that it almost reads as an extended footnote to that dialogue" (Chanter 1988: 49), although in her own footnote to this passage she notes that "Levinas says that the Platonic interpretation 'completely fails to recognize the role of the feminine.'" (55). This is a case in which, I would argue, reading both Levinas's "Greek" and "Hebrew" writing is important, for it enables the interpreter to understand how Levinas could make this claim, despite the resonances within his writing of Platonic metaphysics. Later in this essay I will suggest how to account, at least in part, for this contradiction in Levinas's writing on eros and "sexual difference."

primordial masculine relation to God and the Holy because sexuality only enters the scene with the feminine, that is, with the second creation of Woman from Man. The feminine thus is made secondary and subordinated to the masculine so as to preserve the primordial relation of Man to the Divine and to the Universal through the masculine alone.[17]

Furthermore, if God had in the beginning created Man and Woman as two separate and equal beings, instead of an original unitary being, according to Levinas these two "principles" would have issued in an unending state of war. In order to avoid war in the *polis* and "family scenes" at home, then, Levinas argues that God created Woman so that she is subordinated to Man, knowing that this arrangement produces— indeed, relies on—injustice. It is an injustice that is for Levinas "justified" in as much as the "part," that is, Woman, suffers injustice for the sake of peace for the whole, that is, Man and Woman joined in marriage and society (this part-whole relation functions here despite Levinas's views as represented in note 18 below).

Levinas draws on *Berakhot* 61a in these terms as follows:

> Our text asks itself, however, in what way the idea of two equal beings—man and woman—in the first man is "the most beautiful idea." Does the image of God mean from the outset the simultaneity of the male and the female? Here is the answer of Rav Abbahu: God wanted to create two beings, male and female, but he created in God's image a single being. He created less well than his original idea. He would then—if I may venture to say so—have willed beyond his own image! He wanted two beings. In fact, he wanted that from the beginning there should be equality in the creature, no woman issuing from man, no woman who came after man. From the beginning he wanted two separate and equal beings. But that was impossible; this initial independence of two equal beings would no doubt have meant war. It had to be done not strictly according to justice, which would demand two separate beings. To create a world, he had to subordinate them one to the other. There had to be a difference which did not affect equity: a sexual difference and, hence, a certain preeminence of man, a woman coming later, and as woman, an appendage of the human. We now understand the lesson in this. Humanity is not thinkable on the basis of

---

17 Levinas is aware of the dangers of the very temptation to which he ultimately succumbs: "The various relations that can exist in man and being are always judged according to their proximity or distance from unity. What is relation? What is time? A fall from unity, a fall from eternity. There are many theologians in all religions who say that the good life is a coincidence with God; coincidence, that is, the return to unity. Whereas in the insistence on the relation to the other in responsibility for him or her the excellence of sociality itself is affirmed; in theological terms, proximity to God, society with God" (1998: 112).

two entirely different principles. There had to have been a *sameness* that these *others* had in common. Woman was set apart from man but she came after him: *the very femininity of woman is in this initial "after the event."* Society was not founded on purely divine principles: the world would not have lasted. Real humanity does not allow for an abstract equality, without some subordination of terms. What family scenes there would have been between the members of that first perfectly equal couple! Subordination was needed, and a wound was needed; suffering was and is needed to unite equals and unequals. (1990c: 173)

In what sense is this a thinking of "sexual difference" otherwise than in the Eleatic notion of Being? Is Woman's temporal difference from Man her "coming after the event," that is, her having been created second? Is this "coming after," lagging behind Man, the "very femininity" of Woman? Is this what Levinas means by thinking "sexual difference" otherwise? It would appear so.

Levinas's turn to biblical and rabbinic rather than to Greek sources does not seem to have affected the subordination of Woman to Man, especially as regards her "sexual difference" from Man. While Woman is not here equated with matter or to the receptacle of Being, as for Plato, the injustice marking Woman's temporality as "coming after the event" and as requiring her subordination to ensure peace may merely be a somewhat softer version of this gendered Eleatic metaphysics. Further, Levinas's siding, in this essay, with the interpretation that Woman derives from the "tail " of Man is in tension not only with his critique of the Eleatic notion of being but with another—although much more brief and fragmentary— reading of *Berakhot* 61a found in his essay,"Judaism and the Feminine" (1990b: 30–38). There Levinas (provisionally) differentiates between the rabbis and Plato on "sexual difference,"[18] whereas here he collapses this

---

18 "If woman completes man, she does not complete him as a part completes another into a whole but, as it were, as two totalities complete one another—which is, after all, the miracle of social relations. The discussion between the schools of Rav and Shmuel on the creation of Eve can be viewed from this perspective. Did she come from Adam's rib? Was this rib not a *side* of Adam, created as a single being with two faces that God separated while Adam, still androgynous, was sleeping? This theme perhaps evolved from Plato's *Symposium,* but it is one which in the Doctors takes on a new meaning. The two faces of the primitive Adam from the beginning look towards the side to which they will always remain turned. They are faces from the very outset, whereas Plato's god turns them round after separation. Their new existence, separated existence, will not come to punish the daring of too perfect a nature, as in Plato. For the Jews, separated existence will be worth more than the initial union" (1990b: 35.) However, in the same essay, Levinas counters this view, emphasizing the priority of the masculine in the following terms: "These ideas are older than the principles in whose name modern woman struggles for her emancipation, but the *truth* of all

distinction. Also, Levinas wishes to claim that "sexual difference" does not
affect the equity between Man and Woman. This does not account, however, for his rationalizing the injustice of hierarchy and the subordination
of Woman to Man as necessary.[19] How, then, may we account for this
apparent failure to think sexual difference otherwise?

4. KEEPING UP APPEARANCES

In order to address this question, I now turn to a consideration of the
inscription of the feminine, deception, and idolatry in Levinas's writing
as tied especially to the deformations of appearance. While he seeks to
undo the negative association of the feminine with matter, plurality, and
change as well as her subordination to masculine form, Levinas necessitates subordinating Woman to the masculine, a principle he regards as
prior to the feminine. Levinas, I suggest, institutes a gender hierarchy
within his ethics in part as a consequence of his continued attachment to
certain residues of the Eleatic notion of Being. For example, in repeating
Plato's negative feminizing of rhetoric as deception, Levinas reintroduces
the very metaphysics he would wish to think otherwise. Further, in
appropriating biblical and rabbinic feminizings of idolatry and sorcery in
terms of appearance, he treats them—like rhetoric—as constitutionally
deceptive. Rhetoric, Idolatry, and Woman, as I will show, are all tied to
appearance understood as opposed to the Real.

For example, Levinas treats Woman as having been created by God,
at least in part, through the arts of appearance and illusion. His views on
this matter become clear in his discussion of the following midrash in
Berakhot 61a:

> For the text "He fashioned the rib into woman," it has to be understood
> that the Holy One, Blessed be He, plaited Eve's hair into braids and took
> her to Adam, for in other countries plaiting is called *binyatha* (building).
> (1990c: 174)

---

these principles lies on a plane that also contains the thesis opposed to the image of initial
androgyny and attached to the popular idea of the rib. It upholds a certain priority of the
masculine. The latter remains the prototype of the human and determines eschatology....
The differences between masculine and feminine are blurred in this messianic age" (ibid.).

19 Levinas elsewhere describes the successful creation of equals outside God's Self in
the creation of Man and Woman: "The true paradox of the perfect being has consisted in
wanting to create equals outside himself, a multiplicity of beings, and consequently action,
beyond interiority. It is here that God has transcended creation itself" ("Simone Weil against
the Bible"; 1990b: 141).

Levinas interprets this passage, focusing on the connection between the feminine, artifice, appearance, and deception, as follows:

> In the feminine, there is face and appearance, and God was the first hairdresser. He created the first illusions, the first make-up. To build a feminine being is from the outset to make room for appearance. "Her hair has to be done." There is in the feminine face and in the relation between the sexes this beckoning to the lie, or to an arrangement beyond the savage straightforwardness of a face-to-face encounter, bypassing a relationship between human beings and approaching each other in the responsibility of one for the other. (Ibid.)

In this midrashic reading, Levinas invites an association between rhetoric and deceptive femininity. God functions for Levinas not only as the "first hairdresser" but as the "first make-up" artist. The always already made-up face of the feminine, thus, is associated with artifice, deception, and the lie. These feminized tropes for appearance reinscribe in the heart of his thought the very pernicious gender ideology that Levinas would otherwise undo.

Levinas casts his suspicion of appearance in gendered terms that resemble Plato's view of rhetoric, in particular in his *Gorgias*.[20] Levinas repeatedly draws upon Plato's views of rhetoric in his work, treating it as a seduction of the other's freedom. Like Plato, he considers rhetoric a deceptive and shadowy knack with speech that imitates, haunts, and would supplant being or truth. In its attempt through ruse to seduce the neighbor into a "bad proximity," rhetoric is synonymous with injustice. As Levinas writes in his *Totality and Infinity*:

> Rhetoric, absent from no discourse, and which philosophical discourse seeks to overcome, resists discourse. ... It approaches the other not to face him, but obliquely.... Truth is bound up with the social relation, which is justice.... Justice is ... access to the Other outside of rhetoric, which is ruse, emprise, and exploitation. And in this sense justice coincides with the overcoming of rhetoric. (1969: 70–72)

Levinas seems even less optimistic than Plato about the ability within discourse finally to separate and distinguish between rhetoric and philosophy when he suggests:

---

20 For more on the importance of Plato's *Gorgias* in forming the predominant negative view of rhetoric in (Jewish) philosophy, see Shapiro 1994; 1997. For a more extensive treatment of the shifting views of rhetoric in Levinas's philosophy, see Shapiro 2000.

This threatening ideology hides in the core of the Logos itself. Plato is
confident that he can escape it by means of good rhetoric, but he soon
hears within discourse the simian imitation of discourse. ("Ideology and
Idealism"; 1989b: 241)

In Levinas's writings, the difficulty and importance of distinguishing
between rhetoric and philosophy—and, as we will see, of demarcating
between the proximities of idolatry or sorcery and metaphysical or
ethical desire—is inscribed in gendered oppositions and terms. The
stakes of "telling the difference" between bad and ethical proximity to
the Other, like distinguishing between idolatrous and proper love of
God, could not be greater. Further, distinguishing between these two
forms of proximity is as difficult as—according to Levinas, even more
difficult than—was distinguishing between rhetoric and philosophy
for Plato.

This near incapacity to distinguish between two forms of proximity,
the unjust and the ethical, is a problem that haunts Levinas throughout
his writings (1981). When this entanglement between closely related, but
opposed, discourses is taken up in Levinas's thought in explicitly religious terms, the role of gender in disciplining this difference emerges
most strongly.

5. SORCERY, SISTER OF THE SACRED

In Levinas's talmudic essay, "Desacralization and Disenchantment,"
a commentary on *b. Sanhedrin* 67a–68a, the ability to distinguish between
appearance and reality is registered and put into question—now, however, in the context of discerning the differences between the Sacred and
sorcery as well as between the Sacred and the Holy. Levinas writes of
the difficulty of distinguishing sorcery from the Sacred in a manner
strikingly reminiscent of the problem of deceptive appearance in Plato's
and Levinas's views of rhetoric (as well as, of course, in those of many
philosophers temporally between them). Levinas writes,

> Sorcery, first cousin, perhaps even sister, of the sacred, is the mistress of
> appearance. She is a relative slightly fallen in status, but within the
> family, who profits from the connections of her brother [the Sacred],
> who is received in the best circles. (1990c: 141)

As the "mistress of appearance," sorcery is feminized. Furthermore, she
trades on her connections to "her brother," the Sacred, to gain credibility.
Sorcery appears to be what she is not. She appears like and confuses herself with the Sacred, her brother. In order to undo this sorcery,
appearance must be separated from the true.

The problem of distinguishing appearance from the true is addressed by Plato in his *Gorgias* when he describes rhetoric as masquerading as that which she is not. Plato describes rhetoric as follows:

> Now of these four [gymnastics, medicine, legislation, and justice], which always have the greatest good of the soul or the body in view, the art of flattery takes note—I won't say with full knowledge, but by shrewd guessing—and divides herself into four, entering secretly into each of the branches, and pretends that she has become what she has entered, caring nothing for the greatest good, but seeking to entrap ignorance with the bait of pleasure of the moment. And she accomplishes her deceitful design to the extent that she has come to be considered of the highest value. (*Gorgias* line 465; Helmbold: 25)

The similarity between these descriptions is not accidental. Rhetoric, Sorcery, Idolatry, and the Feminine are all figured through each other as deceptive uses of appearance. And appearance is understood as other than—even as opposed to—the true and the real.

The feminization of appearance in Levinas's thought draws on several genealogies—those pertaining to the creation of Woman (as in *Berakhot* 61a), the history of the feminine figuration of rhetoric in relation to logic and philosophy, and the association of women with sorcery and idolatry in the Jewish tradition. Indeed, Levinas reserves his most negative treatment of the feminine in terms of Woman's association with idolatry and sorcery.

In "Desacralization and Disenchantment," Levinas examines the following text from the Gemara in *Sanhedrin* 67a:

> The sorcerer, if he performs an act, etc, There is a *baraita:* The text says "sorceress" whether it be man or woman; but one says "sorceress" because the vast majority of women engage in sorcery. (1990c: 142)

After assuring his audience that "This text cannot be taken literally" and that "Sarah did not engage in sorcery, nor did Rebecca, Rachel, Leah, Ruth, or Bathsheba," Levinas tells us that we should "Rest assured of the dignity of the biblical woman" and "of the dignity of the feminine in itself" (ibid.). However, Levinas will further suggest that

> It is on the basis of a certain degradation of the feminine—but each essence is responsible for its own modes of degradation—that the charm of sorcery would function: appearance in the *very heart* of the real, dissolution of reality through the ungraspable resources of appearance, the non-real received in its unreality, as a trace of the surreal; equivocations perceived as enigmas; and, in the "fling" experienced as an ecstasy of the sacred, the law suspended. (1990c: 143; emphasis in original)

As I have already indicated, this characterization of sorcery fits not only Plato's treatment of rhetoric but Levinas's view of rhetoric as well. The problem of rhetoric is that it appears to be true and takes the place of philosophical discourse. However, disentangling the two—appearance and reality or rhetoric and philosophy—is (near) impossible. This is what makes both rhetoric and sorcery so dangerously potent. Indeed, the philosophical problem Levinas addresses in "Desacralization and Disenchantment" has to do with the problem of distinguishing appearance and reality, sorcery and the sacred:

> But hence there is a philosophical problem: How is degradation possible? How can holiness be confused with the sacred and turn into sorcery? How can the sacred transform itself into enchantment, into power over human beings? (1990c: 146–47)

These are questions for which there are no direct or easy answers. Indeed, as I have already suggested, gender plays an important role in giving the appearance of answering these questions (and others like them). Thus, gender is used, in the first instance, to cover up the insufficiencies within these discourses, definitively to separate between such closely related, but opposed, terms and ways of life. Relatedly, gender also provides images, terms, and practices ready-to-hand for the further disciplining and the keeping in place of these opposed—but, dangerously, indistinguishable—discourses and experiences. As I will demonstrate, Levinas even splits the "Face" into two in such gendered terms.

6. Two Faces

As I have noted, in his essay "And God Created Woman," Levinas interprets the creation stories of Genesis as supporting the view that Woman was made out of the tail, not the Face, of Man. Further, he considers that there are two Faces, one feminine and the other masculine. The feminine is always already made-up, while the masculine is direct and unadorned, even to the point of a certain savagery. In this context Levinas asks,

> Which of the two faces, the masculine or the feminine, leads? Here equality would end in immobility or in the bursting apart of the human being. The Gemara opts for the priority of the masculine. A man must not walk behind a woman, for his ideas may become clouded. The first reason stems perhaps from masculine psychology. It assumes that a woman bears the erotic within herself as a matter of course. (1990c: 174–75)

Given that the Face is, perhaps, the ethical term par excellence in Levinas's thought— referring to the infinite alterity of the other person for whom "I" am responsible—this is a very troubling split. Although there is a trace of awareness in his thought that the feminine is a projection of what Levinas here terms "masculine psychology," it does not undo this split between faces in which the masculine is prior. In the conclusion of his essay, Levinas explains that the Gemara prefers a man to choose to walk behind a lion rather than behind a woman because "The text of the Gemara prefers the danger of the lions to this intimacy" (1990c: 175). After Woman comes idolatry, showing—according to Levinas—that the Gemara "still prefers the sentimental road [of following Woman] to that of idolatry" (176). Then comes a passage in this essay that brings one to question again what Levinas might mean when he refers to thinking "sexual difference" otherwise:

> You see: the feminine is in a fairly good position in this hierarchy of values, which reveals itself when choices become alternatives. It is in second place. It is not woman who is thus slighted. It is the relation based on sexual differences which is subordinated to the interhuman relation—irreducible to the drives and complexes of the libido—to which woman rises as well as man. Maybe man precedes—by a few centuries—the woman in this elevation. From which a certain—provisional?—priority of man. Maybe the masculine is more directly linked to the universal, and maybe masculine civilization has prepared, above the sexual, a human order in which a woman enters, completely human. (177)

It is as if Levinas, in locating the creation of Eve from a subordinate part of Adam, makes Woman subordinate to Man in the present, in space, in our imperfect world, but also as capable of "coming after" Man and eventually returning fully to the human from which she came. In so doing, Levinas imagines Woman as eventually—that is, in time—transcending and leaving behind her feminine sexuality, joining Man on a higher plane to which he has both preceded her and paved the way in terms of a masculine Universality.[21] Levinas regards this version of "sexual difference" as an improvement on the Eleatic notion of Being. However, in thus thinking sexual difference, Levinas seems to associate the feminine and the "bad proximity" of rhetoric, idolatry, or sorcery in terms of space and the deformations of appearance. In thinking sexual difference in terms of time, he also allows for an ethical proximity to the

---

21 The priority and constitutive character of the masculine in the human as regards both creation and eschatology, the end of days, is evident elsewhere in Levinas's writing as well. See my discussion of this issue and these other texts below.

other in which Woman can eventually be included in as much as she leaves behind and transcends her feminine sexuality into a sort of Universal masculinity. This eschatological solution to thinking sexual difference otherwise, however, is continually haunted by the ontological way in which Levinas reads the Genesis stories of creation and by the residues of the Eleatic notion of Being he would elude.[22] While succumbing to the temptation of reading Genesis ontologically is certainly understandable, it is lamentable that Levinas did not, rather, begin with an ethical interpretation of that text.

That Levinas succumbs to the use of gender stereotypes in order to institute, enforce, and govern the differences between ethical and bad proximity is most disappointing in one who has set out to think "sexual difference" otherwise as a basis for ethics. Further, temporalizing sexual difference still locates it not only within a heteronormative and essentialized understanding of Man and Woman, male and female, but exclusively within the feminine and Woman. Levinas, thus, fails adequately to think identity through "sexual difference" otherwise. Again, I ask, how are we to account for these systematic failures, so as not simply to dismiss Levinas's thought, especially his turn to ethics as first philosophy? Can we think "sexual difference" otherwise?

7. The Parable of "The Moon That Makes Itself Little"

While I have focused on the residues of hierarchy infiltrating Levinas's thought from the very Eleatic metaphysics he would think otherwise, it is clear that some hierarchical thought is present within the talmudic texts he reads in his biblical exegeses. For example, as I have before noted, in "And God Created Woman" Levinas assures his readers that

> the feminine is in a fairly good position in this hierarchy of values [as drawn out in *Berakhot* 61a].... It is in second place. It is not woman who is thus slighted. It is the relation based on sexual differences which is subordinated to the interhuman relation.... Maybe the masculine is more directly linked to the universal, and maybe masculine civilization has prepared, above the sexual, a human order in which a woman enters, completely human." (1990c: 177)

---

22 This despite Levinas's clear statements elsewhere disavowing the desire of a return to a primordial unity in the following terms: "One last thing that is very close to my heart. In this whole priority of the relationship to the other, there is a break with a great traditional idea of the excellence of unity. The relation would already be a deprivation of this unity. That is the Plotinian tradition. My idea consists in conceiving sociality as independent of the 'lost' unity" (1998: 112).

In order to better understand why Levinas preserves gendered hierarchical thinking in both his "Greek" and "Hebrew" writings, I will turn to another talmudic reading in which this orientation is affirmed. In his reading of tractate *b. Hullin* 60a, Levinas finds an articulation of the "theme of the conduction of elevation and descent, of the greatness of humility or the humility of greatness ... in the parable of 'The Moon that makes itself little'" ("Judaism and Kenosis"; 1990b: 116). Rabbi Shimon be Pazi's account of this parable, in *Hullin* 60b, is as follows:

> Immediately after the creation of the two great lights [as recounted in Gen 1:16], one of them, the Moon, said to the Creator: "Sovereign of the world, can two kings wear the same crown?" And God answered: "Go, therefore, and make yourself smaller!" (Ibid.)

Levinas inquires after the reason for the Moon's question and God's answer to her, thus:

> Was the Moon unable, out of pride or vanity, to share the greatness of the Sun? And was not the order she was given, "to make herself smaller," the just punishment for such pretentiousness? Or was the Moon, troubled by a precocious philosophical concern, affirming the necessity of a hierarchical order in being? Did she already intuit the "negativity" between equals and discern that greatness cannot be shared—that the sharing of greatness is war? Rather than commanding a punishment unjustly imposed, perhaps what the voice of God proposed was the greatness of smallness—of humility, of the abnegation of night. The nobility of the best ones: smallness equal to greatness, and compatible with it. (1990b: 117)

This passage resonates strongly with the concerns expressed by Levinas, in his "And God Created Woman," that two equal principles (masculine and feminine) would have issued in an unending state of war, necessitating hierarchy for the sake of peace at home and in the *polis*. In this talmudic essay, however, the feminine, as it were, talks back in a dialogue with God about her apparently shrunken status. Another difference appears here as well: the humility of the Moon is associated with the "smallness"—perhaps, even, the persecution—of Judaism in the larger world, thus associating the feminine with Judaism itself. Following the course of this "dialogue" further will be instructive for understanding the problems of gender and hierarchy elsewhere in Levinas's thought, as in his essay, "And God Created Woman."

The Moon asks God, "I just expressed a sensible idea: is that any reason to make me smaller?" (ibid.) Levinas glosses this question as follows:

Hierarchy is necessary, but I [the Moon] already see that it is necessarily unjust. The ontology of the creature is contradictory. It is dangerous to utter truths! As for the greatness of smallness, I do not at the outset see it as being as great as greatness. Is not the "glorious lowering" a scandal to reason? (Ibid.)

The insights Levinas ventriloquizes in the name of the Moon are clearly his own. Levinas puts into the mouth of the Moon a more contemporary, perhaps even "feminist" concern with equality and the injustice of hierarchy. However, he also has the Moon acknowledge that hierarchy is both necessary and "necessarily unjust." God's offered solution to this injustice—like Levinas's—is a turn from spatial to temporal difference: "Thou shalt reign day and night," says the Lord, "while the reign of the Sun will be limited to the day" (ibid.). Levinas elaborates as follows: "There are lights without brilliance whose lustre the Sun cannot dim: there are insights of the intuitive mind that systematic reasoning, in its glorious clarity, cannot refute. The wisdom of the night remains visible during the day" (ibid.).

The Moon, however, is not satisfied. She asks,"What would be the advantage of shedding light in full daylight?" (ibid.). In an attitude similar to that toward Woman in his "And God Created Woman"— "the feminine is in a fairly good position in this hierarchy of values"—Levinas notes: "The role of second brilliance cannot heal the wounded ego."

God's response now draws an even tighter connection, for Levinas, between the Moon, the feminine, temporality, and Judaism:

> "By you," the Eternal says to the undaunted Moon, "Israel will be able to reckon the days and nights." This consideration opens a new dimension, which makes the inevitable hierarchy fairer, and helps the Moon understand the possible greatness of making-oneself-little. The Sun and Moon are not just lights, but movement, time—history. To the solar calendar of the nations is added Israel's lunar calendar: universal history, and individual history. (Ibid.)

Levinas once again draws a connection between the particular (instead of the universal) and "Hebrew" (rather than "Greek"). Further, Israel's temporality is tied to messianic history. The feminine lunar calendar is read by Levinas as signifying Israelite history:

> The biblical history of Israel: drawn in upon itself, lateral, yet Messianic history. Perhaps it was necessary that among the categories of ontology— or despite these categories—the category "Israel" should arise, in order that the notion of a smallness as great as—or greater than—greatness should take on meaning. (1990b: 117–18)

However, universal history ("Greek") and, even, politics and "visible history" may be required "in the long run" as well,[23] Levinas determines, in response to the Moon's further questioning of God: "It is impossible ... to reckon the cycle of the seasons without recourse to the Sun. Does not Scripture say in *Genesis* 1:14: 'They (Moon *and* Sun) will serve as signs to mark the seasons, the days, and years?'" (1990b: 118). God makes one last, apparently unsuccessful, effort to console and persuade the Moon of the "greatness of humility" but is met with "a dissatisfied silence." It is for this final "ambiguity that surrounds the greatness of the saintly and humble who risk being taken for failures" that "Holiness takes on the responsibility." For it is God who is both most humble and great:

> Here is the humility of God assuming responsibility for this ambiguity. The greatness of humility is also the humiliation of greatness. It is the sublime kenosis of a God who accepts the questioning of his holiness in a world incapable of restricting itself to the light of his Revelation. (118)

I am, of course, not questioning the greatness of humility. Rather, I am interested in the ways in which this particular dynamic of saintliness is driven by and inscribed in gendered terms in Levinas's thought. In order better to understand the sources of this dynamic in "Hebrew" and not only "Greek," I turn now to a brief consideration of Levinas's appropriation of the thought of the Rabbi Hayyim of Volozhin in his *Nefesh Ha-Hayyim* in these terms.

8. Kenosis in *Nefesh Ha-Hayyim*

In a consideration of "the cosmology or general ontology" of Reb Hayyim of Volozhin's *Nefesh Ha-Hayyim*, Levinas finds a pluralism of entities, worlds—and, perhaps, "individual persons, and collectivities and ideal realities"—in which "there is the possibility of being-toward-being, of alterity" (1990b: 123). In this pluralistic context, however, there is hierarchy:

> Among these entities or worlds there is a hierarchical order. It is a hierarchy of holiness and dignity, and thus an intertwining or a concatenation with strands of the holiness and light of God, who is the summit and principle of that concatenation. In this [kabbalistically informed] order, the higher is the soul of the lower: the height is the

---

23 A comparison of Levinas's and Franz Rosenzweig's views on the relations between Jewish history and universal history in these terms would be illuminating, although beyond the scope of this essay.

animation, the depth the "body" or "clothing" of the height. The height is also called the root of the depth: the roots, in this case, grow upward, so to speak. The height is the inside, the upper is what gives movement to the lower.... *Elohim*, at the top of the hierarchy, is the soul and animation of all the worlds; through their hierarchical interconnection the master's energy is transmitted to all, by lowering itself from the higher to the lower, but also by raising the lower toward the higher ... in a continuous creation, ongoing every moment. (Ibid.)

The resonances with Levinas's treatment of the parable of "The Moon That Makes Itself Little" are striking.[24] These resonances will grow as Levinas argues that this hierarchy is different from that of "Greek": "But the creature is not reducible to that hierarchy in its simplicity, in which it might still resemble a Greek cosmos" (124). This is analogous to Levinas's claim in "And God Created Woman" that "It is not woman who is thus slighted [by being in second place in the hierarchy]" (1990c: 177). But in this essay, "Judaism and Kenosis," "The last to be created and raised to the highest by the divine breath that gives him life, [carrying] within his being a residuum of all the levels of the creature," is not Woman, but Man.[25] Although Man—and not Woman as such—is associated with the body and matter as at the "lowest level" of creation in *Nefesh Ha-Hayyim*, the lowest rises to the highest. "Elevation ... does not depend solely on its place in the cosmological hierarchy" (1990b: 124) and is, thus, not like Eleatic metaphysics, in which matter is irrevocably subordinated to form as is particular to universal. The subordination of the feminine to the masculine does, however, persist in Levinas's reading of *Nefesh Ha-Hayyim* and, indeed, in his own thought.

> Everything depends on him, even the outpouring of God, which confers being and light on the entire hierarchy of worlds.... Hence, there is a privileged relationship between ... man and the manifold entirety of the creature on the one hand, and a special intimacy between man and *Elohim* on the other.... Man is, like the Creator himself, at the apex of the hierarchy of the worlds, the soul of the universe.... And this, not in the name of any pride or diabolical pretension, but by the will of God himself who did not recoil from that equality with the human, or even from a certain kind of subordination to the human. (124–25)

---

24 Indeed, both the parable of the Moon and this turn to *Nefesh Ha-Hayyim* appear in the same essay, "Judaism and Kenosis."

25 1990b: 124. Phyllis Trible (101) has remarked on how the creation of Woman can be understood as the apex of the hierarchy of creation in that she was created after Adam, the "Earth Creature," at which point "he" was separated into two sexes.

In turning here to a consideration of *Nefesh Ha-Hayyim*, I do not address its overall importance for Levinas's thought. Rather, I am interested in how Levinas's reading of *Nefesh Ha-Hayyim* informs his understanding of the difference between "Hebrew" and "Greek" and of "sexual difference" in that context. The creation story on which *Nefesh Ha-Hayyim* relies in this cosmology is the first creation of Man, that of Gen 2:7, in which *Elohim* breathes into matter, into the nostrils of Man, bringing him to life.[26] This is the account of the creation of Man *before* the creation of Woman from him. Had Rabbi Hayyim of Volozhin contextualized his reading in the second, not the first, account of the creation of Man and Woman, Levinas would have had to confront problems related to "sexual difference" that are elided here.

The gender hierarchy in "And God Created Woman" is more fixed than is the account of creation in Levinas's reading of *Nefesh Ha-Hayyim*. While Levinas claims that the hierarchy in which Woman follows Man is not a slight to Woman but is a "relation based on sexual differences which is subordinated to the interhuman relation ... to which woman rises as well as man," Levinas still enforces a hierarchy in which Woman "in her sexuality" is subordinated. She is lower than Man, but the elevation of the feminine as such—perhaps, even beyond the masculine, as the masculine is made by Levinas to surpass the feminine—remains, for the most part, unimagined by Levinas. This is so even though the elevation of the feminine would have been consistent with that logic of elevation of the individual and matter put forward in *Nefesh Ha-Hayyim*. Indeed, on the transformation of hierarchy, *Nefesh Ha-Hayyim* seems to offer some possible resources not, however, taken up by Levinas as regards "sexual difference": "In subordinating God's action of the world to the possibility for the least powerful creature to be *for* the whole of creat[ion], the (one-way) cosmological hierarchy is broken, without being replaced by any other new hierarchy, or the reverse of this hierarchy, or anarchy."[27] Instead, as in the parable of

---

26 In his essay, " 'In the Image of God', according to Rabbi Hayyim Volozhiner," Levinas reproduces and expands much of his reading of *Nefesh Ha-Hayyim*: "The humanity of man in *Nefesh ha-Hayyim* is understood not in light of the rational animality of the Greeks but in light of the biblical notion of man created in the image of God. More precisely, the biblical expression set out in Genesis 1:27: 'in the image of Elohim' " (1994a: 156). "Human souls come from the divine breath: is it not written in Genesis 2:7 that 'God breathed into [man's] nostrils the breath of life'?" (158).

27 1994a: 162. Levinas may, of course, consider the subordination of masculine to feminine as a problematic reversal of this hierarchy, or anarchy. However, this reversal is regarded as problematic only if the masculine and feminine are essentialized as irreducibly opposed principles. This, in part, is what I understand Levinas to mean by "sexual

"The Moon That Makes Itself Little," there is only a dissatisfying silence
that remains.

9. "AND GOD SAID TO ABRAHAM ... 'ALL THAT SARAH HAS SAID TO THEE, HEARKEN TO HER VOICE'"

There is one instance in Levinas's "Jewish writings" where God subordinates a male to a female. In accounting for the implication of Sarai's
name change into "Sarah" in Gen 17:15, Levinas asks,

> Will the woman's condition forever remain inseparable from the posses-
> sive that contains—or deforms—the second syllable of a word meaning,
> in the case of Abraham's wife, the sovereignty of a princess? The sover-
> eignty of a princess or of a human person! But also the sovereignty of a
> woman, who, in a masculine world, always runs the risk of being taken
> as a thing to be owned.... Henceforth, dignity of the person that has
> regained her fullness and accedes to the highest vocations of the human.
> This ontological correction is announced by God precisely to the hus-
> band. Abraham will soon hear (*Genesis* 21:12): "And in all that Sarah
> says to you, obey her voice." In prophecy itself, a possible subordination
> of the male inspiration to the female. (1994b: 86)

This provocative instance will remain an isolated and, alas, undevel-
oped possibility in Levinas's thought. However, juxtaposing even this
bare but illuminating fragment to Levinas's otherwise pervasive reading
of the subordination of feminine to masculine in the hierarchy of things,
one is brought up short. For example, while Levinas seems to authorize
this hierarchy as God's, in reading *Berakhot* 61a in such an unnuanced
way, Levinas bears responsibility for his interpretation. As I have indicated, other avenues of interpretation were—and are—possible. And, as I
have noted, while the weight of tradition in *Berakhot* 61a would seem to
support his hierarchical reading of "sexual difference," Levinas's
hermeneutic elsewhere seems to take the counternarratives within the
Talmud more seriously than he does in his "And God Created Woman."
    I have examined Levinas's views on gender in some of his other
"Jewish writings" so as better to understand his resistance to hearing more
vividly, more strongly, and more persuasively the counternarratives

---

difference." However, subordinating justice to these not only opposed, but hierarchically
arranged, principles is both a problematic subordination of eschatology to ontology, infinity to totality, and other to the same. It is the undoing, in short, of ethics as first
philosophy. Justice is explicitly compromised by Levinas's preservation of this gender-
hierarchy in the name of "peace."

about Woman in *Berakhot* 61a. I have found that this subordination of the feminine to the masculine is evident in these other writings on Hebrew cosmology and ontology and, even, as I will now demonstrate, in Levinas's gendered understanding of eschatology.

10. Eschatology and the Feminine

In his essay "Judaism and the Feminine," Levinas emphasizes the priority of the masculine in the following terms:

> These ideas are older than the principles in whose name modern woman struggles for her emancipation, but the *truth* of all these principles lies on a plane that also contains the thesis opposed to the image of initial androgyny and attached to the popular idea of the rib. It upholds a certain priority of the masculine. The latter remains the prototype of the human and determines eschatology.... The differences between masculine and feminine are blurred in this messianic age. (1990b: 35)

Indeed, the feminine is not simply blurred but erased as the masculine—indeed, the virile—reemerges at the End of Days. The ontological "priority of the masculine" in the creation of Woman from the "rib" of Man ("opposed to the image of initial androgyny") returns and is "the prototype of the human and determines eschatology." (I will treat this problematic reversal of the ethical relation between eschatology and ontology in Levinas's thought on gender later in this essay.) While the feminine opens the dimension of intimacy, transcendence remains exclusively the province of the masculine. As in Levinas's philosophical writings, in which the dangers of the dyad—following Buber in this regard—are treated in feminine terms as the problem of the privacy and exclusivity of romance with the other, the "third party" is the introduction of the other man.[28] Justice does not pertain to the dyad but only

---

28 Another critique of Buber's dyadic "I-Thou" relation pertains to its reciprocity, rather than the asymmetry of my responsibility for the other. See the explication of the "third party" above, as both beyond the other before me as well as already reflected in the eyes of that other. Therefore, the split between the domain of intimacy and that of the public sphere in which justice pertains cannot be rendered absolute in this latter understanding of the "third party," except if the feminine other, the Woman, is scandalously not regarded as evoking the "third party" in her gaze, her eyes. What would a relation not of Man to Woman, but of Woman to Woman constitute? Would the appearance of a feminine "third party" open the relation to the public and justice, or would it return one (her) to the intimate realm? In other words, is the subject unerringly masculine in Levinas's thought? Does Levinas's heteronormative relation of Man to Woman allow women to be subjects? These are

emerges in relation to the "third party" and the public.[29] The public
sphere is masculine, whereas the home is the domain of the feminine,
whether or not a woman is present. The feminine, thus, never represents anything other than the intimate, even when it signifies the ethical
in her welcoming.

> In the rabbinic interpretation of love, maternity is subordinate to a
> human destiny which exceeds the limits of "family joys." ... The forms
> of romance that one finds in the Bible are at once interpreted by the
> *midrash* in such a way as to bring out the eschatological side of the
> romance.... Poetic images of amorous life are discrete in the Bible, out-
> side the Song of Songs, which is soon interpreted in a mystical sense....
> [T]he feminine will never take on the aspect of the Divine [in
> Judaism].... The dimension of intimacy, not the dimension of loftiness,
> is opened up by woman. Doubtless the mysterious interiority of femi-
> nine existence will be used to experience, like a betrothed, the Sabbath,
> the Torah itself, and sometimes the divine Presence in the nearness of
> men, the *shekhinah*. The images do not in any way become feminine fig-
> ures. They are not taken seriously. Amorous relations in Scripture are
> interpreted symbolically and denote mystical relations. (1990b: 35–37)

Woman only represents romance, intimacy, and sexuality for Man. Thus,
feminine figures "are not taken seriously." In Levinas's eschatology, the
masculine appropriates that which had previously been associated with
the feminine, in surpassing this world into the world to come at the End
of Days.[30]

> True life, joy, pardon and peace no longer belong to woman [at the End
> of Days]. Now there rises up, foreign to all compassion for itself, spirit in

---

some of the questions both raised by and implied within my examination of Levinas's
understanding of "sexual difference" in both "Hebrew" and "Greek."

29 This exclusion of the feminine from the public domain in which justice pertains
problematically registers the exclusion from principles of justice of the feminine, of Woman
defined through and in relation to the feminine, and, perhaps, even of women. The "necessity of injustice" in the subordination of the feminine and Woman to the masculine and Man
in Levinas's ontology of creation is a troubling correlate of both the feminizing of the dyad
and the masculinizing of the "third party" in Levinas's thought.

30 This appropriation, indeed, the entire description of the role of gender in Levinas's
eschatology, utterly resonates with Eliot Wolfson's analysis of gender symbolism and
dynamics in Kabbalah and Jewish mystical traditions generally (see esp. 1994; 1995). The
importance of *Nefesh Ha-Hayyim* for Levinas may not, thus, be insignificant in this regard.
The feminine is appropriated by the masculine and even becomes a figure within God, for
Levinas. For example, "Mercy—the *rachamim* (the trembling of the womb where the Other
is in gestation in the Same, maternity within god, so to speak)—attenuates the rigours of the
Law" ("Revelation in the Jewish Tradition"; 1994a: 142).

its essence, virile, superhuman, solitary. It recognizes itself in Elijah, the prophet without pardon, the prophet of anger and punishment, a suckling of crows, inhabiting deserts, without kindness, without happiness, without peace.... But the biblical figure which haunts Israel on the paths of exile, the figure that it invokes at the end of the Sabbath [instead of the Sabbath Queen, *the shekhinah*, at the beginning of the Sabbath], in the dusk where it will soon remain behind without help, the figure in whom is stored up for the Jews all the tenderness of the earth, the hand which caresses and rocks his children, is no longer feminine. Neither wife nor sister nor mother guides it. It is Elijah, who did not experience death, the most severe of the prophets, precursor of the Messiah. (1990b: 38)

This masculinist eschatology, alas, is both symptomatic of and compatible with Levinas's failure to think "sexual difference" otherwise than the Eleatic notion of Being, in which the end is a return to the beginning and difference is absorbed in the Same. And, as I have been suggesting, the sources of this failure are not only within "Greek" but within Levinas's reading of "Hebrew" as well. Can Levinas's thought be read otherwise so that justice to women becomes possible—perhaps, is even demanded—in accord with his most fundamental claims: the regard for the face of the other person(s) and ethics as first philosophy?

11. Reconfiguring Rhetoric

I have argued that the gendered configuration of the relationship between rhetoric and philosophy (and in Jewish philosophy the related feminizing of idolatry) is a crucial locus for both the constituting and regulation not only of these disciplines and forms of life but of "sexual difference." As Levinas argues, the history of the Eleatic philosophy of Being has demonstrated a systematic subordination of matter as passive and feminine to form as constitutive and masculine. In order to think "sexual difference" otherwise so as to institute the possibility of ethics, including that of gender justice, I argue, a reconfiguration of the gendered character of the relationship between rhetoric and philosophy must be undertaken. A critique and reconfiguration of representations of gender is important as well for those genealogies of the sacred and idolatry that, as in Jewish philosophy, have developed out of and along the same lines as those of rhetoric. This is necessary because these feminized views of rhetoric and idolatry are remains of an Eleatic metaphysic that negatively configures and subordinates woman and the feminine to man and the masculine.[31]

---

31 This is not to say, however, that only "Greek"—in particular, the Eleatic philosophy of Being—is responsible for the negative figuration of rhetoric and idolatry in these terms.

The reinscription of gender stereotypes through the appropriation of rhetoric in these terms repeats the problematic subordination of difference to the same and the other to the self. Contrary to Levinas's insistent identification of justice with the "overcoming of rhetoric," therefore, I believe that at stake in the revaluing of the relationship between rhetoric and philosophy is precisely the very question of justice.

Without such a critique of this negative feminine figuration of both rhetoric and idolatry, Jewish (and not only Jewish) philosophy and theology will inexorably repeat the marginalization of women, the feminine, and the body. When not treated as simply the other of philosophy—that is, as the bearer of error, delusion, and prejudice—rhetoric offers resources for, and methods of, critical reading that will enable us both to uncover and reconfigure otherwise the pernicious gender ideology within philosophy itself (for more on the importance of re-reading philosophy rhetorically, see Shapiro 1994; 1997). We may, thus, undo the problematic rendering of the feminine, the other, body, and woman in the Eleatic notion of Being by a "thinking otherwise" that Levinas both calls for and, alas, fails to perform. Levinas may have left unfulfilled the promise to think sexual difference otherwise, a challenge that I choose to pick up. However, we must ask whether notions of "sexual difference" will provide a way toward gender justice or whether, as in Levinas's case, they will prove to be yet another ethical cul-de-sac.

12. Toward a Re-reading of "And God Created Woman" Otherwise

In virtually every other talmudic essay by Levinas, his interpretations are consistently so nuanced that the reader is often not certain where he stands on the issues under debate. Indeed, most often, Levinas seems to stand in several places at once. In the essay "And God Created Woman," however, he leaves almost no ambiguity as to where he stands. He follows the interpretation that Woman was created out of the tail, not the face nor the side, of Adam. Furthermore, he justifies the creation of Woman as subordinated to Man, at least in the meantime. For, to have two equal principles would constitute endless war; thus, according to Levinas, God scrapped his original plan to create beyond himself, as it were, that is, to create two equal creatures.[32] Instead, according to Levinas

---

The Tanakh and Talmud also negatively feminize idolatry (and seductive, garrulous, or indiscrete speech as well), though in somewhat different terms. See Shapiro 1998.

32 The masculine gendering of God, thus, does not seem to be contingent, since God's first desire to create two equal but different principles, Man and Woman, "beyond Himself" seems to signify not simply an issue of the "surpassing"—or undermining—of God's unity

following the argument of *Berakhot* 61a, God in creating Woman instituted injustice as a necessary part of creating a world with the possibility of peace. In the meantime, therefore, there must be hierarchy and inequality, at least until the End of Days.

But, surely, as I have suggested, there are other readings possible of this creation narrative, especially in light of an ethical and not ontologically determined eschatology. Beside the gendered, ultimately masculine versions of eschatology rehearsed above, Levinas has made a number of comments about eschatology that emphasize its open-ended and always unfinished character. Unlike ontology that is closed in a totality, eschatology points to the infinite: "a world to come in an inexhaustible future of love itself, an eschatology paradoxically endless or precisely infinite" ("Contempt for the Torah As Idolatry"; 1994b: 60). In this relation to the future, a re-reading of ontology as for-the-other is made possible. The connection between ontology and eschatology is itself reversed. In this reversal, eschatology is not understood as the return of a primordial ontology—and thus the return of the masculine in the first story of the creation of Man in Genesis—at the End of Days. Rather, eschatology's infinite openness to the future opens as well the closed totality of ontology to the other and the otherwise than being.

Indeed, in his *Totality and Infinity*, Levinas describes creation in terms that put in question his ontological interpretation of the creation of Man and Woman in "And God Created Woman."

> Theology imprudently treats the idea of the relation between God and the creature in terms of ontology. It presupposes the logical privilege of totality, as a concept adequate to being. Thus it runs up against the difficulty of understanding that an infinite being would border on or tolerate something outside of itself, or that a free being would send its roots into the infinity of a God. But transcendence precisely refuses totality, does not lend itself to a view that would encompass it from the outside.... What embarrasses the traditional theology, which treats of creation in terms of ontology—God leaving his eternity, in order to create—is incumbent as a first truth in a philosophy that begins with transcendence: nothing could better distinguish totality and separation than the difference between eternity and time.... For the idea of totality, in which ontological philosophy veritably reunites—or comprehends—the

---

(because, for example, Levinas sees plurality and this radical unity as compatible in "Hebrew" ontology), but of God creating beyond, as it were, his masculine self another, separate, and equal feminine principle. According to Levinas, God decides not to create equality but rather the injustice of the subordination of the feminine to the masculine and of Woman to Man for the sake of "peace."

multiple, must be substituted the idea of a separation resistant to synthesis. To affirm origin from nothing by creation is to contest the prior community of all thing[s] within eternity, from which philosophical thought, guided by ontology, makes things arise as from a common matrix. The absolute gap of separation which transcendence implies could not be better expressed than by the term creation, in which the kinship of beings among themselves is affirmed, but at the same time their radical heterogeneity also, their reciprocal exteriority coming from nothingness. One may speak of creation to characterize entities situated in the transcendence that does not close over into a totality.... The I's form no totality, there exists no privileged plane where these I's could be grasped in their principle. There is an anarchy essential to multiplicity.... But a principle breaks through all this trembling and vertigo when the face presents itself, and demands justice. (1969: 293–94)

Although in *Totality and Infinity* Levinas speaks of the fault of theology's interpreting creation in ontological terms, it is the ontology of totality that he refuses. The reversal of ontology into ethics—in which being-for-the-other characterizes existence rather than the desire of the self to persist in being—is another understanding of ontology that is consonant with Levinas's critique of ontology as totality. This latter understanding of the reversal in the relation between eschatology and ontology opens the possibility—indeed, the necessity—of reconfiguring gender relations both in a re-reading of Genesis and in eschatology. This "reversal of ontology into ethics" opens the text of "And God Created Woman" to other interpretations. As Levinas instructs, the claims of the text are to be heard not only in the profound resonances of the past but in attending as well to "my" neighbors today. By reading the text in regard to the faces of those others who face "me" now and in terms of our contemporary moment in which gender justice is an increasing concern both within and beyond Judaism, a number of questions are raised that must be posed in relation to Levinas's thought, especially in relation to Levinas's claim that ethics is first philosophy.

One of the ways in which Levinas's clinging to gender hierarchy, even into the End of Days, can be understood is in terms of the problems of the reversal or inversion of principles when they are treated abstractly. The "struggle with the Angel" is to help guard against just such inversions. When the principle is not watched and safeguarded from the vantage point of the particular, it may slip into its opposite. I would suggest that Levinas's ideological blind spot about Woman and the feminine keeps him from realizing that his instituting of gender hierarchy—even into eschatology—reinscribes the injustices of both totality and Eleatic metaphysics in his thought. (Indeed, Levinas does seem willing to institute [provisional] injustice into his understanding of the ontology of "sexual difference.") In reading Genesis solely in ontological terms—and in terms in which being-for-the-other cannot include Woman as such as this Other—Levinas undercuts his understanding elsewhere of both ethics and eschatology.

In fact, an argument can be made that it is from the vantage point of the particular—that is, the "feminine" or "Woman"—that the ethical reading of the Bible can best be undertaken. Levinas articulates a similar position in his reading of *Nefesh Ha-Hayyim,* in which one begins not with the universal but with Man as matter and individual, for the sake of elevation. As I have noted, however, this individual is Man created before the creation of Woman as a separate being. Indeed, the vantage point of Woman and the feminine is precisely eclipsed in "And God Created Woman." Levinas is explicit about the injustice of hierarchy to Women, although, as in the parable of "The Moon That Makes Itself Little," he sees it as both a necessary and a temporary injustice. From the vantage point of the "Woman," however, it appears as more than a temporal or, indeed, temporary problem, but rather as injustice *simpliciter.* Why someone so attuned to alterity is also systematically deaf to the claims of Woman and, especially, women (as such) is a question I cannot address, let alone answer, here. Rather, the question I pursue here is whether, once having clarified the contours of this "systematic distortion" in Levinas's thought, a redemptive critique is possible and, if so, how.

13. METHODOLOGICAL POSTSCRIPT

I have suggested two possible approaches: one, the reconfiguring of the gendered relationship between rhetoric and philosophy that Levinas reappropriates and through which he, thereby, reinscribes Eleatic metaphysics in his thought; two, the re-reading of his talmudic essay, "And God Created Woman," from the vantage point of the particular, the excluded, the exception, that is, from the location(s) of the "feminine," "Woman," and, indeed, women.

If Levinas's treatment of ethics as first philosophy is not to be marred, indeed inverted, by the treatment of Woman, a "struggle with the Angel" is crucial. For, Levinas treats regard and responsibility for the "face" of the other(s) paradigmatically in terms of "my" obligation to the stranger, the widow, the orphan, including women thereby at least in some instances of deprivation and suffering. While the "widow" may be treated as only a figure, surely Levinas also means to include actual widows in this responsibility for the other person(s). However, only in Levinas's treatment of Abraham's "subordination" to the prophetic voice of Sarah does Levinas indicate an understanding of the tragic consequences of systematic injustice toward Woman and women

intrinsic to the masculine hierarchy that, however, he treats as necessary to peace.

For the most part, a sense of lamentation, repentance, or even responsibility for the suffering of women necessitated in such rationalizing of
the peace of totality through subordination is absent in Levinas's writing.
Rather, Woman is treated as ambiguously posing a threat in her embodiment both of great modesty and radical immodesty.

> The feminine presents a face that goes beyond the face. The face of the
> beloved does not *express* the secret that *Eros* profanes; it ceases to
> express, or, if one prefers, it expresses only this refusal to express, this
> end of discourse and of decency, this abrupt interruption of the order of
> presences. In the feminine face the purity of expression is already trou-
> bled by the equivocation of the voluptuous. Expression is inverted into
> indecency, already close on to the equivocal which says less than noth-
> ing, already laughter and raillery. (1969: 260)

The negative seductiveness of femaleness is found within the "essence"
of Woman; however, the "feminine" as welcoming the other does not at
all require the presence of a woman or women. Women can attain universality prepared by the "masculine" only to the extent that they leave
behind their potentially disruptive "female sexuality." (Levinas takes this
position despite his awareness that this threatening view of "female sexuality" is a product both of specifically male projection and desire.) While
men must limit their virility to welcome the other, becoming feminine,
Levinas is not only ambivalent about this limitation of virility (as evidenced, for example, in his praising of the "brutal directness" of the male
"face to face" relation), but he allows the virile importantly to reappear—
and to "disappear" the feminine—in the eschatological figure of Elijah.
Thus, re-reading the narrative of the creation of Woman and Man in Genesis requires an ethical or eschatological interpretation that does not
reinstitute a totalizing and masculine ontology but rather one that is a
reversal in/of ontology of one-for-the-other, including the other woman.

The example of Levinas's exegesis of rabbinic texts pertaining to the
creation, character, and role of Woman in the Tanakh is a very difficult
and troubling one. In many ways, it is not paradigmatic of Levinas's
engagement with the plurivocity of rabbinic texts. However, it is instructive as to the ways in which the notion of "sexual difference" in Levinas's
philosophical and "Jewish writings" significantly intersect in their sup-
positions about the feminine and Woman. In this instance, alas,
"Hebrew" does not function in Levinas's readings to guard the principles
of justice, among others, against reversal. Even though Woman as "feminine" *rachamim*, mercy, may be considered as both prior to and more
perfect than justice, that position becomes hard to distinguish from the

"injustice" of subordination. She does not attain a significance outside of the intimacy of the dyad. Her entrance into the public domain as a/the "third party" remains to be theorized, indeed, to be thought. As I have indicated, however, there are sparks that may be blown into embers that may enlighten interpretation otherwise:

> Jewish identity is inscribed in these old documents. It cannot be annulled by simply ignoring these means of identification, just as it cannot be reduced to its simplest form of expression without entering into the discourse of the modern world.... In this way the flame traverses History without burning it. But the truth illuminates whoever breathes on the flame and coaxes it back to life. More or less. It's a question of breath. (1989b: 266)*

---

* I wish to thank Harvard University for a fellowship in the study of Women and Religion during 1997–98 that made the research for this essay possible. Aspects of this essay were presented in lectures at Harvard University Divinity, at the Association of Jewish Studies in 1998, and at the Lehigh Conference on Jewish Postmodernisms in 1999. I thank Hannan Hever, Laura Levitt, Miriam Peskowitz, Larry Silberstein, Deborah Valense, and Lauren Winner for their various critical engagements with this essay. I thank Rebecca Kraweic in particular for her especially insightful comments on this paper.

RESPONSE

Catherine Chalier
Nanterre University, Paris

In her contribution to this volume on *Levinas and Biblical Studies*, Tamara C. Eskenazi points out the role of the "Here I am" (*hinneni*) in Levinas. In thinking the birth of human subjectivity in the mode of the "Here I am" said to the other, Levinas alerts us to the extent to which the Hebrew Bible, especially in the Torah, reflects an ethics calculated to safeguard persons from encroaching upon others, that is, a precaution against either assimilating or dominating the other. But are we talking about a simple precaution, albeit one that is obviously desirable, in order to avoid the violence provoked by a person's submission to the intimidation or to the threats of the other? Must one not pay particular attention to how the categories of the philosopher shed light on *election's* stake in the Bible?

In thinking the birth of human subjectivity in the mode of the "Here I am" (*hinneni*) said to the other, Levinas establishes a relationship that is of a very demanding nature in terms of this subjectivity and the other. Now this relationship signifies the defeat of the egotism not only of those inclined to serve themselves off the other or to live at another's expense but also of those enslaved to the desire for the other and subject to the other, consciously or unconsciously. The philosopher often describes it from the perspective of Abraham's response—"Here I am"—to the God who demands that he rise up and go to an unknown land (Gen 12:1) or, according to the traditional reading, to go *toward himself* (*lekh lekha*). To rise, to leave there what holds one captive to the past, which does not give—and even sometimes forbids—the impulse of living; then to go without nostalgically turning back toward the alienating ties of the past that are, despite it all, reassuring, constitutes a major teaching of the biblical text and a message of liberation. It is a message that is transmitted to particular individuals but also to the entire people, since it is renewed at the moment of the liberation from Egypt at *Pesach.* Now this is the excellence of *election.* Indeed, the one who hears this call, or the people who cross the sea while tyrannical powers of the past do not cease from stalking their prey and tormenting, do not decide it in an autonomous gesture of revolt or emancipation. In the Bible, it is the answer to the call that is liberating and that causes subjectivity to come about in its irreducible oneness. The call prevails both upon the temptation to stay there, subject to the forces that alienate, even if they cause pain, and upon the desire to be the only master of one's liberation.

The "self," to discuss it now according to Levinas's categories, does not constitute the prerequisite but the object itself of the promise. While the philosophies of reflexivity, or of the return to oneself, try to figure out how a subject constitutes *itself*, and how, in its liberty, it accepts or rejects commitments, Levinas teaches how the self emerges outside of the sorry hold of the being's neutrality at the moment of its answer to the call. The call of the other, which in its weakness and its strength demands that one find within oneself the resources of life that permit one to respond. Some take exception to Levinas and argue that this structure of subjectivity resembles an alienation, which is correct from a strictly formalistic perspective. But, lest we engage in a disastrous contradiction, this also calls for a clear distinction between alienation and election. The alienation from the call and the desire of the other, or from what one thinks to perceive as the word of God, is almost always the corollary of fear, of distress, or of anticipation, recognized or masked, and which, though they mislead themselves, are nonetheless concerned: What will happen to me if I do not submit? What can I gain from this? Election, to the contrary, signals a defeat of the omnipresence of such a question in the life of the psyche; it liberates one from one's anxiety by submitting to the *risk* of an answer for the *other*. Now, paradoxically, by lightening the weight of worry *for oneself*, it makes me discover its most inalienable and dynamic internal liberty: its uniqueness of subject when facing the other. In the Bible, the "I" does not exist prior to the answer; it is awakened within oneself—in a self charmed by the marvels of idolatry—by the call of the Eternal to the elect. Now the word par excellence that announces the good news of election has the simplicity of the word "You." If someone should call me—should say You—and, doing this, awaken the "here I am" in myself, if the caller engages me to rise up, despite the temptation of torpor or comfort, and to find for myself resources—then even though I seek to preserve myself from all alterity, ignoring all the while that I had them [the resources] within me—this is election. The life that is saved—the life that leaves Egypt, still now—is not the one that takes care of itself; it is the one that hears the "You," the one that is able to answer. No precaution is in play here; it is about election and its daily miracle or even the renewal of life (*hitkhadshut*).

But how can one think along these lines after the Shoah? This major question asserts itself, and Tod Linafelt's text causes one to confront it. "Even Titus, wicked as he was, could venture into the Holy of Holies, slash both veils, and go forth in peace. But Aaron's sons, who came into the Tabernacle to present an offering, were taken out burnt" (*Lev. Rab.* 20:5). Reading the biblical passage Lev 10, we are forbidden, according to the writer, from continuing to ask, as many traditional commentators have, what were the faults of Nadab and Abihu, sons of Aaron, to have been subjected to this fate. We can no longer say that "God never acts unjustly" (citing Bamberger: 804), and all theodicy is indecent, as Levinas maintains. This is why, according to the writer, it is appropriate to interpret Aaron's silence, after the death of his sons, not as a silence of acceptance: "it signals anger and unwillingness to acknowledge the decree of Moses." Indeed Moses wanted them transported outside of the camp and wanted no one to mourn them: "Uncover not your heads, neither rend your clothes" (Lev 10:6). Unless the silence of Aaron, the writer suggests further, is the one of the survivors of the Shoah "simply struck dumb by the horrific magnitude of the event." But whatever the explanation for this silence, can one say that Nadab and Abihu disappeared without leaving any trace?

This question expresses the painfully haunted memory of those who survived their brothers, who died without a burial; it comes from the necessity incumbent upon them to watch over these traces in order not to become *themselves* the cenotaph of these deaths. But how does one watch over these traces if it is true that the fire consumed their bodies? We know that these traces exist, nonetheless, in the psyches of the survivors, but watching over them does not mean to find some pleasure in it, to maintain despair and to subscribe to morbidity. On the contrary, one must fight against the temptation of death, as the Eternal requires in the Bible: "I have set before you life and death, blessing and cursing: therefore choose life, that both you and your seed may live" (Deut 30:19). For a religious Jew, watching over these traces and choosing life are not contradictory; on the contrary. In fact it is the only way not to compromise oneself with the mighty forces of darkness within oneself. However, this means also, as Levinas says, that religion has lost, for the faithful, any illusion of consolation. Thus, the one who continues to recite the *Shema Israel* discovers, at the heart of his or her distress and anguish, that the words pronounced promise no help, except that the saying of them during the night is in itself a help. Indeed, by requiring that the faithful continue to listen to the call of God, even when it seems that the darkness must prevail over the desire for life, the *Shema* obligates one to be alert to the presence, in the deep recesses of one's soul, of an alterity that commands one to love. Now this commandment of love obviously makes no sense unless it originates in love itself, a love that, even though it does not manifest itself in a tangible way, even when human pain becomes extreme, still has not disappeared. This is obviously the whole difficulty for humankind: to believe that one is loved, to hear oneself called to love, and to observe the dark night—the same [night] that has buried one's brothers and the one that does not cease to torment. But this also means entry into a more demanding faith, awaited already by Maimonides, as much in the *Mishneh Torah* as in the *Guide of the Perplexed,* of Job himself, and thus thought of in our days by Levinas when he speaks of "faith without consolation": to serve God out of love and not out of the expectation of gratification.

Nonetheless, this also implies that human beings have the strength to make this call from God within them live—or to let it die. The God, who is described in the prayer preceding the *Shema* as a "merciful father" (*av harakhaman*), does not have the power to impose himself. From that time onward, the pain that oppresses God's sons and daughters runs the risk of rendering them deaf to his call and inciting them to say, as Linafelt's text suggests, that "God acts unjustly," that God has abandoned them. This is not, however, the answer that Levinas has to the tragic contradiction between the thought of God's love and the all too visible abandonment of his faithful. God, he says, is not the All-powerful that our distress seeks out; indeed, thinking that God has abandoned us entails such a belief. Against the temptation to think like this, which is a characteristic of weakness and anger, but mainly of dereliction, the philosophy of Levinas teaches that the road to God requires that one pass through the answer that, despite the night one is traversing, a person continues to give when called by the face of the other who is even weaker than oneself. Now, perhaps miraculously, it is at this moment, sometimes through tears, that this person discovers that he or she is loved. The nearness of the call—finding whom to respond to as an opening to the saved life, the previous analysis suggested—is still heard in this desert that the world often becomes. But one must, in order to see the weakness and the strength, rise up and go toward those who, without even knowing it, are within the trace of the God whose goodness does not save according to the criteria of human desire. "He is good in just this eminent sense; He does not fill me up with goods but compels me to goodness, which is better than goods received" (Levinas 1996a: 141).

In her contribution, by reflecting on the words of the sages in the Talmud, Annette Aronowicz writes: "The rabbis are no longer alive, but their voices, recorded in the text, still address us, still confront us with the vulnerability of the other, the one who is not me, who is not us. To respond to that vulnerability is to answer those voices, thus keeping them within the community of the living." This assertion, which ties the weakness of the rabbis who have henceforth disappeared, and the strength of their voices which commands us, still today, to listen to them, that is to say, to interpret their dicta, so that they might continue to live within us and make us live, leads the reader to ask about the proximity, which is so insistent in the work of Levinas, between the statute of the biblical verse and that of the face. Indeed, the one like the other calls the reader to responsibility; the one like the other, in its weakness and in its strength, demands that the life within oneself arise to help it by making itself responsible. Now the paradox resides in that it is precisely by arising to answer that a human being discovers that one is alive, in one's most irreplaceable singularity.

Not to abandon the verse to its death by leaving it to congeal in a dogmatic opinion, in a proposition that results from a history that is henceforth obsolete, or by forgetting it altogether, and not to abandon the face to its mortal vulnerability, are two actions of the same scale. To prevent the death of the verse means to question it, to give it the sap of one's life, along with the joys and the sorrows that cause a question to rise to one's lips that no one, before us, was perhaps ever able to ask and, by doing this, to discover a new aspect of the verse's "power to speak," which, in this way, comes back to life. For the biblical texts extend to within our lives; they are the contemporaries of each one of us, of each generation, on the condition, of course, that the readers make for themselves "space" for them. Now the grace of encountering a teacher who, in the present, helps to make this journey is of primary importance here if one is to avoid letting the reading lose itself to pure subjectivism, on the pretext of escaping dogmatism. Indeed, if the interior life involves the reading of the Book, beginning with the questioning specifically suited to each person, it also demands that one know how to frame this questioning within the tradition of the sages, not in order to repeat it purely and simply, but to make it come alive, by renewing it. The teacher is precisely the one who transmits, who directs one's attention to the level at which the letter entreats the reader, and who makes it [the letter] instructive. Just like the image of Aaron's rod that begins to bloom (Num 17:23 [ET 17:8]), the teacher enables the words that have been considered dead for too long to regain life. But the teacher, Aronowicz underlines, does not impose anything, and to answer the teacher does not imply at all that one submits to the content of the interpretation. It implies simply—which is obviously essential—"an acquiescence to the possibility of being taught." Not to abandon the face to its mortal distress is equivalent to hearing its call, a call that nevertheless has no more power to impose itself than does the verse, even though Levinas insists on the Height from which it originates. But Height does not mean power. Height conjugates precisely with weakness. We know that, in the Talmud (b. Meg. 31a), R. Yohanan points out that, in Scripture, when the power of the Saint, blessed be he, is exalted, his humiliation is associated immediately with this power. Now the face—just like the verse—is found in the *trace* of the Infinite, says Levinas. It is not a phenomenon that adjusts itself to the line of sight that I would like to take; it is situated in the *trace* of God who, in the Bible, only shows himself to Moses "from the back" (Exod 33:23). But this God exerts power no more to impose the biblical verses on people who prefer the deafness than to constrain a person to answer to the face. God lowers Godself, in speech, and it is this speech—only it in its weakness and its strength—that God gives to human beings in order that they hear in these words, so ancient and always so new, the loftiness of the call to responsibility. Levinas says that the human face speaks, that it commands this responsibility towards itself, from which each one of us often wants to relieve oneself, in order to be at leisure to pursue one's business and to build up one's power to be, without having to be burdened with such a worry. But this speech of the face, would it be audible without the instruction of the verses? Would it be audible without the descent of God (*vayered haShem*) to Sinai? It is not certain, and the plan to exterminate the Jewish people—to whom this Speech was entrusted so that it might live and be transmitted—demonstrates that it was also this Speech that the Nazis wanted to annihilate by annihilating the flesh of all the children of Israel. But it is also why, in a world that, so often still, prefers to celebrate death rather than to answer the face, it is important not to let oneself become weary, not to let oneself be intimidated by the modem tenets of nihilism and, patiently, to turn oneself toward the Book that commands that one watch over one's brother or one's sister, up until the final moment. The emergence of the human in the being does not occur, for Levinas, by increasing the power of being that we each have; it begins on the road of this responsibility.

(Translated by Suzanne Singer)*

---

* The translation has been conformed to Semeia Studies style in some small particulars (eds.).

BIBLIOGRAPHY

Ansley, Alison. 1988. Amorous Discourses: "The Phenomenology of Eros" and Love Stories." Pages 70–82 in *The Provocation of Levinas: Rethinking the Other*. Edited by Robert Bernasconi and David Wood. London and New York: Routledge.

Aronowicz, Annette. 1994. Translator's Introduction. Pages ix–xxxix in Levinas 1990c.

Bal, Mieke. 1991. The Politics of Citation. *Diacritics* 21:25–45.

Bamberger, Bernard J. 1981. Leviticus. Pages 731–975 in *The Torah: A Modern Commentary*. Edited by Gunther Plaut. New York: UAHC.

Bassler, Jouette M. 1986. Cain and Abel in the Palestinian Targums: A Brief Note on an Old Controversy. *JSJ* 17:56–64.

Beal, Timothy K. 1994. The System and the Speaking Subject in the Hebrew Bible: Reading for Divine Abjection. *Biblnt* 2:171–89.

Beal, Timothy K., and Tod Linafelt. 1995. Sifting for Cinders: Strange Fires in Leviticus 10:1–5. *Semeia* 69/70:19–32.

Benjamin, Jessica. 1988. *The Bonds of Love: Psychoanalysis, Feminism, and the Problem of Domination*. New York: Pantheon.

Bernasconi, Robert, and Simon Critchley, eds. 1991. *Re-reading Levinas*. Bloomington: Indiana University Press.

Blanchot, Maurice. 1995. Do Not Forget. Pages 245–49 in *The Blanchot Reader*. Edited and translated by M. Holland. Oxford: Blackwell. [Orig. 1988]

Bledstein, Adrien Janis. 1993. Was Eve Cursed? (or Did a Woman Write Genesis?). *BRev* 9/1:42–46.

Blumenthal, David. 1993. *Facing the Abusing God: A Theology of Protest*. Louisville: Westminster John Knox.

Bongmba, Elias. 2002. Intertextuality in Cheikh Hamidou Kane's *The Ambiguous Adventure:* Multiple Readings of the Motif of Death. In *Re-imagining Africa: New Perspectives on African Literature*. Edited by Sue Kossew and Dianne Schwerdt. New York: Nova Science.

Boyarin, Daniel. 1993. *Carnal Israel : Reading Sex in Talmudic Culture*. Berkeley and Los Angeles: University of California Press.

Brooks, Roger, and John J. Collins, eds. 1990. *Hebrew Bible or Old Testament? Studying the Bible in Judaism and Christianity*. Notre Dame, Ind.: University of Notre Dame Press.

Brueggemann, Walter. 1982. *Genesis*. IBC. Atlanta: John Knox.

Burggraeve, Roger. 1991. *Emmanuel Levinas: Une bibliographie primaire et secondaire (1929–1985) avec complément (1985–1989)*. 3d ed. Leuven: Center for Metaphysics and Philosophy of God.

Burnham, Frederick B., ed. 1989. *Postmodern Theology: Christian Faith in a Pluralist World*. San Francisco: Harper & Row.

Busenitz, Irvin A. 1986. Woman's Desire for Man: Genesis 3:16 Reconsidered. *Grace Theological Journal* 7:203–12.

Calloud, Jean. 1995. Figure, Knowledge and Truth: Absence and Fulfillment in the Scriptures. *Semeia* 69/70:61–81.

Caputo, John D. 1993. *Against Ethics: Contributions to a Poetics of Obligation with Constant Reference to Deconstruction*. Bloomington: Indiana University Press.

Celan, Paul. 1988. The Straightening. Pages 137–49 in *Poems of Paul Celan*. Translated by M. Hamburger. New York: Persea.

Chalier, Catherine. 1991. Ethics and the Feminine. Pages 119–29 in Bernasconi and Critchley.

Chalier, Catherine, and Miguel Abensour, eds. 1991. *Emmanuel Levinas*. L'Herne 60. Paris: Editions de l'Herne.

Chanter, Tina. 1988. Feminism and the Other. Pp.32–56 in *The Provocation of Levinas: Rethinking the Other*. Edited by Robert Bernasconi and David Wood. London and New York: Routledge.

———. 1991. Antigone's Dilemma. Pages 130–46 in Bernasconi and Critchley.

Clements, Ronald. 1970. Leviticus. Pages 1–73 in vol. 2 of *The Broadman Bible Commentary*. Nashville: Broadman.

Cohen, Richard A. 1994. *Elevations: The Height of the Good in Rosenzweig and Levinas*. Chicago: University of Chicago Press.

Conrad, Joseph. 1971. *Heart of Darkness*. Edited by Robert Kimbrough. New York: Norton.

Damrosch, David. 1987. Leviticus. Pages 66–77 in *The Literary Guide to the Bible*. Edited by Robert Alter and Frank Kermode. Cambridge: Harvard University Press.

Davis, Colin. 1996. *Levinas: An Introduction*. Notre Dame, Ind.: University of Notre Dame Press.

Derrida, Jacques. 1978. Violence and Metaphysics: An Essay on the Thought of Emmanuel Levinas. Pages 79–153 in *Writing and Difference*. Chicago: University of Chicago Press.

———. 1991a. At This Very Moment in This Work Here I Am. Pages 11–48 in Bernasconi and Critchley.

———. 1991b. *Cinders*. Translated by N. Lukacher. Lincoln: University of Nebraska Press.

———. 1999. *Adieu to Emmanuel Levinas*. Stanford: Stanford University Press.

Descartes, René. 1968. *Discourse on Method and the Meditations*. Translated by F. E. Sutcliffe. New York: Penguin.

Ellul, Jacques. 1973. *Hope in Time of Abandonment*. Translated by Edward Hopkin. New York: Seabury.

Fackenheim, Emil. 1990. *The Jewish Bible after the Holocaust: A Re-reading*. Bloomington: Indiana University Press.

Fewell, Danna Nolan, and David M. Gunn. 1993. *Gender, Power and Promise: The Subject of the Bible's First Story*. Nashville: Abingdon.

Fokkelman, J. P. 1991. *Narrative Art in Genesis*. Sheffield: Sheffield Academic Press. [Orig. 1975]

Foucault, Michel. 1972. *The Archaeology of Knowledge and the Discourse of Language.* Translated by A. M. Sheridan Smith. New York: Barnes & Noble.

Fowl, Stephen. 1995. Texts Don't Have Ideologies. *BibInt* 3:15–34.

Gibbs, Robert. 1992. *Correlations in Rosenzweig and Levinas.* Princeton, N.J.: Princeton University Press.

Görg, Manfred. 1994. Kain und das "Land Nod." *BN* 71:5–12.

Greenberg, Irving. 1977. Cloud of Smoke, Pillar of Fire: Judaism, Christianity, and Modernity after the Holocaust. Pages 7–55 in *Auschwitz: Beginning of a New Era?* Edited by E. Fleischner. New York: Ktav.

Greenstein, Edward L. 1989. Deconstruction and Biblical Narrative. *Prooftexts* 9:43–71.

Grosz, Elizabeth. 1989. *Sexual Subversions: Three French Feminists.* Sydney: Allen & Unwin.

Gunn, David M. 1990. Reading Right. Reliable and Omniscient Narrator, Omniscient God, and Foolproof Composition in the Hebrew Bible. Pages 53–64 in *The Bible in Three Dimensions: Essays in Celebration of Forty Years in Biblical Studies in the University of Sheffield.* Edited by David J. A. Clines, Stephen Fowl, and Stanley Porter. JSOTSup 87. Sheffield: Sheffield Academic Press.

Gunn, David M., and Danna Nolan Fewell. 1993. *Narrative in the Hebrew Bible.* OBS. Oxford: Oxford University Press.

Gutiérrez, Gustavo. 1983. *The Power of the Poor in History.* Maryknoll: Orbis.

Handelman, Susan. 1991. *Fragments of Redemption: Jewish Thought and Literary Theory in Benjamin, Scholem, and Levinas.* Bloomington: Indiana University Press.

Haran, Menahem. 1960. The Uses of Incense in Ancient Israel. *VT* 10:113–29.

Hauser, Alan Jon. 1982. Genesis 2–3: The Theme of Intimacy and Alienation. Pages 20–36 in *Art and Meaning: Rhetoric in Biblical Literature.* Edited by David J. A. Clines, David M. Gunn, and Alan J. Hauser. JSOTSup 19. Sheffield: JSOT Press.

Heidegger, Martin. 1961. *An Introduction to Metaphysics.* Translated by Ralph Mannheim. New York: Doubleday.

———. 1962. *Being and Time.* Translated by John Robinson and Edward Macquarrie. New York: Harper & Row.

———. 1993. A Letter on Humanism. Translated by Frank A. Capuzzi and J. John Gray. Pages 213–65 in *Basic Writings.* Edited by David Farrell Krell. London. Routledge. [Orig. 1947]

Hendel, Ronald S. 1991. When God Acts Immorally. Is the Bible a Good Book? *BRev* 7/3:35–37, 46–49.

Herion, Gary A. 1995. Why God Rejected Cain's Offering: The Obvious Answer. Pages 53–65 in *Fortunate the Eyes That See: Essays in Honor of David Noel Freedman in Celebration of His Seventieth Birthday.* Edited by Astrid B. Beck et al. Grand Rapids: Eerdmans.

Hodgson, Peter. 1994. *Winds of the Spirit: A Constructive Christian Theology.* Louisville: Westminster John Knox.

Ingraffia, B. 1995. *Postmodern Theory and Biblical Theology: Vanquishing God's Shadow.* Cambridge: Cambridge University Press.

Irigaray, Luce. 1980. When Our Lips Speak Together. Translated by Carolyn
    Burke. *Signs: Journal of Women in Culture and Society* 6:69–79.
———. 1981. And the One Doesn't Stir without the Other. Translated by
    Hélène Vivienne Wenzel. *Signs: Journal of Women in Culture and Society*
    7:60–67.
———. 1991. Questions to Levinas: On the Divinity of Love. Pages 109–18 in
    Bernasconi and Critchley.
Jabès, Edmond. 1989. *The Book of Shares.* Translated by R. Waldrop. Chicago: Uni-
    versity of Chicago Press.
Jameson, Fredric. 1988. Imaginary and Symbolic in Lacan. Pages 75–115 in *Situa-
    tions of Theory.* Vol. 1 of *The Ideologies of Theory and Essays 1971–1981.* London:
    Routledge.
Jobling, David. 1986. *The Sense of Biblical Narrative II: Structural Analyses in the
    Hebrew Bible.* JSOTSup 39. Sheffield: Sheffield Academic Press.
———. 1994. Hannah's Desire. *Bulletin of the Canadian Society of Biblical Studies*
    53:19–32.
Kant, Emmanuel. 1965. *The Critique of Practical Reason.* Translated by L. Beck. Indi-
    anapolis: Bobbs-Merrill.
———. 1987. *Critique of Judgment.* Translated by W. Pluhar. Cambridge: Hackett.
    [Orig. 1790]
Kearney, Richard. 1986. *Dialogues with Contemporary Continental Thinkers.* Man-
    chester: Manchester University Press.
Keller, Catherine. 1985. *From a Broken Web: Separation, Sexism and Self.* New York:
    Crossroads.
Kierkegaard, Søren (Johannes de Silentio). 1941. *Fear and Trembling and The Sick-
    ness unto Death.* Translated by Walter Lowrie. Princeton, N.J.: Princeton
    University Press. [Orig. 1843]
Kirschner, Robert. 1983. The Rabbinic and Philonic Exegesis of the Nadab and
    Abihu Incident. *JQR* 73:375–93.
Kisiel, W. 1988. The Missing Link in the Early Heidegger. Pages 1–40 in *Hermeneu-
    tic Phenomenology: Lectures and Essays.* Edited by Joseph Kockelmanns.
    University Press of America.
———. 1993. *The Genesis of Being and Time.* Berkeley and Los Angeles: University
    of California Press.
Krasovec, Joze. 1994. Punishment and Mercy in the Primeval History (Gen 1–11).
    ETL 70:5–33.
Kugel, James L. 1990. Cain and Abel in Fact and Fable: Genesis 4:1–16. Pages
    167–90 in *Hebrew Bible or Old Testament? Studying the Bible in Judaism and
    Christianity.* Edited by Roger Brooks and John J. Collins. Notre Dame, Ind.:
    University of Notre Dame Press.
Lacan, Jacques. 1985. God and the Jouissance of the Woman. A Love Letter. Pages
    137–61 in *Feminine Sexuality: Jacques Lacan and the école freudienne.* Edited by
    Juliet Mitchell and Jacqueline Rose. Translated by Jacqueline Rose. New
    York: Norton.
Lanzmann, Claude. 1985. *Shoah: An Oral History of the Holocaust (The Complete Text
    of the Film).* New York: Pantheon.
Laughlin, J. C. H. 1976. The Strange Fire of Nadab and Abihu. *JBL* 95:559–65.

Levenson, Jon. 1988. *Creation and the Persistence of Evil: The Jewish Drama of Divine Omnipotence*. San Francisco: Harper & Row.

Levi, Primo. 1961. *Survival in Auschwitz: The Nazi Assault on Humanity*. Translated by Stuart Woolf. New York: Macmillan.

Levinas, Emmanuel. 1946. IL Y A. *Deucalion* 1:141–54.

———. 1947. *De l'existence à l'existant*. Paris: Vlin.

———. 1961. *Totalité et infini: Essai sur l'extériorité*. The Hague: Nijhoff.

———. 1966. On the Trail of the Other. Translated by Daniel Hoy. *Philosophy Today* 10:34- 36.

———. 1969. *Totality and Infinity: An Essay on Exteriority*. Translated by Alphonso Lingis. Duquesne Studies Philosophical Series 24. Pittsburgh: Duquesne University Press. [Orig., see 1961.]

———. 1975. Ideology and Idealism. Pages 121–38 in *Modern Jewish Ethics: Theory and Practice*. Edited by Marvin Fox. Columbus: Ohio State University Press.

———. 1976. *Noms propres*. Montpellier: Fata Morgana.

———. 1977. *Du sacré au saint: cinq nouvelles lectures talmudiques*. Paris: Minuit.

———. 1978a. *Existence and Existents*. Translated by Alphonso Lingis. Boston: Kluwer. [Orig., see 1947.]

———. 1978b. Signature. Edited and translated by Adriaan Peperzak. *Research in Phenomenology* 8:175–89.

———. 1979a. *Le Temps et L'autre*. Montpellier: Fata Morgana. [Orig. 1947]

———. 1979b. To Love the Torah More Than God. Translated by Helen A. Stephenson and Richard I. Sugarman. *Judaism* 28:216–20.

———. 1981. *Otherwise Than Being or Beyond Essence*. Translated by Alphonso Lingis. Boston: Nijhoff. [Orig. *Autrement qu'être ou au-delà de l'essence*. Dordrecht: Nijhoff, 1974.]

———. 1982a. *De l'évasion*. Introduction and annotations by Jacques Rolland. Paris: Fata Morgana.

———. 1982b. *L'au-delà du verset*. Paris: Minuit.

———. 1984. *Israël, le Judaïsme et l'Europe*. Paris: Gallimard.

———. 1985. *Ethics and Infinity*. Translated by Richard Cohen. Pittsburgh: Duquesne University Press. [Orig. *Ethique et L'infini*. Paris: Fauard, 1982.]

———. 1987a. Humanism and Anarchy. Pages 127–39 in *Collected Philosophical Papers*. Translated by Alphonso Lingis. Boston: Nijhoff.

———. 1987b. Language and Proximity. Pages 109–26 in *Collected Philosophical Papers*. Translated by Alphonso Lingis. Boston: Nijhoff.

———. 1987c. *Time and the Other*. Translated by Richard Cohen. Pittsburgh: Duquesne University Press. [Orig., see 1979a.]

———. 1989a. God and Philosophy. Translated by Richard A. Cohen and Alphonso Lingis. Pages 166–89 in Levinas 1989b.

———. 1989b. *The Levinas Reader*. Edited and translated by Seán Hand. Oxford: Blackwell.

———. 1989c. Revelation in the Jewish Tradition. Pages 190–210 in Levinas 1989b.

———. 1989d. Suffering and Death. Translated by Richard A. Cohen. In Levinas 1989b. [Orig. 1946–47]

———. 1989e. There Is: Existence without Existents. Translated by Alphonso Lingis. Pages 29–36 in Levinas 1989b. [Orig. 1946]

————. 1990a. And God Created Woman. Pages 161–77 in Levinas 1990c.

————. 1990b. *Difficult Freedom: Essays on Judaism.* Translated by Seán Hand. Baltimore: Johns Hopkins University Press. [Orig. *Difficile liberté,* 1963.]

————. 1990c. *Nine Talmudic Readings.* Translated and with an introduction by Annette Aronowicz. Bloomington: Indiana University Press.

————. 1991. Wholly Otherwise. Translated by Simon Critchley. Pages 3–10 in Bernasconi and Critchley.

————. 1993a. *Collected Philosophical Papers.* Translated by Alphonso Lingis. Dordrecht: Kluwer.

————. 1993b. *Outside the Subject.* Translated by Michael B. Smith. Stanford, Calif.: Stanford University Press.

————. 1994a. *Beyond the Verse: Talmudic Readings and Lectures.* Translated by Gary D. Mole. Bloomington: Indiana University Press. [Orig., see 1982b]

————. 1994b. *In the Time of the Nations.* Bloomington: Indiana University Press.

————. 1994c. On the Jewish Reading of Scriptures. Pages 101–15 in Levinas 1994a. [Reprinted pp. 17–31 in this volume.]

————. 1996a. God and Philosophy. Pages 129–48 in *Basic Philosophical Writings.* Edited by A. Peperzak, S. Critchley, and R. Bernasconi. Bloomington: Indiana University Press.

————. 1996b. *Proper Names.* Translated by Michael B. Smith. Stanford, Calif.: Stanford University Press. [Orig., see 1976]

————. 1998. Philosophy, Justice, and Love. Pages 103–21 in *Entre Nous: Thinking-of-the-Other.* Translated by Michael B. Smith and Barbara Harshav. New York: Columbia University Press. [Orig. 1982]

Levine, Baruch. 1989. *The JPS Torah Commentary: Leviticus.* Philadelphia: Jewish Publication Society.

Linafelt, Tod. 1994. Reading the Hebrew Bible after the Holocaust: Toward an Ethics of Interpretation. Pages 627–41 in *The Holocaust: Progress and Prognosis, 1934–1994.* Lawrenceville, N.J.: Holocaust Resource Center of Rider College.

————. 1995a. Surviving Lamentations. *HBT* 17:45–61.

————. 1995b. The Undecidability of ברך in the Prologue to Job and Beyond. *BibInt* 4:1–19.

Lyotard, Jean-François. 1990. *Heidegger and "the jews."* Minneapolis: University of Minnesota Press.

MacQuarrie, John. 1994. *Heidegger and Christianity.* New York: Continuum.

Magonet, Jonathan. 1991. *A Rabbi's Bible.* London: SCM.

Manning, Robert Shefler. 1993. *Interpreting Otherwise Than Heidegger: Emmanuel Levinas's Ethics As First Philosophy.* Pittsburgh: Duquesne University Press.

Mbiti, John. 1969. *African Religions and Philosophy.* London: Heinemann.

————. 1971. *New Testament Eschatology in an African Background: A Study of the Encounter between New Testament Theology and African Traditional Concepts.* Oxford: Oxford University Press.

Megill, Alan. 1985. *Prophets of Extremity.* Berkeley and Los Angeles: University of California Press.

Meskin, Jacob. 1989. From Phenomenology to Liberation: The Displacement of History and Theology in Levinas's *Totality and Infinity. Philosophy and Theology* 4:119–44.

Micklem, Nathaniel. 1953. Leviticus. *IB* 2:1–134.

Miclot, Brian. 1993. Thinking the Ethical out of Time: A Pre-ethical Investigation of Temporality. Ph.D. diss. University of Notre Dame.

Milgrom, Jacob. 1970. *Studies in Levitical Terminology*. Berkeley and Los Angeles: University of California Press.

———. 1991. *Leviticus 1–16*. AB 3. New York: Doubleday.

Miller, James B. 1989. The Emerging Postmodern World. Pages 1–19 in *Postmodern Theology: Christian Faith in a Pluralist World*. Edited by Frederic B. Burnham. San Francisco: Harper & Row.

Moltmann, Jürgen. 1988. *Theology Today*. Translated by John Bowden. Philadelphia: Trinity Press International.

Morgenstern, Julian. 1963. *The Fire upon the Altar*. Chicago: Quadrangle Books.

Néher, André. 1981. *The Exile of the Word: From the Silence of the Bible to the Silence of Auschwitz*. Philadelphia: Jewish Publication Society.

Pagis, Dan. 1981. Footprints. Pages 29–37 in *Points of Departure*. Translated by S. Mitchell. Philadelphia: Jewish Publication Society.

Penchansky, David. 1992. Up for Grabs: A Tentative Proposal for Doing Ideological Criticism. *Semeia* 59:35–42.

Peperzak, Adriaan. 1983. Emmanuel Levinas: The Jewish Experience in Philosophy. *Philosophy Today* 27:297–306.

———. 1993. *To the Other: An Introduction to the Philosophy of Emmanuel Levinas*. West Lafayette, Ind.: Purdue University Press.

Peters, Ted. 1992. *God—the World's Future: A Systematic Theology for a Postmodern Era*. Minneapolis: Fortress.

Phillips, Gary A. 1994a. Drawing the Other. The Postmodern and Reading the Bible Imaginatively. Pages 403–31 in *In Good Company: Essays in Honor of Robert Detweiler*. Edited by David Jasper and Mark Ledbetter. Atlanta: Scholars Press.

———. 1994b. The Ethics of Reading Deconstructively, Or Speaking Face-to-Face: The Samaritan Woman Meets Derrida at the Well. Pages 282–325 in *The New Literary Criticism and the New Testament*. Edited by Elizabeth Struthers Malbon and Edgar V. McKnight. JSNTSup 109. Sheffield: Sheffield Academic Press.

Plato. 1952. *Gorgias*. Translated by W. C. Helmbold. New York: Bobbs-Merrill.

Plaut, Gunther. 1995. Cain and Abel: Bible, Tradition, and Contemporary Reflection. Pages 11–16 in *Preaching Biblical Texts: Expositions by Jewish and Christian Scholars*. Edited by Fredrick C. Holmgren and Herman E. Schaalman. Grand Rapids: Eerdmans.

Quinones, Ricardo J. 1991. *The Changes of Cain: Violence and the Lost Brother in Cain and Abel Literature*. Princeton, N.J.: Princeton University Press.

Rad, Gerhard von. 1972. *Genesis: A Commentary*. OTL. Philadelphia: Westminster.

Rashkow, Ilona N. 1993. *The Phallacy of Genesis: A Feminist-Psychoanalytic Approach*. Literary Currents in Biblical Interpretation. Louisville: Westminster John Knox.

Riemann, Paul A. 1970. Am I My Brother's Keeper? *Int* 24:482–91.

Rosenblatt, Naomi H., and Joshua Horwitz. 1995. *Wrestling with Angels: What the First Family of Genesis Teaches Us about Our Spiritual Identity, Sexuality, and Personal Relationships*. New York: Delacorte.

Rosenzweig, Franz. 1953. *Franz Rosenzweig: His Life and Thought.* Edited by Nahum Glatzer. New York: Schocken.

Roskies, David. 1989. *The Literature of Destruction: Jewish Responses to Catastrophe.* Philadelphia: Jewish Publication Society.

Roth, John K., and Michael Berenbaum. 1989. *Holocaust: Religious and Philosophical Implications.* New York: Paragon.

Rowlett, Lori. 1992. Inclusion, Exclusion and Marginality in the Book of Joshua. *JSOT* 55:15–23.

Scholem, Gershom. 1954. *Major Trends in Jewish Mysticism.* New York: Schocken.

Schüssler Fiorenza, Elisabeth, and David Tracy, eds. 1984. *The Holocaust As Interruption.* Edinburgh: T&T Clark.

Shapiro, Susan E. 1994. Rhetoric As Ideology Critique: The Gadamer-Habermas Debate Reinvented. *JAAR* 62:123–50.

———. 1997. A Matter of Discipline: Reading for Gender in Jewish Philosophy. Pages 158–73 in *Judaism Since Gender.* Edited by Miriam Peskowitz and Laura Levitt. New York: Routledge.

———. 1998. The Feminization of Idolatry. *Harvard Divinity Bulletin* 27:27–28.

———. 2000. Rhetoric, Ideology, and Idolatry in the Writings of Emmanuel Levinas. Pages 254–78 in *Rhetorical Invention and Religious Inquiry: New Perspectives.* Edited by Walter Jost and Wendy Raudenbush Olmsted. New Haven: Yale University Press.

Sheehan, Thomas. 1979. Heidegger's Introduction to the Phenomenology of Religion, 1920–21. *The Personalist* 20: 313–24.

Soyinka, Wole. 1975. *Death and the King's Horseman.* London: Methuen.

Spina, Frank Anthony. 1992. The "Ground" for Cain's Rejection (Gen 4): 'adamah in the Context of Gen 1–11. *ZAW* 104:319–32.

Trible, Phyllis. 1978. *God and the Rhetoric of Sexuality.* OBT. Philadelphia: Fortress.

Twersky, Isadore. 1980. *Introduction to the Code of Maimonides (Mishneh Torah).* Yale Judaica Series 22. New Haven: Yale University Press.

Visotzky, Burton L. 1991. *Reading the Book: Making the Bible a Timeless Text.* New York: Doubleday.

Waltke, Bruce K. 1986. Cain and His Offering. *Westminster Theological Journal* 48:363–72.

Wenham, Gordon. 1979. *The Book of Leviticus.* Grand Rapids: Eerdmans.

West, Gerald. 1990. Reading "the Text" and Reading "behind the Text": The "Cain and Abel" Story in a Context of Liberation. Pages 299–320 in *The Bible in Three Dimensions: Essays in Celebration of Forty Years of Biblical Studies in the University of Sheffield.* Edited by David J. A. Clines, Stephen E. Fowl, and Stanley E. Porter. JSOTSup 87. Sheffield: Sheffield Academic Press.

———. 1992. Interesting and Interested Readings: Deconstruction, the Bible, and the South African Context. *Scriptura* 42:35–49.

———. 1994. Difference and Dialogue: Reading the Joseph Story with Poor and Marginalized Communities in South Africa. *BibInt* 2:152–70.

———. 1995. And the Dumb Do Speak: Articulating Incipient Readings of the Bible in Marginalized Communities. Pages 174–92 in *The Bible in Ethics: The Second Sheffield Colloquium.* Edited by John W. Rogerson, Margaret Davies, and M. Daniel Carroll R. JSOTSup 207. Sheffield: JSOT Press.

Westermann, Claus. 1982. *Genesis 1–11: A Commentary*. Translated by John H. Scullion. Minneapolis: Augsburg.

Wiesel, Elie. 1972. *Souls of Fire: Portraits and Legends of Hasidic Masters*. New York: Summit.

———. 1976. *Messengers of God: Biblical Portraits and Legends*. New York: Random House.

———. 1978. *A Jew Today*. New York: Vintage.

———. 1979. *The Trial of God: A Play in Three Acts*. New York: Schocken.

———. 1981. *Five Biblical Portraits*. Notre Dame, Ind.: University of Notre Dame Press.

———. 1991. *Sages and Dreamers: Biblical, Talmudic, and Hasidic Portraits and Legends*. New York: Summit.

Williams, James G. 1991. *The Bible, Violence, and the Sacred: Liberation from the Myth of Sanctioned Violence*. San Francisco: Harper.

Wolde, Ellen van. 1991. The Story of Cain and Abel: A Narrative Study. *JSOT* 52:25–41.

Wolfson, Eliot. 1994. *Through a Speculum That Shines*. Princeton, N.J.: Princeton University Press.

———.1995. *Circle in the Square*. Albany: SUNY Press.

Wright, Tamra, Peter Hughes, and Alison Ainley. 1988. "The Paradox of Morality: An Interview with Emmanuel Levinas." Pages 168–80 in *The Provocation of Levinas: Rethinking the Other*. Edited by Robert Bernasconi and David Wood. New York: Routledge.

Wyschogrod, Edith. 1974. *Emmanuel Levinas: The Problem of Ethical Metaphysics*. The Hague: Martinus Nijhoff.

———. 1989. "Interview with Emanuel Levinas." *Philosophy and Theology* 4/2:105–18.

———. 1992. Who Is Emmanuel Levinas? *Sh'ma: A Journal of Jewish Responsibility* 22/429 (March 6):65-67.

———. 2000. *Emmanuel Levinas: The Problem of Ethical Metaphysics*. 2d ed. New York: Fordham University Press.

Ziarek, Ewa. 1993. "Kristeva and Levinas: Mourning, Ethics, and the Feminine." Pages 62–78 in *Ethics, Politics and Difference in Julia Kristeva's Writing*. Edited by Kelly Oliver. New York: Routledge.

CONTRIBUTORS

Annette Aronowicz is Robert F. and Patricia G. Ross Weis Professor of Judaic Studies in the Religious Studies Department of Franklin & Marshall College. She is the translator of *Nine Talmudic Readings* by Emmanuel Levinas (Indiana, 1990) and the author of *Jews and Christians on Time and Eternity: Charles Peguy's Portrait of Bernard Lazare* (Stanford, 1998). Her interests lie in the process of secularization and in the interrelationship of religion and politics. She can be reached at Annette.Aronowicz@fandm.edu.

Timothy K. Beal is Harkness Professor of Biblical Literature and Director of the Baker Nord Center for the Humanities at Case Western Reserve University in Cleveland, Ohio. He is co-editor of the book series Afterlives of the Bible with University of Chicago Press and author, most recently, of *Religion and Its Monsters* (Routledge, 2002). He can be reached at bealhemoth@cwru.edu.

Elias Bongmba is Associate Professor of Religious Studies at Rice University. His areas of specialization include African and African Diaspora religions, contemporary theology and ethics, hermeneutics, nineteenth-century theology, and African studies. He is author of *African Witchcraft and Otherness: A Philosophical and Theological Critique of Intersubjective Relations*, in which he employs the philosophy of Emmanuel Levinas. He has published articles in *African Studies Review, Theology and Literature,* and *Religion and Theology.* He is currently working on a monograph on humanistic responses to the sociopolitical crisis in Africa. He can be reached at bongmba@rice.edu.

Catherine Chalier is Professor of Philosophy at the University of Paris, Nanterre, and the author of numerous books on Levinas. Her most recent book (in English) is *What Ought I to Do: Morality in Kant and Levinas* (Cornell University Press, 2002).

Tamara Cohn Eskenazi is Professor of Bible at Hebrew Union College-Jewish Institute of Religion, in Los Angeles. She is the author of several works, including *In an Age of Prose: A Literary Approach to Ezra-Nehemiah.* She is completing a commentary on Ezra-Nehemiah for the Anchor Bible series and is also the Editor-in-Chief of the newly launched Women of Reform Judaism Commentary on the Torah. She can be reached at teskenazi@huc.edu.

Jione Havea is lecturer at Charles Sturt University's School of Theology, and at United Theological College, NSW, Australia. He specializes in cross-cultural studies. His *Elusions of Control* will shortly be published by the Society of Biblical Literature. He can be reached at jioneh@nsw.uca.org.au.

Scott Hennessy is a graduate student in Religious Studies at the University of Virginia. His dissertation is entitled: Emmanuel Levinas and the Shoah: Towards a Christian Theology of Rescue. An Episcopal priest, he is currently the rector of St. Thomas's Parish, Orange, Virginia. He can be reached at fsh7@earthlink.net.

Tod Linafelt is associate professor of biblical literature at Georgetown University in Washington, DC. He is the author of *Surviving Lamentations: Catastrophe, Lament, and Protest in the Afterlife of a Biblical Book* (Chicago, 2000) and a commentary on the book of Ruth (in the Berit Olam series, Liturgical Press, 1999). He is editor of *Strange Fire: Reading the Hebrew Bible after the Holocaust* (NYU/Sheffield, 2000), *A Shadow of Glory: Reading the New Testament after the Holocaust* (Routledge, 2002), and, with Timothy K. Beal, of a Festschrift for Walter Brueggemann, *God in the Fray* (Fortress, 1998). He can be reached at linafelt@georgetown.edu.

Susan E. Shapiro is Associate Professor in the Department of Judaic and Near Eastern Studies at the University of Massachusetts, Amherst. Her recent work has been in the areas of post-Holocaust philosophy, feminist Jewish philosophy, and the Jewish Uncanny. Her writings on topics related to the essay in this volume are "A Matter of Discipline" in *Judaism since Gender* (ed. Miriam Peskowitz and Laura Levitt, Routledge, 1997), "On Thinking Identity Otherwise" in *Mapping Jewish Identities* (ed. Laurence Silberstein, New York University Press, 2000), and "Rhetoric, Ideology, and Idolatry in the Writings of Emmanuel Levinas" in *Rhetorical Invention and Religious Inquiry* (ed. Walter Jost and Wendy Olmsted, Yale University Press, 2000). She can be reached at shapiro@judnea.umass.edu.

Martin Srajek holds a Ph.D. in philosophy of religion from Temple University, where he focused on the Jewish-ethical elements in the work of Jacques Derrida and Emmanuel Levinas. He is the author of *In the Margins of Deconstruction: Jewish Conceptions of Ethics in Emmanuel Levinas and Jacques Derrida* (Duquesne University Press, 2000). He has taught at several academic institutions, including Princeton University, Swarthmore College, and Illinois Wesleyan University. He is a licensed clinical social worker in the state of Illinois, where he has been a psychotherapist in private practice for the last five years. He is a contributing editor to the newsletter of the American Association for Pre- and Perinatal Psychology and Health. He may be reached at srajek@infant-parent.com.